Visual Storytelling in the 21st Century

David Callahan
Editor

Visual Storytelling in the 21st Century

The Age of the Long Fragment

palgrave
macmillan

Editor
David Callahan
Department of Languages & Cultures
University of Aveiro
Aveiro, Portugal

ISBN 978-3-031-65486-2   ISBN 978-3-031-65487-9 (eBook)
https://doi.org/10.1007/978-3-031-65487-9

© The Editor(s) (if applicable) and The Author(s), under exclusive license to Springer Nature Switzerland AG 2024

This work is subject to copyright. All rights are solely and exclusively licensed by the Publisher, whether the whole or part of the material is concerned, specifically the rights of translation, reprinting, reuse of illustrations, recitation, broadcasting, reproduction on microfilms or in any other physical way, and transmission or information storage and retrieval, electronic adaptation, computer software, or by similar or dissimilar methodology now known or hereafter developed.
The use of general descriptive names, registered names, trademarks, service marks, etc. in this publication does not imply, even in the absence of a specific statement, that such names are exempt from the relevant protective laws and regulations and therefore free for general use.
The publisher, the authors and the editors are safe to assume that the advice and information in this book are believed to be true and accurate at the date of publication. Neither the publisher nor the authors or the editors give a warranty, expressed or implied, with respect to the material contained herein or for any errors or omissions that may have been made. The publisher remains neutral with regard to jurisdictional claims in published maps and institutional affiliations.

Cover credit line: © Eoneren / Getty Images

This Palgrave Macmillan imprint is published by the registered company Springer Nature Switzerland AG.
The registered company address is: Gewerbestrasse 11, 6330 Cham, Switzerland

If disposing of this product, please recycle the paper.

Acknowledgements

Initial support for this project was received from the Portuguese Foundation for Science and Technology (FCT), the Centre for Languages, Literatures and Cultures in the Department of Languages and Cultures at the University of Aveiro, and at the Centre for Intercultural Studies, the Polytechnic University of Porto.

Although it seems obvious, the openness and helpful receptiveness to specialized academic work at Palgrave Macmillan, and in especial the kind guidance of Camille Davies and Esther Rani, should be explicitly mentioned as having provided the conditions and helpfulness that make such a collection of specialized chapters possible. To this should be added the anonymous peer reviewers who participated in shaping the collection.

Personal thanks are owed to my colleague over many years Anthony Barker, to our research partner Clara Sarmento at the Centre for Intercultural Studies in Porto, to colleague Marie-Manuelle Silva for intellectual prodding from French studies, as well as to my PhD students Edmilson Miranda Jr, Luís Branco, and André Silva for being the hard core of a stimulating research group focused on issues in popular culture, and finally to my wife Andreia Sarabando for having aided at every stage of this project.

About the Book

The initial impetus for this book came from a conference at the University of Aveiro in Portugal, with the title "Visual Storytelling: From the Mural to the Digital." In the event, almost all of the papers dealt with contemporary and recent forms of visual storytelling, there being a sense that twenty-first-century technological and social developments were unique and pressing enough that attention had to be given to current exemplifications rather than to everything from cave paintings onwards. Accordingly, it was decided to reproduce this focus by way of a selection of the papers developed into chapter-length arguments. Thanks must therefore go to all of the participants in the conference—from five continents—who contributed to the friendly and participative environment of the conference, as well as to those authors who responded to the challenge to expand their ideas into fully fledged research findings. These range from video games through several types of art practices, the use of social media, commercial movies, television programmes of more than one type, illustrated books for children, and comics. All of these cultural venues for visual storytelling will be found to be politically engaged in the sense of evidencing self-aware interventions in contemporary debates, as now typifies storytelling of all types. More surprisingly, they may all be conscripted into an argument, suggesting that the fragmentation of current cultural forms and attention spans can be seen from a different angle if we reroute the perception of fragmentation towards a vision of rhizomatic connection instead of atomization and disconnection.

Contents

1. Introduction: Visual Storytelling in the Age of the Long Fragment   1
   David Callahan

2. Forms and Order: Making the World More Just Through Video Games?   13
   David Callahan

3. Video Games as Animation: Inquiries into the Animatic Nature of Playable Images   33
   Víctor Navarro-Remesal

4. Wonder, Awe and Negative Emotions in *What Remains of Edith Finch*   55
   Bartosz Stopel

5. Look Behind You, Orpheus: Queer Archeology and Mythical Lesbians in Contemporary Film   73
   Ana Bessa Carvalho

6. "All These Things into Position": Intermedial Storytelling via Radiohead's "Street Spirit," the Novels of Ben Okri, and Feminist Dystopia   91
   Alena Zhylinskaya

7 What's the Story? How Hybrid Comics Against Gender
   Violence Rework Narrative and Support Artivism   109
   Nicoletta Mandolini

8 Voices of Graffiti in Urban Settings: Symbolic
   Contestation and Political Narratives   131
   Patrícia Oliveira, Carlos Vargas, and Cristina Montalvão
   Sarmento

9 Bourne-Again Bond: Retooling the Spy Story in the
   New Millennium   153
   Anthony Barker

10 Monsters in Animation and Related Nightmares in
   Contemporary Popular Culture   175
   Rebeca Cristina López-González

11 The Graphic Self of Public Intellectuals: Chinese
   Tiaoman as Digital Practices of Self-Representation
   on WeChat   195
   Chen Li

12 Through Etched Glass: Representing Urban Place in
   Christina Fernandez's Photographic Series *Lavanderia* 219
   Sheila Brannigan

13 The Artwork in Geological Time   245
   Roger Davis

Index   265

Notes on Contributors

Anthony Barker recently retired from the University of Aveiro, Portugal, where he had been head of its Research Centre, coordinator of the Cultural Studies research group, and director of the PhD in Cultural Studies. He has also been the president of the Portuguese Anglo-American Studies Association. His publications include edited and co-edited collections on *Europe: Fact and Fiction* (2003), *The Power and Persistence of Stereotyping* (2005), *Television, Aesthetics and Reality* (2007), *Identity and Cultural Exchange in Travel and Tourism* (2015), *Personal Narratives, Peripheral Theatres: Essays on the Great War* (2018), and *Body and Text: Cultural Transformations in New Media Environments* (2019). Recent publications include articles on television drama and comedy, and the representation of business in film culture.

Sheila Brannigan is a lecturer and PhD researcher in the Department of Modern Literatures and Cultures at NOVA University Lisbon, Portugal, after studies in the History of Art and Applied Linguistics in Middlesbrough, London, and Birmingham. Her interests centre on representations of the urban landscape in photography, with a particular focus on social values in portrayals of a place and its people. Her dissertation examines three photographers whose works pose the question of their own positionality regarding the American urban communities they photograph. She is a member of the multi-university Centre for English, Translation, and Anglo-Portuguese Studies. She is also a keen photographer of urban landscapes.

David Callahan is Associate Professor and head of English at the University of Aveiro, Portugal. Formerly Chair of the European Association for Studies on Australia, his work has mostly concentrated on postcolonial topics and appeared in journals such as *Inks: Journal of the Comics Studies Society*, *Postcolonial Studies*, *Arizona Quarterly*, and *Game Studies*, along with book chapters and books or edited books such as *Contemporary Issues in Australian Literature* (2002), *Australia: Who Cares?* (2007), *Rainforest Narratives: The Work of Janette Turner Hospital* (2009), and most recently the co-edited *Body and Text: Cultural Transformations in New Media Environments* (Springer, 2019).

Ana Bessa Carvalho is an Invited Assistant Professor in the Department of English and North American Studies at the University of Minho, Braga, Portugal, where she completed a PhD thesis in comparative literature and queer studies on representations of family-making and queer kinship in contemporary literature and photography. She is a member of the research group Gender, Arts, and Postcolonial Studies (GAPS), and of the Centre for Humanistic Studies (CEHUM) at the University of Minho. In addition, her poetry has been published in several recent anthologies.

Roger Davis is the head of English in the Department of Humanities and Social Sciences at Red Deer Polytechnic, Red Deer, Alberta, Canada. His research interests include cannibalism, dystopian literature, poetry and poetics, and academic integrity.

Chen Li is a PhD researcher in the Department of Culture Studies at Tilburg University, Netherlands. She also writes for *Diggit Magazine*, an academic platform affiliated with Tilburg University. Her current research focuses on the phenomenon of Chinese public intellectuals within contemporary digital environments, investigating how intellectuals (re)present and position themselves in digital public spheres by examining their digital practices and communicative strategies, in particular the shifting roles of public intellectuals who engage in debates encompassing gender issues, cultural heritages, and the attention economy in the context of globalization and digitalization.

Rebeca Cristina López-González is Associate Professor in the Department of the Translation and Linguistics at the University of Vigo, Galicia, Spain, after having completed a PhD in Translation and Interpreting. Her thesis deals with the dubbing of intertextual humour in commercial animated films. She has written numerous articles in national and international journals and chapters in books about children's and YA literature as well as animated film and its interrelationship with other fields such as literary translation, dubbing, and gender theories. She is a member of the research group Anglo-German Children's/YA Literature and its Translation, and collaborates with the TALIS (Teaching and Learning International Survey) research group at the University of Valencia. Her research interests are centred on specialized translation, ranging from audiovisual to economic/tourism, legal, and literary translation.

Nicoletta Mandolini is FCT (Portuguese Foundation for Science and Technology) Junior Researcher at the Centre for the Study of Communication and Society at the University of Minho, Braga, Portugal, as a member of the project "Sketch Her Story and Make It Popular: Using Graphic Narratives in Italian and Lusophone Feminist Activism Against Gender Violence" (https://www.sketchthatstory.com/). She was a post-doctoral researcher at the Catholic University of Leuven, Belgium, and did her PhD at University College Cork, Ireland. She is the author of the monograph *Representations of Lethal Gender-Based Violence in Italy Between Journalism and Literature:* Femminicidio *Narratives* (Routledge, 2021) and of numerous articles on sexist abuse in contemporary literature and media. She is a founding member of SnIF (Studying 'n Investigating Fumetti [Comics]).

Víctor Navarro-Remesal is a senior lecturer at Tecnocampus, Pompeu Fabra University, Barcelona, Spain, and a founding member of DiGRA Spain. There he teaches history of video games, cultural industries, and interactive narrative, and his research interests are games/play and cinema, Zen and slow gaming, Japanese games, and game preservation. He is the author of *Libertad dirigida: Una gramática del análisis y diseño de videojuegos* (Shangrila, 2016) and *Cine Ludens: 50 diálogos entre el juego y el cine* (Editorial UOC, 2019), as well as the editor of *Pensar el juego. 25 caminos para los game studies* (Shangrila, 2020) and *Perspectives on the European Videogame* (Amsterdam University Press, 2021). Currently, he is one of the two lead investigators of the project "Ludomythologies: Myths and Ideology in Contemporary Video Games."

Patrícia Oliveira completed her PhD in Political Science at the Institute of Social and Political Sciences, University of Lisbon (ISCSP-ULisboa), Portugal, with a dissertation entitled "Political Culture and Documentary

Film in Portugal (1974–2012)." She is a Guest Professor in the Department of Communication, Philosophy and Politics at the University of Beira Interior, Covilhã, Portugal. Since 2016, she has been vice-coordinator of the Political Observatory (http://observatoriopolitico.pt/), a member of the editorial board of the *Revista Portuguesa de Ciência Política* ("Portuguese Journal of Political Science") and a researcher at the Centre for Arts and Communication, University of the Algarve (CIAC-Ualg), Portugal.

Cristina Montalvão Sarmento is Associate Professor of Political Theory at the Institute of Social and Political Sciences, University of Lisbon (ISCSP-ULisboa), Portugal, with *aggregation in Global Studies* from the Universidade Aberta (Distance Learning University, Lisbon, Portugal); head-coordinator of the Political Observatory (http://observatoriopolitico.pt/); editorial chief of the *Revista Portuguesa de Ciência Política* ("Portuguese Journal of Political Science"); secretary-general of the International Association of Portuguese Language Universities (AULP); and vice-president of the International Association of Universities (IAU-UNESCO).

Bartosz Stopel is Associate Professor of Literary Studies at the University of Silesia, Poland. His current research focuses on cognition and emotion in the experience of narratives in various media. Recent work has been published in *The Routledge Companion to Literature and Emotion* (2022), as well as in *Projections* and the *Journal of Literary Theory*, after earlier publications on literary theory and aesthetics. His first book, *From Mind to Text* (Routledge, 2018), explores the affective underpinnings of the aesthetic interpretation of literature.

Carlos Vargas is a Visiting Professor in the Department of History at the NOVA University Lisbon, Portugal, and a member of the History, Land Use and Communities research centre (HTC) at the NOVA University Lisbon, as well as of the Functional Ecology Centre—Science for People and the Planet (CFE) at the University of Coimbra, Portugal, along with the Political Observatory, Lisbon. He holds a PhD in Political Science, specializing in public policies. His main research interests include cultural theory, cultural policies, and cultural practices in Europe and the Americas.

Alena Zhylinskaya is a PhD student in the Department of Foreign Literature at the Belarussian State University, Minsk, Belarus. In 2021 she received a scholarship from the International Visegrad Fund to conduct research at the Institute of English Studies, Jagiellonian University, Krakow, Poland. Her research interests include postcolonial Nigerian literature, the discourse of hybridity, studies on identity and nationality, and the theory of narrative.

List of Figures

Fig. 7.1	*Luchadoras* on the walls of Rome. Source: Lucha y Siesta's Facebook page: https://www.facebook.com/lucha.ysiesta/photos/2556500114628395?locale=es_LA	115
Fig. 7.2	Matrioskas made available online by *Non una di meno*. Source: *Non una di meno*'s website: https://nonunadimeno.wordpress.com/2017/03/04/matrioske-parlanti-senza-sfondo/	123
Fig. 8.1	"While art entertains, money acts." Ginjal Street, Cacilhas, Portugal. June 15, 2013. Photograph by Pedro Fidalgo	136
Fig. 8.2	"Hold on, hold on." Deutsche Bank. 100 Pascoal de Melo Street, Lisbon, Portugal. March 31, 2013. Photograph by Pedro Fidalgo	137
Fig. 8.3	"Low wages, Unemployment, Precariousness, Theft of the Christmas allowance, Increase in gas, Increase in VAT, Sacrifices, Increase in work hours, General strike, Participate!, It's for everyone." Sete Rios Train Station, Lisbon, Portugal. June 16, 2013. Photograph by Pedro Fidalgo	140
Fig. 8.4	"Solidarity to the struggle of people for dignity. After Greece comes Portugal. Everybody onto the Streets." 154 Luz Soriano Street, Lisbon, Portugal. October 4, 2012. Photograph by Pedro Fidalgo	142
Fig. 8.5	"Sold to the Troika." University City. Old Canteen main entrance, Lisbon, Portugal. June 13, 2013. Photograph by Pedro Fidalgo	143
Fig. 8.6	"Hail Markets, who art in heaven. Speculate with us consumers. From now until the hour of our death. Ah mother." 146 Luz Soriano Street, Lisbon, Portugal. October 12, 2012. Photograph by Pedro Fidalgo	147

Fig. 11.1	The map of China's fight against the pandemic (中国抗疫图鉴). Image resource: *People's Daily*, April 15, 2020. https://mp.weixin.qq.com/s/mrljz1K7-mWQvfy9ZpehVA	196
Fig. 11.2	One example of Uncle Lion in Xu's *Uncle Lion Diary*. Image resource: https://www.sohu.com/a/489190668_611314	202
Fig. 11.3	Uncle Lion observing teen idols from behind a curtain. Image resource: https://mp.weixin.qq.com/s/-uY32x9O4K3VKgWE1ZxqYQ	204
Fig. 11.4	Xu Zhiyuan speaking with teen idols on an egalitarian physical level. Image resource: https://v.qq.com/x/cover/mzc00200ql6hmqx/r32634hv8q8.html	205
Fig. 11.5	The cartoon cuteness of Uncle Lion. Image resource: https://www.sohu.com/a/489190668_611314	207
Fig. 11.6	In the text box, Uncle Lion asks his readers "who is your idol?" Image resource: https://mp.weixin.qq.com/s/-uY32x9O4K3VKgWE1ZxqYQ	211
Fig. 11.7	A photo of *Thirteen Bar*. Image resource: https://zhuanlan.zhihu.com/p/400905411	212
Fig. 11.8	The screenshots of thirteen posters posted by the WeChat account Onewaystreet on 1 September 2021. My translation is provided below each poster. Image resource: https://mp.weixin.qq.com/s/VLQEiLUCfhB3LxjIv1F_TA	213
Fig. 11.9	The promotion package of flip-flops and a book written by Xu Zhiyuan. Image resource: https://www.sohu.com/a/327613569_611314	214
Fig. 11.10	Xu Zhiyuan's style. Image resource: https://www.sohu.com/a/327613569_611314	215
Fig. 12.1	Christina Fernandez. Lavanderia #1. 2002–2003. Archival pigment print. 76.2 × 101.6 cm (30 × 40 in.) Web. Gallery Luisotti Web site. https://galleryluisotti.com/images/lavanderia-2002/ Courtesy of the artist and Gallery Luisotti, Los Angeles	222
Fig. 12.2	Christina Fernandez. Lavanderia #11. 2002–2003. Archival pigment print. 76.2 × 101.6 cm (30 × 40 in.). Gallery Luisotti Web site. https://galleryluisotti.com/images/lavanderia-2002/ Courtesy of the artist and Gallery Luisotti, Los Angeles	223
Fig. 12.3	Christina Fernandez. Lavanderia #6. 2002–2003. Archival pigment print. 76.2 × 101.6 cm (30 × 40 in.). Gallery Luisotti Web site. https://galleryluisotti.com/images/lavanderia-2002/ Courtesy of the artist and Gallery Luisotti, Los Angeles	224

Fig. 12.4	Christina Fernandez. Lavanderia #2. 2002–2003. Archival pigment print. 76.2 × 101.6 cm (30 × 40 in.). Gallery Luisotti Web site. https://galleryluisotti.com/images/lavanderia-2002/ Courtesy of the artist and Gallery Luisotti, Los Angeles	225
Fig. 12.5	Ray Torres of Victory Outreach program speaking with youths in East Los Angeles. August 9 1976. Photograph by Gary Ayala from black and white 35mm negative. University of California, Los Angeles, Library, Department of Special Collections Web site. https://digital.library.ucla.edu/catalog/ark:/21198/zz0002r153 The Regents of the University of California. Licensed under Creative Commons Attribution 4.0 International License. https://creativecommons.org/licenses/by/4.0/	239

CHAPTER 1

Introduction: Visual Storytelling in the Age of the Long Fragment

David Callahan

ACCELERATION

We live in a visual age, but we also live in a narrative age. Despite doomsday warnings that attention spans have shrunk down to the size of a TikTok video, there is also a widespread appetite for storytelling that offers immersive intensity over much longer periods. The two tendencies are related through phenomena such as extremely fast-paced movies, as series that are so involving we might consume them in a weekend, as video games designed in such a way that we cannot stop playing them, or as the micro-narratives on social media platforms that quickly ramify via others' comments into vast, multi-faceted processing of some event or feeling, usually accompanied by or launching off an image or images.

Counterintuitively to the generalized fear that our attention span is now hopelessly shredded by this acceleration and the media-hopping promoted by the ease of digital access, the proposal here is that it is longer storytelling experiences that now dominate, even if their consumption is

---

D. Callahan (✉)
Department of Languages & Cultures, University of Aveiro,
Aveiro, Portugal
e-mail: callahan@ua.pt

© The Author(s), under exclusive license to Springer Nature
Switzerland AG 2024
D. Callahan (ed.), *Visual Storytelling in the 21st Century*,
https://doi.org/10.1007/978-3-031-65487-9_1

fragmented across multiple sessions and forms. We now dip in and out of streaming services, for instance, or are constantly faced with our individual decisions about just how many of the 30,374 comments to read after watching or listening to a video on YouTube (the number is the real number attached to just one version of Mazzy Star's "Fade Into You"), not to mention the high-octane challenge to our concentration embodied in the transmedial iterations of a -verse such as the Marvel Cinematic Universe (now the MCU multiverse).

While fragmentation is an acknowledged feature of our attention ecology, perhaps the suggestion that the fragments are longer than expected, and may even be very long, may surprise. One reason that we cannot focus in such a concentrated form is supposed to be the fact that the visual beckons to us everywhere and ceaselessly in contemporary life, or so we are led to believe. This sounds like the sort of thing that might not occasion argument, and yet a moment's reflection will lead us to realize that the visual has always been everywhere for most people. The fact that there are advertisements assailing us wherever we are, that the vast majority of us live our lives looking at screens, and that our daily appearance is so overwhelmingly important that perceived failure can lead to permanent anxiety and suicide, none of this proves that life is any more visual now than at any stage in history. Most of us spend our days looking at things from the moment we open our eyes in the morning until the moment we close them at night, as human beings always have. Looking at your iPhone is no more visual than looking at the fields as you till them, or looking at a conveyor belt from morning to night, or reading a book for that matter.

Yet what we look at and how we relate to it have changed. And as John Berger put it on the first page of his classic *Ways of Seeing*, "The relation between what we see and what we know is never settled" (Berger 1972, 7). Reading the movement of bison across the prairie is not the same as reading the stream of responses to a video we have placed on YouTube, but in both cases it is a changing process, every minute, every hour, every day, adjusting to the conditions, responding to what came before and planning for what we think will come after. Our seeing of whatever kind is modulated via other concerns and priorities. We rarely see anything in isolation, even if we think we do. Apart from what peripheral vision is adding, or announcing, or discounting from what we think we are seeing front on, our focus is filtered by what we had been expecting, or not, what has just happened to us, what we want, and what we believe about the world and what is important. Fragmentation is and has always been a constituent part of human perception. On the other hand, haptically, that we now look down more than up cannot be irrelevant; we spend more time looking at screens than at other people, or landscape, or the stars. Not to own a smartphone these days is not merely to indicate a consumer choice but to wield a philosophy of life, one that can be responded to as a sign of quaint old-fashionedness or as a belligerent challenge to others' very identities. When Guy Debord referred at the dawn of the internet age to "the true depth of society's dependence on images" (1995, 140), it was where the images were threatening to assail us from that exercised him, for while human beings may have always been looking at things, now what we look at is increasingly inflected by commercial imperatives and delivered to us whether we want it or not. Despite the venality at the heart of this summoning of our attention, the intense engagement with the visual via technology also has storytelling as one of its core experiences, in a way that looking at the fields or the sea or the clouds generally does not. And stories are something that attempt to capture our natural tendency to ramble and stray.

Since *Star Wars* appeared in 1977 the visual has changed in another way as well, in that the response to the movie has ushered in the impossible images of science fiction as the dominant story mode of the present, but also as the dominant visual mode. *Star Wars* (now entitled *Star Wars: Episode IV–A New Hope*) may be considered as a key starting point for this process on account of the then startling possibilities of computer-generated moving images. The bar scene in the Mos Eisley Cantina that takes place relatively early in the film, filled with what were in 1977 astoundingly well represented aliens of different physiognomies, was a magical, wondrous experience on the big screen, at the time somehow a step further on in the contract that the cinema had and has had with illusion ever since George Mèlies's 1902 expeditions to the moon. Nowadays, we expect the wonders of illusion in our entertainment, and yet, seemingly out of nowhere, the ease with which everyone can now produce visual illusion threatens (once again) the very relationship we have with the visual as some sort of guarantee of truth. The term "eye witness" is central in the story of "what really happened" that we seek in the justice system and in the news item, the documentary, and the autobiography. But it is also inflected by the invention of photography, a medium that fixed "what really happened" we used to believe, and somehow still do believe. Sheila Brannigan outlines here how a series of photographs of a launderette, notwithstanding its seeming old-fashionedness, continues to invoke this relationship, one in which the cumulative power of many single images builds up a trustworthy story of the lives of a community, much as photography has done over the last hundred years. Despite the centrality of editing and altering procedures throughout the entire history of the development of photography with respect to determining what would be captured and what would not be, the profusion of ways to alter the image in the present is rarely seen as a type of continuity in our relation to the recorded image but rather as a radical departure from the contract that we imagined we had with the results of mechanical capture.

A single photograph is apparently a static image, which may seem quaint in an age in which interest appears to be focused on moving images, from streaming services to TikTok videos to YouTube. Storytelling protocols in general have become accelerated across all media. The sheer speed of contemporary films makes movies from the past, as well as movies from film cultures outside Hollywood, seem frustratingly slow. Video games often involve such a demand on response times that one needs a fighter pilot's reflexes to cope. And it is not only in visual media whose time frame is imposed on us, as it were, as an examination of fiction in print reveals related developments that have accompanied the acceleration visible in filmed media. Novels now have much bigger print than in the past. This means that we can finish a page much more quickly and feel that the story must be engaging us because we are proceeding through it so quickly. This sensation is contributed to by the much shorter chapters that characterize so many contemporary works of fiction. To the short chapters can be added a division into sub-sections so that we are constantly being fed the dopamine reward of achievement: we have finished a sub-section, we have finished a chapter, and we have finished a part. This speed relationship is articulated in the first instance by the visual encounter with printed stories in the form of the larger average book size to accommodate these spatial changes.

Even in academic writing this division into smaller sections has made inroads. We are enjoined now to develop arguments via sub-sections, and there is no doubt that this has made reading some types of academic prose easier, even if their storytelling pleasures are few. All of this would seem to reinforce contemporary observations, not to say fears, that our ability to concentrate has become so weakened that we can only be counted on to focus on anything for a brief period at a time. Like any widespread notion, this observation is not coming from nowhere, but it is part of academic work's brief to see whether there might be more ways to configure accepted notions than those that appear obvious. The proposal here is that current visual, but also other forms of storytelling, can be taxonomized as what can be called the long fragment, a seeming oxymoron but once that seems apt for the ways we interface with just about everything in the twenty-first century, in continuum with how we have always looked at, watched, and seen things.

The Long Fragment

Contemporary developments are actually producing ever longer products in the case of many of the most high-profile media. Still, it can be seen that how we consume them ends up breaking them into smaller units of our own devising. For example, movies are often longer, and even much longer, than in the past, but then they are now more frequently consumed at home, where they may be paused, for half an hour or a week or whatever, watched over several smaller sessions to suit our timetable or our mood. This phenomenon is often not seen as positive. For sociologist Rogers Brubaker the "frictionless hyper-accessibility of superabundant digital content tends to diminish the value and significance of any given cultural object. And it tends to diminish our investment in any particular object" (Brubaker 2023, 84). While it is true that our attention span is being curated via smaller and smaller units and sub-units, in other respects these smaller units are woven together or congregate with other units across the same or different media, and also across time. The now well-known phenomenon of transmedial connection clearly has its basis in commercial intent that our attention be retained across a series, across a platform, and across various iterations of a story or theme. That is, that we not be sent careering away elsewhere, restlessly in search of an elusive hit that contributes to "a crisis of desire" (Brubaker 2023, 84), but that our captured concentration alights on related matter, within the same platform.

The supreme example of the conflation of length and fragmentation is that of the video game, the principal commercial storytelling medium of our time. Some video games can take a length of time that seriously challenges the claim that nobody can maintain their attention these days for longer than the time to post a photo of a muffin or dash off an emotional reaction phrase before rushing off to append likes and emoticons to similarly trivial images and opinions. Open-world games can take well over a hundred hours, depending on one's skill and completionist determination. For those who are not familiar with long narrative video games, it is possible to complete the main narrative without bothering with all the side quests, errands, and the like, so that there may be enormous differences between the investment of time in a video game on the part of any two players. But whether you are the sort who attempts to find every collectable item (despite their total irrelevance to the main narrative) or who wants to follow the main story without too many distractions, it does not matter how long the game could potentially be, it is broken up into subunits that supply constant challenges and rewards, from the minor to the significant. At times, game makers' perception of how little we will be able to attend to a video game unless we are bombarded with in-game rewards and achievements can become frankly irritating, to the extent that the relentless interruptions to forward progress by the chance to add this resource, collect that item, improve this skill can drive one away. I am thinking of my experience of the video game *Yonder: The Cloud Catcher Chronicles* (Pridefull Sloth, 2017), which I abandoned after a short while, screaming with surfeit, as I was repeatedly enjoined to accumulate this, find that, pick up something else, and interact with whatever. Perhaps the company's name should have alerted me. If the game gets the balance right, however, it can offer a flow of narrative, challenge, and reward that, although made up of longer or shorter fragments, can overwhelm any tendency to jump and skitter away in search of other pleasures. An example of the latter in my case would be *The Last of Us Part II* (Naughty Dog, 2020).

The video game world, however, has far less attention uniformity than other entertainment environments. Even if we remove pattern-matching and simple repetition mobile games from the mix, there are games that take a very short time, such as the much-praised visual narrative *Florence* (Annapurna, 2018), and others that routinely take up to a hundred hours, even for proficient players, such as *Elden Ring* (FromSoftware, 2022). Lists of the longest games of all time will nevertheless discriminate between completing the main storyline and completing that plus all side quests, stories within stories often, which can lengthen one's engagement substantially. The increasingly bloated story environments of some video games have led one of the *Guardian*'s video game columnists, Keith Stuart, to predict that

> the basic economics of the games industry are going to tempt more developers into thinking about creating shorter, more intense arcade-style adventures. It can take up to six years to make an epic open-world game now, and

with workers unionising and fighting back against crunch culture, that figure could double, with a huge addition to costs. (Stuart 2023)

As can be seen in the cluster of three chapters dealing with video games in this volume, there is no need to focus on deliberately massive games to explore aspects of video games and our experience of them that are just as prevalent. One of these is the overlooked fact that they are almost entirely all forms of animation, which, among other features outlined in detail by Víctor Navarro-Remesal, has the effect of binding extremely different games together in a visual continuum that is far from epitomizing fragmentation but rather a gigantic riff on our relationship with illusion and visual playfulness. David Callahan's chapter attempts to outline how taking a very different approach to grouping aspects of our relationship to video games, derived from Caroline Levine's *Forms* (2015), can free up considerations of how they patch into the rest of our ethical and procedural lives. Bartosz Stopel's paean to one of the most visually and narratively intriguing of the century's games so far, the compact wonder of brief stories nested within other stories that is *What Remains of Edith Finch* (Giant Sparrow, 2017), deals with a stunning visual essay on how fragments are never just themselves. They might be traced through wildly different scenarios and visual narrative devices while being closely related at the same time, in this case through being the stories of the doomed individual members of a numerous family.

In the realm of shorter-form stories than those of movies or video games, streaming services have now become central to the investment of our time in leisure. An episode of a series is shorter than a movie, true, but to watch a series clearly takes longer to consume than a movie, although it can hardly be considered short-form storytelling. Moreover, streaming services cannot be relied on to provide a series lasting many years, unless they are hosting a series made by a regular channel. *The Walking Dead*, for instance, went for eleven seasons and can be seen on Netflix where I live, but it was made by cable channel AMC. A series such as *Blind Spot* on HBO has to be considered an anomaly with its 22–23 episodes for its first four seasons, as these days most series will have a season, or even an entire run, of eight to ten episodes, as Stuart notes in his surmise that video games have reached their upper limit for length. It has also been observed of Netflix that they will rarely prolong a series beyond three seasons and can be quite ruthless even with highly rated series (*Vinyl*, with its one season, comes to mind). While nothing will probably ever again compete with such legends of the small screen as *Coronation Street* (broadcast continuously since 1960) or *General Hospital* (since 1963), watching an eight-episode series does not really seem to be an activity for the attention challenged. Not many contemporary novels take us eight hours to read these days. Indeed, while we can break up our viewing of a series over many sessions, the phenomenon of binge-watching rather suggests the opposite: that we have been captured by the story into a much longer investment of time than almost everything else we do with our day. Watching a series in a day or a weekend seems the opposite of a fragmented attention span. Sometimes though we do the opposite, and it might take us a few sessions to watch one short episode. Why it is evidence of a splintered attention span that we might break up our viewing of an episode in this way seems strange, when nobody thinks that breaking up one's reading of a novel demonstrates an addlepated inability to digest anything whole.

Finally, the well-known transmedial nature of contemporary storytelling (see Elleström 2021; Grampp 2023), in which we can connect and interface across media, actually increases rather than diminishes the need for attention. Following the MCU multiverse requires a high-level ability to hold many storylines in one's head, running over a complicated timeline, and involving many many named characters, often with more than one identity depending on context. For the really adept and willing to put in even more time, there are also series to follow (e.g., *Agents of S.H.I.E.L.D*), while making the connections to the characters and narrative lines as developed in comics is only for those with a truly superior ability to hold a bewildering number of stories in one's head, including stories with alternative versions and that have been developing and ramifying over decades. Popular culture as attention corrosive? Only for those who do not have the attention span to engage with it.

For the more determined or attentive, reverberations can be found in all directions, connecting such things as television series, unexpected novels, and songs, all from different countries and even continents, as Alena Zhilinskaya evidences. Her chain of texts is only one possibility, for by implication many potential networks exist, and this has long been known in literary and new historical studies. The onslaught of available material and media gives the impression of splintering not just our references but our ability to hold on to any of them for very long. On reflection, though, the acceleration and profusion is not so very different from Modernist literary proliferation of allusion and collage as integral to and productive of our relationship with the world. Except that now the allusions and collages are made up of ever larger and larger sources, long fragments it may be.

Conclusion

The visual storytelling that is such a strong feature of contemporary life is also a feature largely experienced digitally, in one form or another. For most people everything comes through their laptops, their tablets, and/or their phones. It is easy to skip from one streaming service to another, then to play a game, then to follow a thread on one or more social media or general sites. It sounds like a nightmare for those people for whom everyone used to spend their days reflectively reading Tacitus, Flaubert, Virginia Woolf, or Toni Morrison, pausing every now and then to consult Hegel or Simone de Beauvoir. A light entertainment break might be taken to watch an Ingmar Bergman movie or attend an opera. Is it possible, though, to see contemporary engagement with the panoply of options as a knitting together across time rather than as a kaleidoscopic fragmentation? The chapters in this volume see all media phenomena as connected rather than isolated, even legacy media such as general release movies, as in Anthony Barker's contribution, are very knowingly in conversation with related exemplars of their genre, as classical film studies has always underlined. Ana Bessa Carvalho further exemplifies how two high-profile recent films dealing with lesbian experience feel the need to examine and invoke the past, partially in order to process the guilt and shame that have accompanied lesbian desire throughout most of European history. Current freedom from this guilt and shame for some is not just something to be unconcernedly enjoyed for the more attentive to history. Desire and satisfied desire resonate against a long history of repression, secrecy, and punishment, transforming each film into an invitation to historicize, to dig like a paleontologist, and to perceive individual experience and its representation as part of a vast rhizome of experience in which each film is one more long fragment.

Nicoletta Mandolini's feminist artivists in Italy have broken down the resources of comics into shorter forms of protest, but they are connected across city spaces in the service of the larger narrative of political protest, with the hope that they will be encountered in more than one location and stitched together by their readers, who thus become spatial participants in keeping the protest energies alive. Patrícia Oliveira, Carlos Vargas, and

Clara Montalvão Sarmento reinforce this political dimension of street art and graffiti, in this case with reference to anger and frustration over austerity measures in Portugal imposed by the IMF. Given that we now live in an environment in which a minuscule number of tech companies want us to see the stories they want us to see, in the way they want us to see them, we need to realize that however much their inventions and processes attempt to narrow us down to the tracks along which they want us to run, there are still venues, such as the street, where they cannot control either the narratives or who sees them. For street art to function more effectively, it needs to be broken up over space, so that it is harder to miss. In this case, there is visual fragmentation, but this only serves to solidify the story of the high capitalist imposition of suffering that is being repeated throughout the city (both the story and the suffering). A concentrated, unified venue for this story would dilute it and restrict it.

Visual media are accordingly more tasked with embodying identities and the representation of ethically meaningful scripts than ever before. Chen Li gives the lively example of knowing Chinese media figure Xu Zhiyuan, who fragments himself into differing persona according to the media avenue being used, whether a type of comic strip on the internet known as *tiaoman*, posted on social media, or in more conventional venues such as interviews, chat shows, and the like. By setting up this contrast, he implicitly asks observers to consider the malleability of a public persona, and, perhaps in buried fashion, the fact that what we see is never unmediated.

Lest we become too carried away, the long fragment may be a convocation to connect, to extend, to deepen, but if the fragments are conjugated out of superficial, limiting, or even dangerous raw materials, their structural connectivity says nothing about how socially helpful they might be. This is one of the reasons why analysis and evaluation of the stories and images that circulate and jostle for our attention needs to be ongoing and critical. This book itself could be considered a long fragment, or made up of long fragments, as it joins with many other assessments of the stories that delight and assail us. Rebeca López-González here writes of how one of the uses of stories for children has been closing down the psychic uses of stories of monsters as traditionally articulated. The development in the direction of withholding fear and danger from children is understandable, but symbolizing the sources of fears was precisely one of the uses of certain types of stories. Her chapter accordingly takes an interventive stance, opposing this tendency. Roger Davis's environmentally engaged visual productions, on the other hand, imagine stories from beyond the end of human time, when the possibility of human beings improving anything will have vanished. To tell such stories obviously asks questions about what appropriate strategies might be, given the impulse to tell a story that should be more than cautionary for those who are alive now, and that might also well remain when all humans have disappeared, but to what end?

Precisely for all of these reasons, our relation to the visual stories through which we approach, and defy, the realities around us, making new realities in the process that then become part of the reality around us themselves, all of this means that there remains a need to continually interrogate new examples of storytelling forms, new cases of the uses of stories in differing formats, and new stories in general. This perpetual need is what this volume aims to respond to by way of its mixture of contemporary storytelling modes, seen here generally optimistically and enthusiastically as progressively engaged with ongoing debates, as well as deputizing a wide range of strategies and media in order to invite people's attention to issues and ethical itineraries, not simply to get a like or a tick in a world of fissiparous attention spans. If the stories we tell do not help us to see otherwise and change constructively, then we probably do deserve to go the way of the dodo.

REFERENCES

Berger, John. 1972. *Ways of Seeing*. Harmondsworth: Penguin.
Brubaker, Rogers. 2023. *Hyperconnectivity and Its Discontents*. Durham, NC: Duke University Press.
Debord, Guy. 1995. *The Society of the Spectacle*. Trans. D. Nicholson-Smith. New York: Zone Books.
Elleström, Lars, ed. 2021. *Beyond Media Borders, Volume 2: Intermedial Relations Among Multimodal Media*. Cham, Switzerland: Palgrave Macmillan.
Grampp, Sven. 2023. Serial Games in a Transmedial World: A Typology for the Digital Age. In *Narratives Crossing Boundaries: Storytelling in a Transmedial and Transdisciplinary Context*, ed. Joachim Friedmann, 121–147. Bielefeld: Transcript.
Levine, Caroline. 2015. *Forms: Whole, Rhythm, Hierarchy, Network*. Princeton: Princeton University Press.
Stuart, Keith. 2023. Pushing Buttons: Why I'm Mourning the Death of the True Arcade Game. *The Guardian*. September 27. https://www.theguardian.com/games/2023/sep/27/pushing-buttons-video-game-arcades. Accessed 25 Nov 2023.

CHAPTER 2

Forms and Order: Making the World More Just Through Video Games?

David Callahan

INTRODUCTION

In her widely noticed book, *Forms: Whole, Rhythm, Hierarchy, Network*, Caroline Levine begins by claiming that "hierarchies of value" concerning "unjust arrangements of power" (Levine 2015, xii–xiii) are embodied in creative forms. As a consequence, to think about the forms of artworks is also to think about these arrangements of power, and not simply to consider abstruse questions of genre or the history of forms over time. Levine is a literary scholar and has nothing to say about video games—which many video games scholars might argue is a good thing too—but her speculations about forms as embodying morality implicitly ask questions about whether video games could be brought into such a discussion. Throughout the book her examples of forms are extremely varied after all, from bureaucratic procedures to laws about what can be classified as art, from television series to canonical literature, so that in principle her observations can be extended to any act or object that can be said to have a form.

D. Callahan (✉)
Department of Languages & Cultures, University of Aveiro, Aveiro, Portugal
e-mail: callahan@ua.pt

© The Author(s), under exclusive license to Springer Nature Switzerland AG 2024
D. Callahan (ed.), *Visual Storytelling in the 21st Century*,
https://doi.org/10.1007/978-3-031-65487-9_2

This chapter will attempt to explore the usefulness or otherwise of Levine's categories to storytelling video games, particularly given the fact that power and morality are not only central to all stories but often invoked in outsiders' vision of what video games are or do as cultural experiences. What I mean by this are two things: (1) a great deal of academic research into storytelling video games in particular is composed of representation studies, and contemporary representation studies focus insistently on such things as gender, ethnicity, history, trauma, and the asymmetries of power in general. In addition, a great deal of informal comment about video games is also addressed to these questions of representation, in somewhat less decorous language than that employed in academia. And (2), when non-gamers talk about video games their terms of reference are frequently connected to their fears—or indeed their rock-solid belief—that video games are bad for you, bad for society, bad as play and bad as morality. And part of what makes them bad is simply that they are video games. For this type of commentary, video games as a technological form are bad, as it appears to be a form that enslaves those who engage with it and provides an experience that, whatever the game, takes time away from other experiences that are supposedly more morally uplifting and beneficial.

Levine does not claim that the creative forms she examines are good for us as forms, or maybe good for everyone, just that they are not simply a background shell to the narratives or ideas or images of works of creativity. "It is the work of form to make order" she says, "[a]nd this means that forms are the stuff of politics" (Levine 2015, 3). When she says "form" she means to destabilize the conventional ways in which this word is used, ways usually derived from genre studies and art history and its conventions. What Levine means by forms is not at all the type of classification that the word immediately suggests, but before we get to what she does mean, even in the more conventional activity of ascribing labels to the formal properties of a creative object, video games operate wildly differently from other storytelling arts.

Something that characterizes commentary on video games is the very different environment of what are considered their forms in this conventional sense. Almost absent are terms we might recognize from not just art history or literary studies but film studies and any other area of visual studies as well. It is not impossible to find that such and such a video game is a bildungsroman, such as *The Legend of Zelda: Ocarina of Time* (Michael James 2021), or that the latest megaproduction is epic, such as *Horizon: Forbidden West* (Wilson 2022; albeit not that it is "*an* epic"), but these are not at all the usual organizing forms through which video game players recognize what they enjoy. The instability and arguments that surround how we classify video games relate in part to the newness of the medium in historical terms, in part to the fact that it is connected to technological developments that we know are constantly evolving, and in part, well, they reproduce our earnest attempts to classify whatever we come into contact with. The terminological situation is also connected to the multiple forms of different types that intersect and combine in a video game, to the extent that labelling this plurality is a shorthand way of convoking a more precise community than do the more limited and sedimented genre forms applied to most books. And yet to say that "video game," tout court, is a form is to refer not to the visual object but to how we access it, via a technological device. It is no more than to say that another well-known story form is "book."

Video games are often said to be things that are recognizable from other creative arts, such as adventure narratives, or science fiction, but the initial starting point for classifying a video game is its gameplay. To say that a game is a science fiction game, for example, does not tell us whether it might provide the sort of experience we enjoy when we play games. There are in fact few equivalents to most video game categories. Such terms as a role-playing game (which itself has different definitions), or a platformer, or a sandbox game, not to mention a roguelike or a soulsborne or a metroidvania,[1] do not clearly reference a game's storytelling aspect or its visual style. Moreover, they are just starter labels. A video game might be termed something along the lines of a Gothic survival-horror action-adventure role-playing game. Perhaps the comparison with respect to genre names should be kept within the bounds of video games and therefore made with other types of games rather than other types of media, but this chapter is not out to solve the verbal and sub-cultural wonders of the

---

[1] Metroidvania games are a subgenre of action-adventure and platformer video games alluding to two iconic video game franchises, *Metroid* and *Castlevania*. Overall, these are often 2D games where players have to explore a relatively large map, instead of progressing through linear levels, but that hardly clears things up. In a Roguelike, from the game *Rogue*, when your avatar dies you have to start over from some distant starting point, unlike most contemporary games, that do not punish the player so severely. A Soulsborne is a challenging third-person action game that relies on lengthy combat, experience points that are lost upon death, and a loose narrative structure. They also tend to be set in dark, oppressive worlds. The name conflates *Bloodborne* and *Demon's Soul*, although many think the latter part of the word references the iconically difficult *Dark Souls* games.

attribution of game forms of such types. It can generally be agreed that video games can be different enough among themselves for people to discriminate among them and arrange them in groups together, but at this point I am going to go on to explore whether Levine's very different sorts of categories make any sense for video games, however they are labelled.

Levine's categories are even less genre types than the labels for video games provided above, but rather the overarching terms: Wholes, Rhythms, Hierarchies and Networks. This has the virtue of treating the same things from different angles, rather than just putting something in its box and saying why it belongs there, and that other things belong in other boxes. Instead of supposedly having this or that form, it can be seen that every cultural product relates, at first sight, to all of these formal categories in some way or ways. Every story is a Whole in some way, even if it is open-ended; every story has a certain Rhythm, or perhaps rhythms in the plural is truer to how narratives move; every story embodies Hierarchies of different types, among the characters and the values they appear to embody, for example, and every story is inserted into hierarchies of value among other stories of the same type and among cultural products in general; and the plot of every story can be considered as a sort of Network of relations that explore the relations among people and in society and among cultural flows. By investigating how video games relate to these concepts is to bring them in with other things that human beings make and do, as opposed to considering them hermetic and alien to those who do not play them.

Wholes

Starting with the notion of a Whole is to encounter a variation on a concept that was exploded by poststructuralism: works are not self-contained and entire, but leaking and multifarious. This is not just a matter of every reader bringing contexts to the encounter that exceed what the text's makers imagined, but a positive characteristic of the human potential to defy "the whole project of Western philosophy," grounded for Derrida on decisions about "what properly belongs and what can be expelled or abjected" (Levine 2015, 25). The observation that written texts were not in fact well-wrought urns or masterful unities became a battleground between traditionalists and enthusiasts for "theory" from the 1970s onward, the latter achieving a hard-fought victory only over many years in semiotics and cultural studies and related areas. In video game studies it has always been obvious that games are not tidy wholes, given that every player's experience can be so very different, much more obviously than that every reader's experience of a narrative will be different. Video games could be said to be the contemporary art that most explodes the notion of creative products being Wholes in any stable way.

Despite this theoretical revolution, for some the suspicion still remains that texts are bounded and therefore there are illicit ways to read a literary story. In my classes I use an example of an interpretation by a South African reader of William Blake's "A Sick Rose," written in 1824, as being about HIV.[2] Before tossing this example out to the students, we have talked about how texts belong principally to their readers, of which the author is one, albeit a highly specialized one. Several contemporary creative figures are quoted supporting this idea, from Abdulrazak Gurnah to David Lynch. Students are receptive to the idea, thrilled to be licensed to move away from the authoritarian simplifications forced on them at high school. But when confronted with the example of the South African reader of Blake's short poem, they are not so sure. It does not seem right; nobody had heard of HIV when Blake wrote, so reading its presence into "The Sick Rose" seems to go too far, even if it does make the poem come alive for that reader. Perhaps the situation is not so binary after all, and sociohistorical knowledge enters the picture alongside the relations of affect that readers have with texts. The problem then becomes: how much of such knowledge is necessary or valuable before it starts taking on authority to arbitrate over the "real meaning" of a text, deadening the possibility of personal relationships of readers with whatever they are contacting with? If this knowledge is necessary or beneficial, and it comes from outside the text, then a text cannot be a bounded whole in and by itself. It requires input, or in a milder form, input will help to make our relation with a text richer and more subtle.

With a video game there is no option. Without the player's input there will be no game. Right from the start the player sets up parameters to suit their preferences, including such major choices as the level of difficulty of the challenges that the game will throw at us or sometimes whether our avatar will be a man or a woman (and what they look like). The Whole of the game is immediately quite different for every player even before they have got past the preface, so to speak, to the extent that it can possess

---

[2] The example is drawn from Myles Holloway, Deirdre Byrne and Michael Titlestad, *Love, Power and Meaning*, Cape Town: Oxford University Press, 2001: 22–29.

quite different aspects between one player and another. Once I was playing a sequence of the game *Far Cry V* (2018) with my son, who was living in a different city. In this sequence, in which my son had to achieve a certain task with another player (me) in order to attain a particular trophy, my avatar would join up with his and we would tackle the challenge together on our separate screens in different cities. My avatar duly travelled to where he was, and suddenly his urgent voice came over the headphones, "Dad, are you a black woman?" I had been playing by myself and had not thought to explain that when I have a choice, I play in a form different to myself, the motivation for which is something of a mystery. As can be seen, this is radically different to a personal interaction with a poem. The fact that in the language of gaming it is common to slip between talking of one's avatar in the first person provides yet another challenge to the idea of a video game being a Whole in a traditional sense.

For a game, in fact, there really is no way to illicitly interact with it, although there are certainly bitter arguments over the interpretations of stories articulated by games. In addition to this type of interpretative experience, common to all stories, a game possesses the very different context of its technology inviting us to explore how we can dynamically, and physically, interact with it, and this experience is part of what it means for us, differently to our interaction with a book. Anyone whose knowledge of hardware and software enables them to seriously subvert a game's rules via the phenomenon known as the speedrun and finish it in an absurdly fast time—even missing out most of the game—is good-humouredly admired. It is respected if anyone can uncover aspects of the game's affordances that permit counterplay, "action taken in games that are within the scope of the designed rules of the game but were not intended to exist or be a significant element of play" (Apperley 2010, 140). Anyone who can proceed through a game without using what it is expected that every player will use is not thought to have failed at experiencing the game "correctly" but is approvingly considered to have revealed possibilities to the rest of us, such as the player who supposedly played the whole of *The Last of Us* without using a gun (except where it is enforced; when the character we are playing as, Ellie, is in a building with the non-playable character David soon after their first encounter, the game apparently forces us to use a gun). Even if this playthrough is an urban legend, it calls forth approbation and a sense of the expanded dimensions of the game, of the "Whole" that we perceived possessing the potential to spill out of what we thought we knew.

Storytelling games have beginnings and ends, so they are wholes in that sense, but the notion that their form patrols "what properly belongs and what can be expelled or abjected" (Levine 2015, 25) is at the very least diluted by their inherent characteristic as ontologically incomplete, achieving a type of wholeness only in individual experience. A hesitant extrapolation could be that video games strongly resist the notion of Wholes as defined, as outside us, and that if this fact is reflected upon, this is morally and socially healthy as it opens up to arguments about the interaction of individuals, groups and supposed cultures as being focused on particular experiences in individual time and not on a fixed and eternal ontological Being. "Being" in this latter sense would mean essentialistic things such as: Germans are X, women are Y, black people are Z, liberals are A, bisexuals are C and so on. Wholes, in other words, that tempting form that so many discourses lazily perceive as a healthy goal in the form of the "whole" person. This challenge to the notion of Wholes would mean asserting not that *Tomb Raider* is X, but rather that my experience of *Tomb Raider* was Y; what was yours? Alas, while this looks good on paper and does correspond to many people's conversations about video games, it is too much to expect that it can fight effectively against the rooted habit of reducing things and people and cultures to their supposed Identity instead of to our Experience of them. Video game forums are full of people angrily telling everyone else what a video game is "really," what it is "really" about, what is "really" bad about it and so on. This provides a chastening lesson, yet another one, that the putatively ethical-behaviour-enhancing aspects of creative arts and stories, along with academic deputizing of them in the service of a more positive relationship with ourselves, with each other and with the world, runs up against precisely the stubbornly hard-wired categorizations that Levine unpacks.

Rhythm

Levine's second category is Rhythm, countering the tendency to privilege spatiality in the approach to creative forms, a tendency inherited from an emphasis on creative forms as something we observe from the position of having consumed them, looking back at them or looking at them from above as, well, wholes. But our initial experience of any story is one of unknowing and of experiencing a time-bound form as we go through it, as reader-response theory pointed out, considerations that tend to be relegated to the background in our critical reflections on our relation to texts. What is the perspective to privilege? That in which we have finished the text and are looking back at it, or that in which we are in the middle of it, not knowing what is coming round the corner? The latter reproduces the form of our life, but who is to say that mimetically mapping onto the time of our lives is what we want or "should get" from creative forms? It may be through their defiance of the fact that we do not know the end of our lives or the narrative our lives will seem to have to observers when we have gone that we get the satisfactions we enjoy from completed narratives. In the case of a video game there is clearly a rhythm to our temporal experience of them, once again one which differs according to our interests and skill but also one that is imposed by the affordances of the game. In a book, or in the way we consume films and television nowadays through technologies we can pause, fast forward, etc., if we are not engaged we can jump forward, skip sections and go right to the end. In a game, unless we are highly skilled technologically, we cannot. We have to respond to at least the central challenges the game presents us with. Games tend to offer us assistance through options to define a difficulty level, to have useful items and locations visually highlighted, to make it easier to aim, move, or see and so forth, but we will still have to achieve X or Y in order to move forward. We cannot simply fast forward or flick through a few pages if we feel like it. The challenges of games and their rhythms—the frequency with which different types of challenges occur and the length of time they interrupt the principal storyline—are centrally bound up with a player's experience of a game's narrative.

Levine's example of Rhythm actually has to do not so much with the modulations of individual creative works but with institutions: the rhythms institutions impose on how we process things, the disciplining rhythms of academic years, semesters, assessment, lessons and their implications: the size of tasks we can ask students to carry out, or ourselves for that matter, a work rhythm that determines choices and priorities, and whose ultimate structuring source is the time we have allotted to us to live (even if we can never know how much that is). This is echoed in the forms used by writers in her view: the rhythms incorporated in literary work comprise a "struggle to impose temporal order" (Levine 2015, 79). To the extent that every form that comes to an end imposes a time-bound order to its imagined reality, then games too impose an order on the flow.[3] Any imposed order

---

[3] There is at least one famous example of a video game that is infinite: *No Man's Sky* (Hello Games, UK, 2016).

could however be seen as a problem: as a restriction, a limitation or a homogenization. In such a view, only a certain amount of disorder and flow best represent resistance to hierarchy and the falsely consoling structures of tidy structures. Levine sensibly points out that extrapolating some sort of dominating hegemony from the rhythms of a work of art is to fail obtusely to recognize that works of art, institutions and work patterns "do not work together, and so in the end are not able to impose a single coherent order on experience" (Levine 2015, 80–81). One way of rephrasing this could be to say that intersectionality operates here as in all social relations, to the extent that rhythms are always already syncopated and unruly.

What institutional rhythms, then, might video games modulate? Here, there is an obvious and growing context: that of the widespread realization that making video games in the largest and most famous companies is to be subjected to a toxic workplace culture in which the creative gains perceived in the finished game come at the expense of crushing overwork, enforced overtime, the destruction of a healthy family life and even of a healthy lifestyle of any type; workers may end up having to live off fast food and dispensing machine sugarbombs in order to keep up with the demands of the job. This phenomenon is known as "crunch." Everyone in both the industry and video game studies is aware of this institutional context, unpacked by Jason Schreier in *Blood, Sweat and Pixels* (2017) and *Press Reset* (2021; also see Cote and Harris 2023). Given that, as play theorist Miguel Sicart reminds us, play is not simply something we do sometimes when we are not working but is valorized as "an attitude, that is, the process of engaging with the world and oneself through play" (Sicart 2017, 84), this attitude clashes with our awareness of the rhythms in the lives of the people who made the games. It lies athwart what video games represent to many who play them and can make for discomfort in enjoying something that has been produced on the back of the mistreatment of workers. This affective response is not to the game as it might be played but to an appreciation of a situation in which a creative work is more than a physical object and more than our individual interaction with it: it is a representation of certain values not just through how it portrays men or women, say, but through how it comes to be in the world in the first place. This knowledgeable awareness is one more thing that distinguishes the environment of video game players from that of, say, book readers. What readers know anything about the workplace culture of publishers, of editors and agents, or of printers and paper factories and the production of ink, and the relation of all of these to each other and to authors?

In this attentiveness to how games come to be there is an ethical relation to background rhythm that seems positive. One response has been to be more open to Indie games, independent games made by a small to minuscule group of friends under conditions that are healthier than those apparent in some of the largest companies. This developing awareness of the rhythms through which video games reach us and a certain attentiveness to the process offer a curious contrast to the reception of books, in which the individual author is the only relevant source of the experience. While the names of a few of the people involved in making a video game will be known, the vast majority will not. When over two thousand people might work on a large commercial video game it would be impossible to accord them the same level of recognition. In lieu of being named, however, they are recognized in their function as the workers who have produced material realities out of the rhythms imposed on them. If such solidarity were extended to all cultural products and processes, this would have the potential to greatly increase social awareness of the operations of power in the supply chains of our pleasures, surely a step forward from treating those pleasures as having arrived from out of a vague market economy that is associated with nobody in particular.

HIERARCHY

Levine's third category is Hierarchy. Hierarchies arrange things and overtly install judgements over their lists and rankings. Hierarchy is definitely a feature of *experiencing* video games, highlighting that games, forms, art and stories are always already social and unable to be objectively categorized. One hierarchy is precisely that of the type of game, its overall form, which calls forth scornful, boastful, dismissive responses when it does not coincide with what are taken to be "higher" forms of a video game by the gatekeepers of every form of contemporary mass culture. Lest this be thought to be a regrettable feature of the febrile, mentally adolescent world of petulant online assertion, something similar operates with written stories, such as conventional romance novels for women, for example, being scorned by readers of Toni Morrison or Salman Rushdie. And in a way the hierarchies are parallel, the video game hierarchy reproducing that of literary studies, even though the two constituencies are still often suspicious of each other.

For many players of video games a game is valuable if it is hard, which just echoes what we have been taught in literary studies since Modernism, that a written story is valuable if it is hard: James Joyce has value where Diana Gabaldon does not. And does this in turn echo dispensations that privilege what is associated with conventional masculinity in a wider sense: activities that are physically hard, supposedly beyond a woman? A game that does not offer punishing and difficult sequences, perhaps also with a dismayingly long return to some point way back in the game if you are unskilled enough to die (the roguelike mentioned above), and that rewards the lightning-fast responses of a twelve-year-old and a fighter pilot's awareness of 3D space, now that's a proper game, while a game that proceeds more slowly, and that is focused on conversation and making choices, for which plenty of time is given, why that is not a real game. It may even be that refuge of the slow-fingered, the walking sim (walking simulator), summed up as "gaming's most detested genre" in one journalist's article (Clark 2017). In the walking sim your avatar moves along choosing conversation and simple gameplay options, as in a game such as *The Walking Dead: A New Day* (Telltale 2012) for example. Praise for *The Walking Dead* focuses on such things as its ethical conundra, its imperfect and human characters, the depiction of an adult caring for an unknown child and its rich voice acting. None of these aspects demand dextrous or overly rapid gameplay skills, hence the scorn evidenced by the gatekeepers of the influential hierarchy of the difficult as representing a hierarchy of value.

Nothing about the hierarchy of gameplay difficulty relates to the moral complexity of the story, the emotional richness of the characters, the empathetic engagement with the evolution of the characters, the creative subversion and play with storytelling or visual conventions, the visual beauty or ingenuity of what we are seeing, but only to the haptic difficulty of the interaction with its gameplay sequences. Hierarchy is a meta-organizing form placed over game forms in this case, which does what hierarchies do: assumes superiority and inferiority, not so much among video games but among the people who play them. For although the video games most people play might be better labelled digital games and include simple sequence games played on mobile phones or computers while we are supposed to be working, games designed to provide frequent rewards, the arguments do not bother with these. Nobody bothers to argue that *Mass Effect* is superior to *Gumboot Glory* (a free pedagogical game you can play on your phone or tablet in which you target noxious animals and plant pests in New Zealand with gumboots and other objects).

The arguments focus on longer, storytelling games, even when the narrative of some of them is actually pretty thin (for a good expansion on this necessarily brief approach to the important topic of difficulty, see Jagoda 2018). However, something that characterizes contemporary arguments about any sort of hierarchy, in most fields dealing with social phenomena, is the contested, unstable nature of all hierarchies.

Any sort of ranking invites intervention and participation, and our digital lives now include constant challenges to our hierarchies in the form of endless lists of, well, everything: the 10 best books on loneliness, David Bowie's 50 top tracks and 124 of the worst gaffes in Boris Johnson's career. These contemporary hierarchies implicitly and playfully challenge us to generate our own lists, not simply to accept them, unlike the impositions of a canon by establishment authority figures. The drive to rank things aligns with Levine's argument that hierarchy is not a dirty word, is not necessarily always a reproduction of the logic of master-slave, and once again this seems like common sense, "because no single hierarchy governs all others, nor do they all work together, successfully reinforcing Western imperialism, or the ruling class, or patriarchy" (Levine 2015, 109). When the UK's *Play* magazine ranks Playstation's greatest games every month, this ranking is implicitly understood to be a game itself, reverberating playfully against all other lists (the top four Playstation 5 games as I write in July 2023 are *Resident Evil 4*, *Deathloop*, *Ratchet & Clank: Rift Apart*, and *God of War Ragnarök*; the centrality of both strong storytelling and attention to realistic visual detail is apparent in three of them). Hierarchy then is not a form of game, but we experience games within hierarchies, as everything else, and this once again dilutes or detonates the idea that a game, or anything, is a hermetic Whole.

Yet hierarchies have consequences, and just as many games are not simply games to their followers or participants, neither is the game of producing hierarchies just or always a game. And video games might often be said to be games of hierarchies at their core, in their insistent appeal to players to stack up alongside other players, or, if we are playing a single-player game, to accumulate trophies, to reach higher levels, and in general to improve every type of quantifiable relation to the story that we can: more weapons, more health, more carrying capacity, more outfits, perhaps more facepaint options. Even the amount of time we have been playing a game is told to us, a visible avenue of comparison with friends and family in which the time spent on a game is seen as evidence of our skill, taste or both (or lack of them). In certain types of games where we have to choose among varying options, at the end of the time we will be told what percentage of players made the same choices we did at a number of the most significant pressure points in the game. One choice we did not make was for our gameplay to be watched and ranked in this way, although it is undeniably interesting to read these statistics at the end of the game or the end of the chapter. They generate a simple sense of community, which is something video game players claim characterizes participation in gameplay. This sense of an active community can no longer be claimed to be exclusive to gamers, however, as generating visible responses to whatever we experience has become generalized via everything from social media to the invitation of comments on as many types of sites as we can think of. Whether explicit or implicit, ranking is at the heart of the digital comments economy and appears as a type of parlour game on the more mature sites, such as *The Guardian*, and a more brutal form of attempted gatekeeping on the sites that allow it, such as anywhere that gives feminist commentator Anita Sarkeesian a forum (until comments are switched off).

Network

Finally, Levine's last category seems tailor-made for a contemporary product, Network. Games played with other players online are obviously networked, but what Levine is interested in is something more everpresent, the fact that human beings operate in terms of connections. The swirl and flow of these connections further undermines the possibility of claiming that anything is ever a Whole, and indeed are video games precisely the form to exemplify the point most convincingly anyway? Even if we take a non-multiplayer game, a game that forces us to move to a pre-determined end, it makes culturally significant challenges to the idea of Wholes through the fact that it has been created by a vast, diverse number of people, probably in more than one country, often using a language that is not the language of the country where they are made or mostly made, and generally representing a culture or cultures that are also not those of the country where they are made. Film and television sound like they do this too, except that film and television are associated culturally with where they are made in a way that many video games challenge. The fact that *The Matrix* (1999) was almost entirely made in Australia does not prevent the film from being considered a hundred per cent American cultural product. And while everybody watches the television series *Borgen* and reads it as telling us things about Danish cultural flows, nobody plays a *Hitman* game, made by Danish company IO Interactive, and thinks: "this is really telling me something about Danish culture, society and history." A game may be made by a French company but be set in the United States, using American voice actors and speaking to us about contemporary or future or past America, as in *Life is Strange* (Dontnod Entertainment), but it is not simply considered a French cultural product the same way a French movie doing such a thing would be. It is a networked form, challenging the ascription of such a creative product to narrow cultural origins. This could be seen as a positive dilution of nationalism as the foundation of cultural activity, although when we look at the video game production of a small country the issues do not seem so clear cut: does it matter if no examples of a creative product refer to the country where they are made, apart from those subsidized by public entities (see Callahan 2019)?

Levine also suggests that certain stories are focused more on networks than characters as individuals, to the extent that network in some sense becomes their form. Her best examples are novels by Charles Dickens and the television series *The Wire*, in which character exists more "as moments in which complex and invisible social forces cross" (Levine 2015, 126). Characters in such stories are not just individuals but nodes which can be read in terms of their connecting functions within the swirl of social forces explored in the work. Of course, many characters in these works are not just the symbolic ciphers that such a description suggests, and they constitute some of the most memorable characters in literature and television in English, but a large part of this occurs precisely because they so insistently enact and suffer the pressures of their place in the social fabric, a fabric in which multiple, finely discriminated lines of connection determine what they can expect, what they can get done, and what can be done to them. The idea of the individual making their own life, the self-made individual, is very distant from the reality of a Dickens character and his horror at what he saw as the delusions and dishonesty of this mantra in American life are clear when he deals with America, as in *Martin Chuzzlewit*, for example.

Now, considering characters as nodes in connecting forces might also be a way to consider the characters in those storytelling video games that include characters, which is most of those of interest to representational analysis. The criticism that video game characters are not complex enough, that their psychology and actions are obvious and simplistic, misses their function as symbolic nodes connecting whatever concepts are in play in that game, revenge, justice and family in *The Last of Us Part II* for instance, but also issues such as social hierarchies, authority and social cohesion, or what meaning there can be for human beings beyond mere survival. But in addition to reading video game characters more in terms of their nodal status, we actually have to produce this nodality through repeated interaction. This repetition alters our experience of story, disallowing us from lazily reading for plot, shall we say. For example, when Ellie and Abby fight in a storeroom in an abandoned theatre in *The Last of Us Part II*, I decided in the second playthrough to let Abby kill Ellie, but if that happens, you have to do the sequence again. You cannot choose for that to be the end of Ellie or the end of the game. The progression in the game requires you to continue the game through the twinned arcs of these two characters, or these two nodes in a network focused on the notion and the act of revenge, one of the most common themes in visual storytelling (more perhaps than in verbal storytelling). For this storytelling theme to emerge more fully, we are forced out of playing as Ellie to play as Abby, whom we have been hitherto trying to kill, and as Abby we are forced to step outside her interaction with Ellie to interact with two members of an enemy group, towards which she becomes more and more protective to the point where she ends up helping that group against her own people. It is not that she transfers her worldview from one group to another, but rather that she begins to see the world in terms of contrasting responses to the post-apocalyptic conditions of social breakdown that they are all in, responses that are nevertheless linked through their being coherent in their own terms. Rather than us against them, Abby starts to see that both groups are in the world together and can be differing points of a network rather than at each other's throats. But these nodes cannot simply understand each other via sitting down and thinking about or talking to each other. Abby is brought to think differently through personal contact with the two members of the other group, brought about when the three of them are involved in conflict with yet another group, enemy to them both. And we the player may be brought to think differently about Abby by being forced to play as her, a far more dynamic version of changing narratorial perspective as might occur in a novel or a film, putting our empathetic potential to the test in multiple ways. Networks may exist, then, but once again, this does not mean that the flows in all directions are constructive or of equal weight. In the end, Abby is unable to repair the connections between the two groups, the result of which is destructive to both of them. And the denouement of the game is somehow dissatisfying in that Ellie, the hero of the *Last of Us* world, is less able to perceive the networked relationship of human beings via the different groups they belong to than Abby has been.

Levine's principal example of a work that benefits from being considered as several forms coming together is the television series *The Wire*. It appears that her forms end up being "social forms" (Levine 2015, 132), not the individual generic identifier we might more readily associate with a creative work, but that is one of her main points: that society and creative works are best considered in terms of the same formal categories, rather than bracketing off creative works via terms that only have meaning within a narrow context. Where else other than academia does it matter if something is considered an epic, or a bildungsroman, or postmodern pastiche? *The Wire* can be seen thus as formally instantiating a network in its storytelling protocols, while also representing its Baltimore society as networked to the extent that rerouting anything in the desire to change things becomes extremely difficult. Characters in the stories are connected "to each other through *multiple* channels" (Levine 2015, 134). Levine then reads *The Wire* in terms of the Wholes that struggle to remain Whole (the role and influence of a traditional Union, for instance), the Rhythms of its storytelling and of each of the social institutions it represents, Hierarchy as everywhere in both the official and unofficial groups that rub against each other and how this trumps individual intentions or moralities, with Network as the overarching storytelling form. This means that countering Baltimore's drug problem and the drug economy "will be doomed to failure, since the crucial fact is that none of these work in isolation" (Levine 2015, 146). All of these aspects in the series mean that it evidences "a social world constantly unsettled by the bewildering and unexpected effects of clashes among wholes, rhythms, hierarchies, and networks" (Levine 2015, 149). This sounds like a recipe for richness of representational energies, but at the same time for despair over the possibility of ever changing anything, so imbricated is everything in multi-directional networks.

CONCLUSION

Stimulating though Levine's book is, has it delivered on its promise that "paying attention to subtle and complex formal patterns allows us to rethink the historical workings of political power and the relations between politics and aesthetics" (2015, xiii)? In terms of the title of my chapter, would thinking about video games via Levine's forms help us to rethink these things in such a way that video games, like serial television or books, could be seen to be contributing to a generalized attention to the workings of power around us and help us to combat them or reshape them in more positive ways?

One answer would be that responses to video games by academics and players already do that, via specific studies of ethical aspects of the gaming industry (Dyer-Witheford and de Peuter 2009, is a crucial example), via familiar representation studies (such as Malkowski and Russworm 2017), and via informed commentary by players on every level of internet forum, so what is the difference? Well, thinking about visual storytelling forms via these categories has a different flavour than the typical gambit of representation studies that is focused on highlighting problems in the representation of gender and ethnicity above all, but also other related categories. Most of these analyses differ little from similar critique of other storytelling forms. These days discussions of formal categories, including genre, are not at the forefront of the experience of literature by readers, but they are a lively part of how players of video games perceive the games they like and the ones they do not. Is this a recognition that Hierarchy governs our openness or resistance to forms and is a starting point for our organizing of what we judge it worthwhile to spend our time on? And through that connection to the Rhythm of our days and weeks video game players are repeatedly asked to justify themselves in ways that users of more traditional forms of stories are not. We are asked by those around us directly why we are "wasting our time" or what we see in such a visual storytelling mode, or we are asked these things implicitly by way of the hierarchies and declarations of official education, culture and politics. To the extent that playing video games involves responding to this permanent questioning—albeit pretty crudely in many cases—it *may* involve us in constant thinking about issues of value, of social worth, of creative presence, of representational issues, and ultimately of "unjust arrangements of power," however these are assessed.

Video games are even unique as a "fictional experience" in their "capacity to evoke actual feelings of guilt" (Isbister 2016, 8), when players make choices, for whatever reason, that go against what they think they would do in everyday life or that go against their values or view of what they think they would do when faced with ethical conundra. This is a deliberate provocation on the part of many video games. The technically simple but brilliantly excruciating game *Papers, Please* (2013) is a famous example. Tasked with making decisions on whether people should be allowed over a fictional border or not, the ethical difficulties become more and more severe until the choices you are forced to make become so harrowing that the only respite is to stop playing. If that does not lead to reflection on the nature of borders, power, compromise and sacrifice, then the player's ability to separate the game from the rest of life is startling indeed. Another famous example is that of killing animals as part of a narrative in which to increase your chances of surviving you have the choice of taking out everything from fish to owls to squirrels, animals that are not doing anything to harm you. Many players are uncomfortable with this, "concerned that the proliferation of digital animal violence may be linked to morally problematic societal attitudes and behaviour towards living animals" (Coghlan and Sparrow 2021, 216), even when the game pushes us in this direction. Once again, the potential for active reflection, for hesitation over the button, appears more dynamic than that when faced with other creative products.

Potential, though, does not guarantee anything. Something that is central to video game studies are arguments around the procedures by which we make our way through games, the degree to which they may afford players agency and the degree to which they are nonetheless so bound by rules that they become the contemporary form par excellence: giving us the illusion of agency and choice while all the time disciplining us through imposed paths and options, surveilling us through the hardware we use to play them, and constantly ranking us and our play against other players and/or various metrics of one kind and another. Network, Hierarchy and Rhythm come together once again. Whole is further challenged by a technology in which our experience is captured and registered by our hardware, most likely by one or more companies over the internet, perhaps followed online by friends as well. Only the friends are easy to ghost (to de-network, as it were). Reflecting on these things may interrupt our assumptions about "our" experience and may also prompt us to further consider "unjust arrangements of power" (Levine 2015, xiii), but after all no forms actually force anyone to reflect on anything, which of course is what hegemonic arrangements count on.

Michael W Clune characterizes Levine's work as coming out of the "new institutionalism," which is "a twentieth-century school of thought in the social sciences that rejects totalizing ideological or economic analyses to focus on how relations between and within institutions shape society" (Clune 2017, 1194–5). Thus it is that Levine's desire is ultimately not to identify better names for anything but rather to suggest overarching formal categories that disturb our labelling tendencies as well as our narrowly separating tendencies. Anything that does that is to be welcomed, even if, alas, the world does not seem to be becoming a more just place on any measurement, despite what video games offer to us as a stimulus to reflection.

References

Apperley, Tom. 2010. *Gaming Rhythms: Play and Counterplay from the Situated to the Global*. Amsterdam: Institute of Network Cultures.

Callahan, David. 2019. Deterritoralisation and the Landscape of New Zealand Video Games. *Journal of New Zealand & Pacific Studies* 7 (1): 63–79.

Clark, Nicole. 2017. A Brief History of the 'Walking Simulator,' Gaming's Most Detested Genre. *Salon*. November 11. https://www.salon.com/2017/11/11/a-brief-history-of-the-walking-simulator-gamings-most-detested-genre/. Accessed 8 Dec 2023.

Clune, Michael W. 2017. Formalism as the Fear of Ideas. *PMLA* 132 (5): 1194–1199.

Coghlan, Simon, and Lucy Sparrow. 2021. The 'Digital Animal Intuition': The Ethics of Violence Against Animals in Video Games. *Ethics and Information Technology* 23 (3): 215–224.

Cote, Amanda, and Brandon Harris. 2023. The Cruel Optimism of 'Good Crunch': How Game Industry Discourses Perpetuate Unsustainable Labor Practices. *New Media & Society* 25 (3): 609–627.

Dyer-Witheford, Nick, and Greig de Peuter. 2009. *Games of Empire: Global Capitalism and Video Games*. Minneapolis: Minnesota University Press.

Holloway, Miles, Deirdre Byrne, and Michael Titlestad. 2001. *Love, Power and Meaning*. Cape Town: Oxford University Press.

Isbister, Katherine. 2016. *How Games Move Us: Emotion by Design*. Cambridge, MA: MIT Press.

Jagoda, Patrick. 2018. On Difficulty in Video Games: Mechanics, Interpretation, Affect. *Critical Inquiry* 45: 199–233.

James, Michael. 2021. Literature in Gaming: The Coming-of-Age, Esports and Game Design Collective. *EGD Collective*. https://www.egdcollective.org/post/literature-in-gaming-the-coming-of-age.

Levine, Caroline. 2015. *Forms: Whole, Rhythm, Hierarchy, Network*. Princeton: Princeton University Press.

Malkowski, Jennifer, and TreaAndrea Russworm, eds. 2017. *Gaming Representation: Race, Gender, and Sexuality in Video Games*. Bloomington: Indiana University Press.

Matrix, The. 1999. Film. Dir. The Wachowskis. Warner Bros, Australia.

Schreier, Jason. 2017. *Blood, Sweat, and Pixels*. New York: Harper.
———. 2021. *Press Reset: Ruin and Recovery in the Video Game Industry*. New York: Grand Central Publishing.
Sicart, Miguel. 2017. *Play Matters*. Reprint. Cambridge, MA: MIT Press,
Wilson, Kyle. 2022. Horizon Forbidden West Review – Epic Yet Encumbering. *The Loadout*. February 28. https://www.theloadout.com/horizon-forbidden-west/review. Accessed 13 Apr 2023.

GAMES

Far Cry V. 2018. Ubisoft, Canada.
Gumboot Glory. 2014. In-Game, for Dairy New Zealand, New Zealand.
Hitman: Codename 47. 2000. IO Interactive, Denmark.
Last of Us, The. 2013. Naughty Dog, US.
Last of Us Part II, The. 2020. Naughty Dog, US.
Life is Strange. 2015. Dontnod Studios, France
Horizon: Forbidden West. 2022. Guerilla Games, Netherlands.
Mass Effect. 2007. BioWare, Canada.
No Man's Sky. 2016. Hello Games, UK.
Papers, Please. 2013. 3909 LLC, US.
Walking Dead, The: A New Day. 2012. Telltale Games, US.

CHAPTER 3

Video Games as Animation: Inquiries into the Animatic Nature of Playable Images

Víctor Navarro-Remesal

INTRODUCTION: VIDEO GAMES, ANIMATION, AND VISUAL CULTURE

Video games are complex, hybrid objects. Their ontology has been the ground for many a debate, and even when their multi-sided nature is acknowledged, the specific weight of each of their components is hardly agreed upon. A founding debate of game studies was the "ludology vs narratology war" (Aarseth 2019), which clashed on the importance of either the ludic or the narrative sides of games and the proper tools to analyse them. Currently, the debates within games studies have been framed as a matter of formalism versus "socially conscious scholarship" (Mäyrä 2020), a combination of contemporary understandings of cultural studies and more or less in-depth sociology, not entirely unlike fan studies.

Scholarly production on video games as visual culture is scarce, discontinuous, and often disconnected. This might have been a necessary step "to establish the video game as an art form in its own right," as Chris Pallant argues: to do so, "the games industry, as well as games

V. Navarro-Remesal (✉)
Tecnocampus, Pompeu Fabra University, Barcelona, Spain
e-mail: vnavarro@tecnocampus.cat

© The Author(s), under exclusive license to Springer Nature Switzerland AG 2024
D. Callahan (ed.), *Visual Storytelling in the 21st Century*,
https://doi.org/10.1007/978-3-031-65487-9_3

commentators, has promoted interactivity above all else as the form's distinguishing feature, thereby setting it apart from live-action cinema, with which games often share common elements, such as visual language, narrative and animated materiality" (Pallant 2018, 204). But that does not mean that the bridges and exchanges between games and cinema have not been explored. As early as 2002, Geoff King and Tania Krzywinska edited a volume on the topic, *Screen/Play* (2002). It has also been explored in culture journalism, with books such as *Generation Xbox: How Videogames Invaded Hollywood* (Russell 2012) and in academia by scholars such as Riccardo Fassone (2017), in Italian, and myself (2019), in Spanish.

In 2002, Aki Järvinen wrote that "the interplay of sounds and images in games has not been studied in any rigorous way" (2002, 113), and while the situation has improved, video games are still rarely discussed as first and foremost visual culture. Martín Núñez has written on the use of the (virtual) camera and focalization in games (2020); Atkinson and Parsayi recently explored video games and aesthetic contemplation, arguing that "in order to open up a space for aesthetic engagement, many of the ludological and narrative demands of the game must recede" (2021, 1). Jesper Juul produced an interactive essay (2021) where he explored "game objects" and how and when we perceive pixels as objects relevant to our actions. The links between Japanese games and the aesthetics of Japan have been explored in some publications (Huber 2007; Navarro-Remesal and Loriguillo-López 2015), while the belonging of games to art, or their uses with artistic intentions, have been covered in *Videogames and Art* (Clarke and Mitchell 2007) or *Works of Game* (Sharp 2015).

Games are sets of complex parts, interdependent and in interplay. Souvik Mukherjee (2015) calls our attention to their narrative side and their connections to literature, while at the same time presenting the medium as a combination of the ludic, the narrative, and the machinic. I believe this triangulation is a very useful description of how the medium works, its origins, and a helpful explainer of its birth. Or, to be more specific, and following Gaudreault and Marion (2005), of its "two births": as a technical possibility and a cultural object. I want to add a fourth vertex to that figure, turning it into a square: the *animatic*. Understanding video games as animatic, and in particular as *playable animatic images*, would be useful both for scholars of games and of media, and to explore them firmly as visual culture.

Animation studies do not deal with video games often. In *Animation*, published by SAGE, we can find just two papers dealing strictly with video games: one in connection to tool-assisted speedruns (Schmalzer 2021) and another on animation in Sierra On-Line's games (Greenberg 2021). A search on *Con A de animación* [With A for Animation], a Spanish journal dedicated to the form and published by the Polytechnic University of Valencia, produces a few more results: a paper on indie games (Rocío Benavent 2019); one on the game *Cuphead* (Studio MDHR, 2017), famous for imitating the visual style of the cartoons of the Fleischer brothers (Criado 2019); a paper on *Life Is Strange 2* and its design of ethical choices (Martín-Núñez and Porta Pérez 2022); a paper on otome games (Montañés 2021); and two on video games as part of transmedia universes, in particular the worlds of Ghibli (García Villar 2019) and *Final Fantasy* (Hernández-Pérez 2019).

Pallant's chapter might be the strongest defence of games as animation: "Fundamentally, all video games are animated texts. However, the way that interactivity serves as the key identifying marker of the video game, results in the (always) animated nature of video games being frequently ignored" (Pallant 2018, 203). If that chapter tried to bring games into animation studies, my intention here is to open the channel in the other direction: to bring animation into game studies. Both movements reveal the need to think of them in terms of visual culture.

Video Games as Images

Video games are implicitly animatic. That much was acknowledged when text-only games, such as text adventures or interactive fiction (IF), branched out of the medium to the extent that they are rarely discussed in gaming spaces, and the IF communities would rarely see themselves as part of it. Text games never disappeared, as Aaron Reed's recent *50 Years of Text Games: From Oregon Trail to A.I. Dungeon* proves (2023); they were just moved to a different space that rarely overlaps with mainstream gaming. In the same manner, so-called live-action footage is rare in video games. The advent of CDs as a storage medium brought many works using that format, which resulted in the need of a specific label to discuss it: FMV (Full Motion Video). Although FMV can also include recorded footage of animation, it often refers to footage captured from reality, with real actors and often real locations. FMV cutscenes were popular for a time, but nowadays they are remembered as tacky products of their era. The style has seen a resurgence in later years, with the works of Sam Barlow and Wales Interactive, for example, and this has led to a resurrected debate on their belonging to the gaming medium.

If we compare, for instance, four contemporary video games: *And the Sun Went Out* (Tin Man Games, 2015), *Telling Lies* (Sam Barlow, 2020), *Death Stranding* (Kojima Productions, 2019), and *TMNT: Shredder's Revenge* (Tribute Games, 2022), we may see that: the first is purely text-based; the second combines live-action footage with a fake computer interface; the third uses photorealistic, 3D graphics; while the last one updates the tradition of pixel-art in a hyper-expressive, cartoony way. If we were to present these productions to people both familiar and unfamiliar with gaming, they would see the first two (text and video) as outliers—perhaps people who did not know them would fail to recognise them as video games. The last two, on the contrary, would be seen as representatives of major styles in game aesthetics and major areas of the gaming industry: AAA games (blockbusters) and indie games.

To further this point, we can use a conceptual experiment: how should we classify a non-interactive video that has been obtained by editing together fragments of a video game? This is not a hypothetical question: in 2001, *Shenmue: The Movie* (Yu Suzuki), a film that put together the cutscenes of *Shenmue* (Sega AM2, 1999) and wove them together with a few bits of recorded gameplay, opened in Japanese cinemas. The special edition of *Metal Gear Solid 3: Snake Eater* (Konami, 2004), called *Metal Gear Solid 3: Subsistence*, included a separate disc with a three and a half-hour cut of *Metal Gear Solid 3*'s cinematics, called *Metal Gear Solid 3: Existence*. It was, to all effects and purposes, a film version of the game. It would be difficult to consider the visual storytelling of *Shenmue: The Movie* and *Metal Gear Solid 3: Existence* something other than animation.

Let's offer another take on that conceptual question. What happens when a film, either short or feature length, is made in full by using video game technology? That is the case of machinima videos, a type of audiovisual fiction made with game engines, or of *The Flying Luna Clipper*, a feature film made in 1987 in Japan by a single creator, visual artist Ikko Ohno, using the gaming microcomputer MSX2. More recently, the film *Away* (Gints Zilbalodis, 2019) was made in similar fashion, by a single creator using gaming technology (in this case, Maya). The movie was unanimously regarded to be animated, was included in the 47th Annie Awards (one of the most important awards in the medium), and won Best Animated Film at the 2019 edition of the Latvian film industry awards Lielais Kristaps.

There is, then, animation in video games, but when it is discussed it is often focused on as a technical aspect, a discussion aimed only at animators. In Jonathan Cooper's manual *Game Anim. Video Game Animation Explained*, he proposes five fundamentals of video game animation: fluidity, feel, readability, context, and elegance. These fundamentals complement the twelve basic principles of animation laid out in Disney animators Ollie Johnston and Frank Thomas's foundational book, *The Illusion of Life: Disney Animation* (1981). There are, of course, technical aspects that only animators would understand, but it seems clear that anyone interested in video games would benefit from having a better understanding of animation and how it manifests in video games, and, by extension, from understanding video games as an animatic form.

Video Games and the Animatic Apparatus

Animation is not just a visual technique. It changes the way images operate and are perceived, how they are created (from being captured from reality to being created from zero), and what they can portray. Of course, this distinction between "realities" is in itself problematic, since every image is real in itself, but here we are dealing with matters of perception and referentiality: animation is not bound by what we can immediately capture from our surroundings but by what we can carry out through several techniques that shape images from zero. More importantly, it creates a new symbolic way of relating to images, a rift between the lifeless and the living. Animation scholar Alan Cholodenko conceptualises this as the "animatic apparatus," referring to all cinema in general and to animation in particular, evoking Agamben's discussion of the concept: an apparatus would be "literally anything that has in some way the capacity to capture, orient, determine, intercept, model, control, or secure the gestures, behaviours, opinions, or discourses of living beings" (Agamben 2009, 14). Cholodenko looks in detail at the "illusion of life" created by this apparatus:

> Animation bedevils definition, even (and especially) 'its' 'own'–double–definition: endowing with life and endowing with movement. By this doubling, this multiplying and dividing, even of 'itself,' animation poses the very question of life itself, movement itself, and their relation, a complicated coimplicated relation in which each of the terms can only be thought through the other, in which each of the terms solicits and replies (to) the other. This is always already double trouble doubled. (Cholodenko 2007, 486)

Cholodenko writes about an "automaton" that complicates the ideal of the organic and the mechanical (2007, 493), while the digital age of cinema, discussed by historians such as Mark Cousins (2011), has further blurred the borders between the real and the animatic. In Deborah Levitt's view of the animatic apparatus, she proposes a definition of "the mediality of the animatic":

> The animatic is any aspect of image production–from animation as such, to digital effects, to extreme camera angles–that does not deploy the cinematic reality effect of the index ... That is, it does not find its raison d'être in representation. It takes up the simulacral dimension of the image, or of audio-visuality, to be more precise. This definition of course complicates any strict boundary between cinema and animation: the two modes consistently exchange and transform one another. (Levitt 2018, 58)

For Levitt, the animatic is "an-ontological," that is, a *non-reality* or a *non-existence*. The animatic is not only something created by different artistic means, opposed to the filmic; it is a way of conceptualising images, life, and movement. It is precisely because the animatic complicates the boundaries with "real images" that emphasising this animatic nature of video games is an urgent task: since we do not see them as fully opposed to reality, we tend to ignore their manufacture, and in their faint boundaries lies a contamination of our side of reality. Through video games, as we will see later, reality becomes tinged by the animatic.

Five Paths for Video Games as Animatic Visual Culture

Adding a fourth vertex to our understanding of video games, as I have argued, is not just a technical detail. The animatic has further impact on different levels of conceptualisation and opens many paths for both visual culture and the game scholar. Five of these levels might be thought of as: (1) history, (2) genealogies, (3) industry and intermediality, (4) ontology and relation to reality, and (5) player experiences.

1. *History*

The roots of video games are usually explored in computer engineering or consumer electronics, but we can also find them in analogue games, in penny arcades (especially in pinball parlours), in (experimental) literature, and many other entertainment objects and creative industries. Understanding video games as animatic helps us expand that vast network and even connect the dots in new and surprising ways.

Cultural critic and Japan specialist Matt Alt has written about the country's specialisation in "fantasy delivery devices" (2020, 11), a range of cultural products that go from the Walkman to anime to cute characters such as Hello Kitty. What these devices have in common is an emphasis on imagination and entertainment, systematised in a way that favours the development of stable cultural industries. Video games are, of course, one of these devices. Under this view, what matters is not so much their technological aspect or how they add new affordances to other media, but how they participate in a general industry and culture of imagination and leisure. Japanese video games are another way for Japan to sell an *animatic world* to itself and to the rest of the world. Not only are they connected materially (as we will see next) to other industries, they share the same fantasy and, to be specific, the same fantasy-as-product.

The animatic roots of video games are even wider and deeper. Meredith Bak (2020) has studied the origins and evolution of optical toys as technology and in society. Bak's proposal is to stop looking at these toys just as "pre-cinema" and imagine them in context, as challenges to the media ecology of their time, meant not only to be looked at but to be *played with*—they were moving images as much as *playthings*. Bak's study also reveals a playful side to the origins of cinema and animation, one that dealt with experimentation, playful manipulation of techniques and technology, and early media as appropriative modulations of the act of seeing.

Cinema was born thus from *playable images,* and in that regard video games continue a long and fruitful tradition. This is not in itself a new argument. It echoes Tom Gunning's exploration of optical toys as a "new technology of the image in the Victorian Era":

> The interactive nature of optical toys makes them direct ancestors of one of the dominant technological images currently, the computer game … Dulac and Gaudreault distinguish between what they call a "player mode of attraction" typical of these toys and a "viewer mode of attraction" that appears as optical devices become theatricalized (as in the projected cinema or, even earlier, Reynauld's *Pantomimes lumineuse*)." (Gunning 2012, 511)

There is a history of this "player mode of attraction" waiting to be written, and it would include the development of video games as playable images. There is, for example, a line connecting nineteenth-century stereoscopic viewers to the ViewMaster toy to contemporary VR headsets. It would also be interesting to see how "pre-video games" such as *Tennis for Two* (William Higginbotham 1958) tried to generate moving, controllable images with the technology that was available to them. Or how the first home console, the Magnavox Odyssey (Sanders Associates, 1972), relied on transparent overlays to add images and meaning to what it could generate in real time, moving dots of light. The creation of sprites was a technological and conceptual leap that made artists necessary and brought iconicity to the forefront of video games, resulting, by the early 1980s, in a cluster of highly recognisable characters such as Pac-Man or Donkey Kong.

In its first issue, the journal on game histories *ROMChip*, inquiring into what its main object of study was, included "The History of Games Could Be a History of Technology" (Giddings 2019) and "The History of Games Could Be a History of What Play Felt Like" (Walker 2019). The history of video games could also be the history of the conquest of the controllable image. This perspective would show us that they belong in a wider family.

2. *Genealogies*

If we go back to the Odyssey overlays, a very simple visual technology that was also used by other machines such as the Vectrex, we can see that Overlays have a wider history in screen media: the advent of colour TV was accompanied by cheap tri-colour TV overlays, such as the Telecolor Filter by Harvard Laboratory or the Colorama Vista Screen, that just added a few fixed bands of colour on top of the black and white images. A game console with overlays might seem like a weird concept in the present, but its original intended audience was most likely familiar with them.

A history of video games as an animatic form, and as part of the animatic apparatus, reveals many relatives, and many of them unusual and strange. For instance, video games appeared in entertainment spaces that were shaped by coin-op automata and moving dioramas (Williams 2017), that is, arcade rooms where the illusion of life became a quick and cheap commercial product. It is easy to go from there to moving toys, to any kind of toy that is based on the pleasure of movement, whether automatized or created by, for example, operating a crank. That would be the case of dolls with automatic movement or automated marble runs. They are also relatives of hand-cranked toy projectors, such as the pre-war models one can see in the Toy Film Museum (Omochaeiga) in Kyoto, or the Spanish toy projectors Cine NIC (1931–1974) and Cinexin (1971–2010). These toys can have little to no interaction and be fully automated or setup-only, but they all share a common source of interest: something artificial is moving in front of us.

Consider, then, a digital version of this: something that does not have the interactivity of video games (based on rulesets, limits, and goals) nor any other function, and is made to make us find pleasure in moving (virtual) objects. Even functional apps can have animatic layers on top of them that do not contribute to their function, which would make them belong, in part, to this group. We could call these programs *video toys* or *digital toys*, and they are an underexplored area of gaming, game studies, and visual culture studies.

Screensavers had a clear function (to prevent phosphor burn-in) but they quickly became exercises in playfulness. And they were successful commercial products that shaped many users' understanding of digital images. Consider the *After Dark* series (Berkeley Systems, 1989–1996). The most famous of its screensavers, "Flying Toasters," became widely popular and had its own theme song, with a karaoke version. *After Dark* later made the jump to video games with the collection *After Dark Games* (Sierra Attractions, Berkeley Systems, 1998), a product that would be hard to understand without the context of screensavers as a mainstay of 1990s computer visual culture.

A similar case would be *Johnny Castaway* (Sierra On-Line/Dynamix, 1992), an ambitious product that featured the tagline "The World's First Storytelling Screen Saver" on its cover. This screensaver consisted of several vignettes featuring a castaway on a deserted island, with many visual gags and some faint narrative that included seasonal events linked to the computer's internal clock. It is no coincidence that *Johnny Castaway* used such a recognisable cartoon trope, since the exploration (and promotion) of computers as a new visual medium benefitted from a familiar frame of reference. With this screensaver, Sierra On-Line was showing continuity with previous popular visual products, which helped highlight the new affordances of the medium. When it comes to media and visual literacy in the 1990s, *Johnny Castaway* belongs in the same broad category as video games.

The so-called desktop pets were also popular after the advent of Windows 95. One example was *Stray Sheep* (Tatsutoshi Nomura 1994), later rereleased as *eSheep*, a cute cartoon sheep that walked around the screen, jumped about, ate flowers, yawned and slept, or looked at the user. A less family-friendly version of desktop pets would be "virtual strippers," live-action recordings of strippers (male or, more usually, female) that sit on the taskbar removing their clothes and performing enticing moves. Both desktop pets and virtual strippers remain practically unexplored to this day.

Digital toys can move between the virtual and the physical. An animated watch face for a smartwatch serves no function other than to entertain and be playful. We can argue that digital toys such as the Tamagotchi inhabit that same space: a digital animated image that is *almost* physical thanks to the object that makes it possible. Tamagotchi, with its low resolution and LCD pixels, its limited two-frame animations, and simple characters, helped shape early emoji, pixel art, and the digitalization of *kawaii* Japanese character design. It also poses an uncomfortable challenge to those that want video games to have a clear ontology: is it a video game? Is it a console? As a toy, it presents a ruleset and goals centred around keeping the virtual pet alive and well, but this system is not strict enough to sit comfortably within a traditional video game model. As many stressed Tamagotchi owners can attest, it does not present purely free play either.

A clearer relative of video games is what has been called *interactive animation*, or animation with game-like interactions but no strict ruleset or goals—in a way, this would be the result of removing the *game* from video games and leaving just playable images. Two cases are noteworthy here: studio Playables and animator Atsushi Wada. Playables is a production company from Zurich founded by Mario von Rickenbach and Michael Frei that creates "strange playful things and help[s] others do so" (official site). They have released *Plug & Play* (Mario von Rickenbach and Michael Frei 2015) and *Kids* (Mario von Rickenbach and Michael Frei 2019), two collections of black-and-white animated vignettes that are connected thematically. They are abstract, surreal, and silent. Atsushi Wada is a Japanese animator who has created several traditional non-interactive short films and released, with the help of Playables, the interactive piece *My Exercise* (2020). In this, players can make a boy do sit-ups with the help of his dog by using the spacebar. A counter shows how many sit-ups we have done, and after a few of them new characters start appearing on screen to help and cheer the boy up. While *Plug & Play* and *Kids* are linear and have endings, *My Exercise* does not have one and cannot be "won." A last element to keep in mind is that all of these pieces are sold on Steam, a digital video games store.

A last relative of video games, within the wider playable images family, would be programmes made to *create animation*, especially in playful and non-commercial ways. That would be the case of *Flipnote Studio* (Nintendo, 2008) and *Flipnote Studio 3D* (Nintendo, 2013), sold for the Nintendo DSi and Nintendo 3DS, respectively. These apps allowed users to create short, simple animations that could be shared as GIFs. When the Nintendo 3DS eShop was about to close, Disney animator Wayne Unten created a short film using exclusively the console with *Flipnote Studio 3D* and other tools. The appeal of this short film, titled *Toadal Disaster* (2023), lies in the tools and how it can be traced visually to their particular gaming hardware.

3. *Industry and Intermediality*

Toadal Disaster shows a link between the video game and animation industries that reveals itself to be broader the more we explore it. For a start, professional animators and character designers can and often do move from one to the other, using mostly the same set of skills.

The aforementioned *The Flying Luna Clipper* is a precursor of the use of game engines in animation film production. In the 2022 edition of the Annecy International Animation Film Market (MIFA), Epic Games, owners of the Unreal engine had a booth where they exhibited their tools and projects made with them and gave talks on real-time animation production. What Ohno or Gints Zibalodis did by themselves is becoming the norm in the industry, and it cannot be stressed enough that game technology is a technology for animation and can be used primarily for that. More importantly, they allow for real-time pipelines and new structures of animation labour. The technical borders between media are being eroded, and scholars of both animation and game production studies need to keep an eye on this.

This crossing between media is not new in Japan. There, we can find many examples of manga artists working as character designers in games. This is famously the case with Akira Toriyama, author of *Dr Slump* (1980–1984) and *Dragon Ball* (1983–1997), who designed characters and created illustrations for *Dragon Quest* (Chunsoft, 1986). Kosuke Fujishima, author of *Oh My Goddess!* (1988–2014), has also designed characters for the roleplaying series *Tales* (Namco, 1995–2021). This results in a professional scene where influences and trends are constantly exchanged and in a visual kinship that brings media together in the eyes of their fans.

On a larger scale, Japanese animation studios frequently create cinematics for video games as work for hire. This industrial collaboration is, again, mostly unexplored. Animation scholar Laura Montero Plata highlighted that lack of research, and showed a selection of cases in a talk for the conference series "Gêmu. Perspectives on the Japanese Video Game," organised by the Japan Foundation in Madrid (2022). We may look at two studios to illustrate different strategies. First, Studio 4° C is one of the few houses that include games in their online portfolio. They have animated cutscenes for games such as *Asura's Wrath* (Cyberconnect2, 2012) and *Catherine* (Atlus, 2011), and their site lists the directors of these cutscenes (Shinya Oihra/Kazuo Nakazawa and Yasuyuji Shimizu, respectively). One can identify certain stylemes of the studio in these works, but they are chiefly produced in the service of a game created by a separate game studio. On the other hand, Studio Ghibli collaborated in the creation of *Ni No Kuni: Wrath of the White Witch* (Level-5, 2011) with cutscenes, character designs, and even a score by frequent Ghibli collaborator Joe Hisaishi. The game was promoted as a Ghibli co-production and the goal was openly to make it recognisable as belonging to the studio's stylistic and thematic preoccupations.

All of this is frequent in the "media mix" model of Japanese popular culture. Marc Steinberg has studied this by focusing on "franchising characters" and describes it as a system of relationality that comes both from marketing and from creativity:

> Since the 1980s, the term media mix has been the most widely used word to describe the phenomenon of transmedia communication, specifically, the development of a particular media franchise across multiple media types, over a particular period of time. … Yet, despite its importance for understanding the present and past of Japanese media, this term is undertheorized and suffers from a surprising lack of historicization. … Though the term continues to be used within contemporary marketing discourse, it is greatly overshadowed by its popular use in describing the circulation of characters and narratives across media types–an essential part of the anime system. (Steinberg 2012, 135)

This results in an "all-consuming, character-driven media environment" in which characters and their "narrative world could be accessed from multiple points at any given time" (2012, 19). But this, Steinberg warns, does not remove medium specificity:

> rather, each manifestation of the character foregrounds the distinct properties of the medium in question: motion–stillness for anime; sequential narrative for manga; interiority and narrative realism for light novels; weight, dimensionality, and physical manipulability for toys; and interaction and interface for video games ... In this respect, the character in its media crossings generates a degree of convergence between media forms around its image, but it also abstracts some of the specificity of each. (Steinberg 2012, 84)

The growing importance of video games in such media mixes motivated DiGRA (Digital Games Research Association) to focus its 2019 conference in Kyoto on what they called "ludo mix":

> [W]e invite contributors to consider the possibility of 'ludo mix' where games and play increasingly occupy the focal point of such a diversified distribution and consumption model. Ludo mixes may include several versions of a game or several different games together with other content thus resulting in novel media ecologies, business models, and development and consumption cultures. (official site, 2019)

Understanding video games as works of an animatic visual culture helps us understand both the material conditions of their creation and the wider framing of their consumption as visual media.

4. *Ontology and Relation to Reality*

The inherent flexibility of the media/ludo mix allows characters to be portrayed in different styles across media. This is the case, for instance, of *Cyberpunk 2077* (CD Projekt RED, 2020), a stylized cyberpunk game with photorealistic character models and textures that somehow gained new life thanks to its spin-off anime series, *Cyberpunk: Edgerunners* (CD Projekt RED, Studio Trigger, 2022). When Järvinen came to categorise visual styles in video games, he concluded they could be divided into three groups: photorealism, caricaturism, and abstractionism. Of these three, photorealism, "a photographic likeness with reality" (2002, 121), is the dominant style in AAA games. While caricaturism is seen as childish, photorealism is associated with an adult style. It can be seen as a result of the search for cultural prestige and technological prowess, the mark of a gaming culture that sees itself in a race to reproduce reality through computer power. The diversity of styles of a franchise like *Cyberpunk*, however, proves that styles can coexist and complement each other, and opens a crack in the monopoly of photorealism.

In gaming cultures, "realism" often equals "visual fidelity," and every hardware jump is seen as getting one step closer to reality. Photorealism is the product of the machinic side of games, not of its animatic side. It is also not a new trend: video games with digitised actors were popular in the 1990s, with the first games in the *Mortal Kombat* series (Midway, Warner Bros Interactive Entertainment, 1992–present) as the main example. What is ironic in that view of video game visual styles is that the pursuit of mimesis would actually be an attempt to replace the cinematic with the animatic. If an animatic form can represent reality and trick the viewer, what need is there for the cinematic? This ontological crisis of the image is an ongoing problem of our time, with the rise of generative programs such as Midjourney or Dall-E.

Motion capture, high-resolution scans of objects to create photorealistic textures, and other similar techniques are common in games. They are a new mutation of the animatic whose novelty lies in trying to hide the an-ontology of the form. The animatic allows abstraction and symbolism, and being aware of the technique is part of its illusion. One example of this would be the game *Tux and Fanny* (Albert Birney, Ghost Time Games, 2021), where certain segments bring changes in visual styles (from pixel-art to cut-out to claymation) with no diegetic justification whatsoever. At the other end of the spectrum, AAA games insist on animating very specific details derived from material reality to foster fascination with the fidelity of its virtual reality, such as the horse testicles that shrink in cold weather in *Red Dead Redemption 2* (Rockstar Games, 2018). It is nonetheless an animatic form in disguise. Game photorealism echoes the movement from "want-see" (giving audiences the images they want) to "can-see" (where computers took cinema beyond photography), a movement that Cousins identifies with the advent of digital cinema (2011, 436). An animatic form that pretends to replace material reality, passing as it, answers to the visual demands of its audience, and the implications of this replacement go beyond video games and the extent of this chapter. The reality of images has been subjected in this process to the viewer's demands.

If we move to more humble and quotidian practices that manifest the gamic animatic in reality beyond the game, first we encounter cosplay, which is in itself a form of play and is not limited to referencing video games. It aims at reproducing a character, often animatic, in the event reality of the cosplayer; the cosplayer tries to enact, in make-believe, that character. Cosplay has been linked, for example, to expressions of fan culture (Chen 2007) and it illustrates how fans do not see animatic forms such as video games as self-contained and separated from the rest of reality. The animatic and the real are not layers that are incommensurable to each other. Visual styles are reproduced with recourse to such interventions as makeup and complex (and expensive) costume production, and it is not uncommon to see cosplayers reproducing the movements of their characters in their routines: the illusion of the illusion of life. In a way, cosplaying is *becoming animatic*.

A second practice of interest would be "scene hunting" tourism, or *butaitanbou* in Japanese, where fans of an animatic work search for the real-world inspirations of settings of their preferred manga, anime, or games (Loriguillo-López 2020). Gamemakers transform recognisable places into animatic spaces and fan tourists transform them back. They know the physical location through the animatic and visit those real places to make the animatic (more) real. It is not uncommon to find people visiting the Japanese neighbourhood of Kabukicho in search of things they recognise from the *Ryu Ga Gotoku* series (Sega, 2005–present), and the city of Yokosuka even distributed a promotional leaflet announcing the locations of *Shenmue*. Susana Tosca has highlighted how these products create a "promised gameland" (Tosca 2021) that tourists have explored virtually before visiting and which they see under a well delimited set of expectations. Photorealistic, anime-like, or with any other visual styles, the animatic side of video games colours our experience of the real world. Through practices in material reality, we *inhabit* these animatic worlds and characters.

5. *Player Experiences*

Following this, the last path I want to present here is the impact of the animatic on player experiences. In particular, looking at video games as (not exclusively) playable images can encourage us to see the player-avatar relation under a new light.

Avatars, a term rooted in the religious tradition of the Indian subcontinent and imported into video game terminology during a period of "appropriation of Eastern culture by Californian tech industries" (de Wildt et al. 2020), were discussed in the early years of game studies as either fictional characters or sets of player tools and mechanics, "heavy heroes" or "digital dummies" (Burn and Schott 2004). But what about the digital object we control? In addition to the interactive essay by Juul mentioned above, Chris Bateman is one of the few theorists to separate the concept from the object. He distinguishes the avatar, as the means through which the player interacts with the gameworld, from the "doll," a *prop* that serves as a visual representation of that avatar (Bateman 2011, 106). We can go further and say that avatars (or their dolls) are also *visual toys* that we control while they offer some degree of autonomy and resistance.

This is, once more, not a fully new argument. Raz Greenberg has studied "gamers as animators" using the Sierra On-Line adventure games as an example and argues that the player-avatar relationship in those games follows the "traditional tension between the animator and the character it animated" (2021, 83). This tension was common in early animated films, such as the Looney Tunes cartoon *Duck Amuck* (Chuck Jones 1953). The machinic side of video games allows that fight to become real, or at least to be fought in real time and with procedural affordances. To further the point, *Duck Amuck* had a video game adaptation (WayForward, 2007) that made us struggle with Daffy Duck in real time, following the film. Or take, for example, idle animations, particularly typical of 2D platformers of the 1990s. A player leaving the controller in *Sonic the Hedgehog* (Sega, 1991) will see an animation of Sonic impatiently tapping his foot while looking at the camera, urging the player to jump back into action. Consider, too, the animations that avatars use in some point-and-click adventures, such as *Gobliiins* (Coktel Vision, 1991) and *Chuchel* (Amanita Design, 2018), to signal that they cannot perform the action we just ordered them to do.

Avatars are, thus, characters we follow and witness as might a literary character, tools we use and roles we play, and also virtual toys we play with. We can think of "avatarness" as a function a virtual object serves by embodying the player within the gameworld, but these virtual objects always have an animatic life of their own. Controlling them is not only a matter of asking ourselves "what do I do" but "what does my character do if I do this?" Avatars do not only react and obey us through animation, they express their personalities, manifesting both the narrative design of the game and the ideas of the animator. Their movement always goes beyond the function of avatarness, of embodiment: they are animatic entities born of the illusion of life.

One last fork that opens in this path is humour. More specifically, humour through control. This is another underexplored area, since "the association with trivialisation brought up by critics of both games and comedy has been hard to shake off" and developers often aim to fight it with "seriousness for legitimacy's sake" (Bonello Rutter Giappone et al. 2022, 5). Nele Van der Mosselaer writes about the dual position of the player that results from the self-division as both actor and observer, between "playing self and played self," both "comic object and the laughing subject" (Van de Mosselaer 2022, 48). We can laugh at what happens to us in the gameworld, and in this regard animation principles like exaggeration can play an important part. Losing hurts less if it comes with funky animation. Or, on the other end of the scale, take the funny dances Kirby does by himself at the end of each level in *Kirby's Dream Land* (HAL Laboratory, 1992): animatic humour can be a reward for the player. A video game like *Wattam* (Funomena, 2019) is built around those pillars: we can control every character on screen (portrayed in a highly caricaturesque, grotesque-cute style) and see what happens when we make them interact. A sentient toilet can take a sentient poop and flush it down itself and a fork, a phone, and a piece of sushi can dance together in circles. In *Wattam*, the answer to "what happens if I do this" is frequently "I get a funny animation" that is intended to make us laugh more than to advance our progress. The visual gag is a central element of visual culture, and video games have a long tradition of constructing them in an interactive manner (Garin 2014). Controlling an animatic slapstick comedian is a source of humour that makes us rethink staples like timing, for example. This understanding of humour is but one way we can explore how animation impacts interaction. If interaction is to be accepted as the defining element of video games, we need accordingly to pay attention to every nuance in the act of playing with animatic entities, as well as to our complex roles as players and puppeteers.

Conclusions

Being animatic goes beyond the formal status of images, even beyond an opposition to the cinematic. It implies a particular type of relation with off-screen reality and with (the illusion of) life. In this chapter, I have tried to expand the study of the complex nature of video games by highlighting their animatic side, which opens many new paths of inquiry. Those discussed here are but a few, and there has only been space to take the first steps in exploring them.

I want to close by insisting on how playable images have their own (an) ontology, a reality that, unlike that of photographed images, shows the artifice and makes the human mediation self-evident, not to reveal the trickery of the playable images but to reinforce the illusion. We play with images in real time, inhabit animatic worlds, and produce movement that we ourselves accept as *living*. The player mode of attraction articulated in manipulating images is a path to engagement with rulesets, goals, characters, and stories. Video games *are* animation: they share a history and a genealogy with that medium, they have material and industrial connections, and they participate in an animatic apparatus that tints our relationship with reality and experiences. Let us (scholars of games, animation, and visual culture) study them as such.

References

Aarseth, Espen. 2019. Game Studies: How to play–Ten Play-Tips for the Aspiring Game-Studies Scholar. *Game Studies* 19 (2).

Agamben, Giorgio. 2009. *"What Is an Apparatus?" and Other Essays*. Trans. D. Kishik and S. Pedatella. Stanford: Stanford University Press.

Alt, Matt. 2020. *Pure Invention: How Japan Made the Modern World*. New York: Crown.

Atkinson, Paul, and Farzad Parsayi. 2021. Video Games and Aesthetic Contemplation. *Games and Culture* 16 (5): 519–537.

Bak, Meredith A. 2020. *Playful Visions: Optical Toys and the Emergence of Children's Media Culture*. Cambridge, MA: MIT Press.

Bateman, Chris. 2011. *Imaginary Games*. Winchester: John Hunt Publishing.

Benavent, Rocío. 2019. El videojuego independiente o 'indie games' made in Spain. *Con A de animación* 9: 42–51.

Burn, Andrew, and Gareth Schott. 2004. Heavy Hero or Digital Dummy? Multimodal Player–Avatar Relations in *Final Fantasy 7*. *Visual Communication* 3 (2): 213–233.

Chen, Jin-Shiow. 2007. A Study of Fan Culture: Adolescent Experiences with animé/manga doujinshi and cosplay in Taiwan. *Visual Arts Research* 33 (1): 14–24.

Cholodenko, Alan. 2007. Speculations on the Animatic Automaton. In *The Illusion of Life, 2: More Essays on Animation*, ed. Alan Cholodenko, 486–528. Sydney: Power Publications.

Clarke, Andy, and Grethe Mitchell, eds. 2007. *Videogames and Art*. Bristol: Intellect Books.

Cousins, Mark. 2011. *The Story of Film*. London: Pavilion.

Criado, José Manuel Palenzuela. 2019. Cuphead y el futuro de la industria audiovisual. *Con A de animación* 9: 14–18.

de Wildt, Lars, Thomas H. Apperley, Justin Clemens, Robbie Fordyce, and Souvik Mukherjee. 2020. (Re-) orienting the video game avatar. *Games and Culture* 15 (8): 962–981.

Fassone, Riccardo. 2017. *Cinema e videogiochi*. Roma: Carocci Editore.

García-Villar, Marta. 2019. Los recursos cinematográficos de *Final Fantasy* y la narrativa transmediática de *Final Fantasy XV*. *Con A de animación* 9: 28–33.

Garin, Manuel. 2014. *El gag visual: de Buster Keaton a Super Mario*. Madrid: Ediciones Cátedra.

Gaudreault, André, and Philippe Marion. 2005. A Medium Is Always Born Twice. *Early Popular Visual Culture* 3 (1): 3–15.

Giappone, Bonello Rutter, Tomasz Z. Krista, and Majkowski and Jaroslav Švelch. 2022. Ludo-comedic Consonance: An Introduction to Video Games and Comedy. In *Video Games and Comedy*, ed. Krista Bonello Rutter Giappone, Tomasz Z. Majkowski, and Jaroslav Švelch, 1–31. Cham: Springer.

Giddings, Seth. 2019. The History of Games Could Be a History of Technology. *ROMchip* 1.

Greenberg, Raz. 2021. The Animation of Gamers and the Gamers as Animators in Sierra On-Line's Adventure Games. *Animation* 16 (1–2): 83–95.

Gunning, Tom. 2012. Hand and Eye: Excavating a New Technology of the Image in the Victorian Era. *Victorian Studies* 54 (3): 495–516.

Hernández-Pérez, Manuel. 2019. 'Branding,' autoría y adaptación transmedia en los productos oficiales de Studio Ghibli: el 'estilo Miyazaki' en los videojuegos de la saga *Ni No Kuni* (2011-2018). *Con A de animación* 9: 102–117.

Huber, William. 2007. Some Notes on Aesthetics in Japanese Videogames. In *Videogames and Art*, ed. Andy Clarke and Grethe Mitchell, 211–218. Bristol: Intellect Books.

Järvinen, Aki. 2002. Gran Stylissimo: The Audiovisual Elements and Styles in Computer and Video Games. In *Proceedings of Computer Games and Digital Cultures Conference*, ed. Frans Mäyrä, 113–128. Tampere: Tampere University Press.

Juul, Jesper. 2021. The Game of Video Game Objects: A Minimal Theory of When We See Pixels as Objects Rather than Pictures. In *CHI Play 21: Extended Abstracts of the 2021 Annual Symposium on Computer-Human Interaction in Play*, 376–381. New York: Association for Computing Machinery.

King, Geoff, and Tanya Krzywinska, eds. 2002. *Screenplay: Cinema/Videogames/Interfaces*. London: Wallflower Press.

Levitt, Deborah. 2018. *The Animatic Apparatus: Animation, Vitality, and the Futures of the Image*. Winchester: John Hunt Publishing.

Loriguillo-López, Antonio. 2020. Scene Hunting for Anime Locations: Otaku Tourism in Cool Japan. In *The Routledge Companion to Media and Tourism*, ed. Maria Månsson, Annæ Buchmann, Cecilia Cassinger, and Lena Eskilsson, 287–296. London: Routledge.

Martín-Núñez, Marta. 2020. Encuadres. Diseñar la escritura audiovisual del videojuego. In *Pensar el juego. 25 caminos para los game studies*, ed. Víctor Navarro-Remesal, 80–86. Valencia: Shangrila.

Mäyrä, Frans. 2020. Game Culture Studies and the Politics of Scholarship: The Opposites and the Dialectic. *GAME: The Italian Journal of Games Studies* 9.

Montañés, María Gutiérrez. 2021. Hamefura o cómo vivir en un juego otome y no morir en el intento. *Con A de animación* 13: 64–77.

Montero Plata, Laura. 2022. *Ready to play? Cinemática vs jugabilidad: interactividad y animación en el gému.* https://www.youtube.com/watch?v=YtL-yh27vTA. Accessed 26 July 2023.

Mukherjee, Souvik. 2015. *Video Games and Storytelling: Reading Games and Playing Books*. New York: Springer.

Navarro-Remesal, Víctor. *Cine Ludens: 50 diálogos entre cine y juego*. Barcelona: UOC Editorial.

Navarro-Remesal, Víctor, and Antonio Loriguillo-López. 2015. What Makes Gému Different? A Look at the Distinctive Design Traits of Japanese Video Games and Their Place in the Japanese Media Mix. *Journal of Games Criticism* 2 (1).

Martín-Núñez, Marta, and Alberto Porta Pérez. 2022. Puzles dramáticos. Decisiones críticas, dilemas éticos y narrativas complejas en el videojuego. *Con A de animación* 14: 40–57.

Pallant, Chris. 2018. Video Games and Animation. In *The Animation Studies Reader*, ed. Nicholas Dobson, Annabelle Honess Rae, Amy Ratelle, and Caroline Ruddell, 203–214. London and New York: Bloomsbury.

Reed, Aaron. 2023. *50 Years of Text Games: From Oregon Trail to A.I. Dungeon*. Oakland, CA: Changeful Tales Press.

Russell, Jamie. 2012. *Generation Xbox: How Videogames Invaded Hollywood*, 2012. Hove: Yellow Ant.

Schmalzer, Madison. 2021. Breaking the Stack: Understanding Videogame Animation Through Tool-Assisted Speedruns. *Animation* 16 (1-2): 64–82.

Sharp, John. 2015. *Works of Game: On the Aesthetics of Games and Art*. Cambridge, MA: MIT Press.

Steinberg, Marc. 2012. *Anime's Media Mix: Franchising Toys and Characters in Japan*. Minnesota: University of Minnesota Press.

Tosca, Susana. 2021. Mediating the Promised Gameland. *Replaying Japan* 3: 151–160.

Van de Mosselaer, Nele. 2022. Comedy and the Dual Position of the Player. In *Video Games and Comedy*, ed. Krista Bonello Rutter Giappone, Tomasz Z. Majkowski, and Jaroslav Švelch, 35–52. Cham: Springer.

Walker, Austin. 2019. The History of Games Could Be a History of What Play Felt Like. *ROMchip* 1.

Williams, Andrew. 2017. *History of Digital Games: Developments in Art, Design and Interaction*. Boca Raton, FL: CRC Press / Taylor & Francis.

CHAPTER 4

Wonder, Awe and Negative Emotions in *What Remains of Edith Finch*

Bartosz Stopel

INTRODUCTION

What Remains of Edith Finch (Giant Sparrow 2017) is an exploration game or a walking simulator, in which players control a character who embarks on a visit to an old, abandoned and desolate mansion in the Northwest of the United States that used to be the residence of the Finch family. The Finches are presumably all dead when the game starts and the player, equipped with Edith Finch's diary, goes to explore the house looking for clues about each family member and their death. From the beginning it is strongly suggested that the Finch family was mysteriously cursed, leading to isolation and tragic, premature deaths. At the same time, Edith's diary frequently touches on the possibility that the family's belief in the curse's existence contributed to their demise and resulted in conflicts between family members over the existence of the curse and the narrative surrounding it that proved to be pivotal for the family history.

B. Stopel (✉)
University of Silesia, Katowice, Poland
e-mail: bartosz.stopel@us.edu.pl

© The Author(s), under exclusive license to Springer Nature Switzerland AG 2024
D. Callahan (ed.), *Visual Storytelling in the 21st Century*, https://doi.org/10.1007/978-3-031-65487-9_4

The story develops linearly and the degree of interaction with the game environment is severely restricted. Yet the game has received widespread acclaim from critics and gamers alike. The review aggregate website Metacritic's score is 89/100 and Steam's rating is 10/10. The game's storytelling, themes, visual imagination and the core aspects of the gaming experience itself, have all been praised. It has been cited as a prime example of environmental storytelling that takes full advantage of what video games as a medium can afford (Bogost 2017). What seems to be most unique in terms of visual storytelling in *What Remains of Edith Finch* is how clues about each family member found in and around the mansion are narrativized to tell a mini-story about their final moments. The stories are triggered by specific items that need to be located by the player first and the exploration of the house involves finding ways inside the rooms that each of the Finches occupied, as the rooms were sealed upon their demises. The player finds that they have been left intact for years after having been abruptly made vacant, leaving us with a sense that the resident has just left for a moment.

While inside the rooms, the player looks for objects that will provide information about each character's final moments. This tends to include forms of visual evidence such as letters, photographs or slides, diaries, comic books, drawings, etc. Each object then initiates an interactive sequence, presumably in the mind of the player-controlled character, depicting the death of whoever it is referring to in an imaginative and unrealistic fashion. There are at least three significant features that almost all of the sequences possess. First, they involve metalepses, when the player-character travels across diegetic levels so as to enact a family member's death. Second, they contain intermedial and combinations (Rajewsky 2005), as the game imitates other media, such as drawings, photographs, comic books and text imposed over landscapes, diaries or other video game genres. Third, every sequence radically departs from the rules and conventions established either by the main game or by earlier sequences in terms of their visual aesthetics, gameplay and the rules of interacting with the environment.

In what follows I wish to explore two issues. First, cognitively, what perspective the game takes on the power of stories and on their connection to human experience. Second, emotionally, how the game is designed to orchestrate affective responses in players and how it offers a gradual working through of traumatic negative emotions, attempting to instil a refreshed and healthy outlook on life. The two issues are closely related, as it is largely through narrativization of characters' biographies that the game attempts to attain its ultimate emotional goals.

With respect to the first point, I will argue that the game takes an ambivalent perspective on storytelling in general, veering between a condemnation of narratives as dangerous fictions that bring the demise of the Finch family, and their celebration as imaginative tools of meaning-making that allow us to make sense out of otherwise meaningless and mundane human existence. This ambivalence is easy to overlook, given how every narrativized segment is carefully designed to elicit a sense of awe and sublimity in the player with its visually imaginative and unreal representation of death, and because the game never explicitly takes the ambivalent stance. However, I do not think of this ambivalence as a flaw reflecting the game's incoherence. I believe the game aims at evoking cognitive dissonance and that accepting this contradictory take is in fact a valuable lesson about the power of narratives that players are supposed to learn from the game.

When it comes to the game's emotional structure, I will showcase how *Edith Finch* attempts to guide players through an emotional journey that starts with acknowledging the Finch family's demise and retelling each member's death in a way that is ultimately about making sense of all the tragedies, healing and attaining a fresh, appreciative outlook on life. The process involves narrativizing every family member's death in unreliable and imaginative ways to inspire a sense of awe and wonder with respect to what mostly seem to be avoidable and tragic accidents. In other words, players are invited to experience all the represented deaths in largely fantastic settings that elevate absurd and avoidable events into mysterious, aesthetically elaborate and unfamiliar scenarios, as well as to reflect on their own cognitive and affective responses to life and death with the help of the series of unusual representations.

This brings to mind both the Aristotelian idea of catharsis understood as clarification (Golden 1976) in terms of a better understanding of one's emotional responses, a process guided by the emotional laboratory of fiction, and Viktor Shklovsky's influential idea of defamiliarization that is at the cornerstone of experiencing any art via deautomatizing everyday perception so as to enrich the experience of the world. By defamiliarizing experiences of death and the loss of family members and by making them strange and unique again, the game encourages players to approach life with a renewed sense of wonder and appreciation, completing the journey from traumatic negative emotions to positive ones that celebrate human existence even when confronting its end.

Storytelling

As mentioned above, the game is structured around interactive and imaginary representations of the Finches' deaths. Every sequence starts when interacting with a specific item attached to a given character and virtually all involve metalepsis, intermedial references and strategies of defamiliarization of the game experience. The game's traversing of the diegetic levels opened up through this process is fairly complex. The player begins by controlling who by the end of the game is revealed to be Christopher, Edith Finch's son, who visits her grave near the old mansion and reads her diary. Upon reading this diary, the player now controls Edith, who herself had gone to visit the house years before in order to uncover the family's secrets and document them.

Throughout the game we frequently hear Edith's voice-over narration with the diary's text superimposed over the physical environment. It is not entirely clear whose fantasies of the Finches' deaths we are enacting—Edith's or Christopher's—but every enaction involves descending yet another diegetic level and controlling a different family member. In some stories (Molly's or Gregory's), the dying Finch imagines becoming another creature, such as a snake, a frog or a video game character, which indicates even further metaleptic transgressions. In one sequence we get to read the diary of Molly, a ten-year-old who died after eating poisonous berries and other inedible substances and who hallucinates turning into a number of ever-more voracious animals. The player first controls a cat jumping across tree branches to hunt down a bird, moving on to being a bird of prey hunting rabbits, a shark hunting seals and a fantastic snake devouring the crewmen of a ship. In another sequence, the player stumbles upon an old-fashioned horror comic book that tells a fictional story of how another family member (Barbara) disappeared. Upon flipping the pages, the story becomes narrated by the grotesque voice of a jack-o-lantern and the player then metaleptically enters the comic book story where they are free to move about the Finch house rendered in the vintage visual aesthetic and reenact the narrative.

Gregory's story involves reading a letter sent between a divorced couple, where the husband consoles his ex-wife after their toddler son drowned in a bathtub. The reenaction of the story takes the toddler's perspective as the letter is read out and imagines a fantastic play activity with toys in a bathtub that ends with the child turning into a frog that dives deeper and deeper to the tune of Tschaikovsky's *Dance of the Flowers*. Sam's story involves browsing old photographs from a hunting trip so as to piece together a story of how he died. In terms of gameplay during this sequence, we control Dawn, Sam's daughter, as she is taking pictures of the hunt, adjusting the lens, framing and looking for specific sights to photograph.

Another example of both metalepsis and intermedial reference can be found in the story of Lewis, who, working in a cannery, drifts more and more into maladaptive daydreaming until he loses his sense of reality and while delusional apparently decapitates himself with one of the cannery tools. His mental breakdown is portrayed in terms of a reality/fantasy split where the player controls Lewis and has to behead fish in the cannery while playing a fantasy adventure video game at the same time. In the final sequence, the cannery disappears and the player only controls Lewis's fantasy game avatar on his way to be crowned king of a magical land.

The list is not exhaustive, but what most of the stories share are clearly intermedial references, where the video game imitates other media (or genres, as with Lewis's story), metalepses and framing stories where the player moves across diegetic levels. This is interwoven with environmental storytelling, leading to rapid changes of gameplay styles, interactivity and visual aesthetics that constantly challenge the norms and conventions of the gaming experience undertaken by the player. With every story, the game subverts its own rules and design, radically altering the sense of narrative immersion and embodiment of the player-character.

I will have more to say on the affective aspect of the game's visual storytelling, focusing on intermediality and defamiliarization in the second part of the chapter, but in the remainder of this section I would like to discuss the cognitive aspect of experiencing the Finch family's stories, as it also has an important bearing on the target effects I believe the game aims to elicit. Towards the end of the chapter I will return to the cognitive, as Edith's final words should be seen as advice on what to intellectually make out of the family's stories and, by extension, out of the game experience.

When it comes to the basic comprehension of the game's narrative structure, the central problems for players' cognition involve the mysteries of the Finches' varying deaths. The narrative macro-questions (Carroll 2019) or the gaps (Bordwell 1985, 48–62) that the players should try to fill would revolve around the issue of the curse: whether it really exists, what its nature is, why the Finches were cursed, if at all, or if there is another explanation for the sequence of mysterious deaths. The microquestions would involve the precise circumstances of each death.

The two converge in the games' climax when after Lewis, Edith's brother, dies their mother gets into an argument with the family matriarch, Edie, who acts as custodian of all the narratives, claiming that her children are dead because of Edie's stories. Edith then gets inside the family library where she begins to read Edie's story but is aggressively interrupted by her own mother who abruptly takes her away and the two leave the house never to return there together. Leaving the house is certainly a pivotal moment in the narrative, but the game suggests it would have been more so if Edith had got to read Edie's story. Unfortunately, we never learn what it was that Edie so desperately wanted to convey to Edith and whether it would fill some of the narrative gaps and uncover more facts about the nature of the curse on the Finches.

Equally mysterious is the short exchange between Edie and her granddaughter (Edith's mother), Dawn. When Dawn interrupts Edith's reading, Edie exclaims that "Edith has a right to know these stories," to which the granddaughter retorts, "my children are dead because of your stories." This can be understood figuratively or more directly. In the former scenario, Edie as the family storyteller and a firm believer in the curse perpetuates the sense of doom and the morbid fascination with death in her family members by telling stories that somehow contribute to their premature demise. The curse then becomes a self-fulfilling prophecy.

In another reading, Edie is more directly responsible for the misery and deaths of her kin. Molly, her firstborn daughter, dies of accidental poisoning as an indirect result of her mother's strict punishment. Walter, her young son, becomes so traumatized on the night of his sister Barbara's disappearance that he spends decades locked in a cellar with his basic necessities provided for by Edie. Calvin, Walter's brother, falls to his death from a swing built dangerously on the edge of a cliff. Taken one by one without the context of the curse or a supernatural mystery, the Finches' deaths show signs of parental neglect, abuse, unaddressed mental health concerns, random accidents or carelessness, all of which are accumulated as generational trauma. Narrativizing them in a supernatural context adds an ideological layer that covers up the actual reasons that made Edie and other parental figures somehow responsible for these deaths.

Finally, Edie herself is obsessed not just with death but with stories and fantasies: with their power, their ability to affect others and to shape reality. It is evident not just through her actions and words recounted by

Edith but also in the artefacts collected in her room. For example, there are newspaper clippings about a moleman living under the Finch house, a story about Walter she must have sold to the press, and various folders with family members' names and the word "concepts" scribbled over them, suggesting her involvement in and labour over a structuring narrativization of their lives. Edith openly says that there were many stories accounting for Barbara's disappearance or death, but Edie decided to focus on and keep a gruesome horror comic book that addresses the issues of earning fame through sensationalized stories that ultimately lead to death, with immortalization via the tawdriness of a popular comic book no compensation for the truncation of young life.

Whatever Edie's connection to the curse and the deaths may be, her preoccupation with narratives indicates dramatically how stories are natural everyday tools for thinking (Herman 2003) and how we routinely engage in conceptualizations of our own and others' experience through stories in order to attain a basic understanding of the world around us, of our past and identities, but also to grasp the significance of everything that happens in a broader picture. In this pursuit, however, lie dangers involving the use of structuring stories, some of which are apparent in the Finch family history. One example is the family curse masterplot (Abbott 2008, 40–54) possibly itself triggering real-life tragic events. Another is the curse mystifying the material reality of the Finch family's deaths and dispersing parental responsibility for neglect and abuse or contributing to a distorted sense-making of random accidents. Interwoven with the above is the danger of being bewitched by the emotional and rhetorical power of stories and by their ability to shape reality, manipulate others and project partisan images and self-images.

Our natural capacity for narrative thinking (Goldie 2011, 8–23) or narrative knowledge (Bruner 1991) in which we aim at causal coherence, meaningfulness and emotional import in our efforts at sense-making is thus always at risk of falling for its own devices, some of which the philosopher Peter Goldie labels fictionalizing tendencies, though I would emphasize that the danger lies in the narrativization of life itself and not in conventions of fictionality.

These four tendencies are more general than the idiosyncratic problems that can be attributed to the Finches and point to deeper issues underlying the putative curse and attempts at narrativizing the events that make up any biography or family history. This does not mean that narrativization will always and necessarily lead to such problems but that they are common risks of tidying family stories into structured narratives. Broadly speaking, two of Goldie's fictionalizing tendencies involve narrative structure and the other two characters and agency. In the first pair, the dangers of storytelling entail the sense that one's life and/or family history are structured like a classic plot with a dramatic structure of introduction, complication and resolution that has a unified thematic thread and tight causality with a meaningful closure. This is evident in Finch family narratives that resemble a cycle of birth, a shortened life plagued with disturbing events and then climactically a tragic death. All of them are bound thematically by the curse that provides closure by seemingly confirming itself with each death.

The whole family history as told by Edith and Edie resembles such a cycle on a collective level. While Edith is supposed to learn Edie's story, this feels, within the scope of the game, as the climax of the family's history. Edie intended to reveal the most significant story to Edith, apparently a major turning point in understanding the family's history as a unified whole. However, a different turning point occurs when Dawn and Edith leave, changing the family history forever and demonstrating to Edie that in the end the unpredictability of life cannot be confined by tidy master narratives. In reality, all of the beliefs in meaningful structure underlying these narrativizing tendencies are false, but we easily fall prey to the dangers they entail because narrative is such a fundamental and instinctive cognitive tool for human beings.

The other category of narrativization tendencies involves the misattribution of agency and a reductive approach to the perception of personality. Again, this is well evident in the Finch family narratives: the role of the curse and suggestions of its supernatural origin are clear cases of shifting agency and responsibility from specific individuals to depersonalized powers that are outside of human control or impact.

Treating people as characters associated with certain narrative genres is a further problematic tendency in which others may be flattened out and perceived as being defined by fixed roles or a narrow range of personality traits, as when categorizing someone as a villain, a tragic hero, a damsel in distress, etc. Such categorizations, inherited from storytelling, not only do not do justice to the complexity of personality but are detrimental to understanding and predicting others' actions, general behaviour or relating to them as complex human beings. In the game, the Finches are very different, but in the eyes of the family history as told by Edie and perhaps in their own fatalistic eyes as well, deep down they are the same set pieces in the family history, doomed to die prematurely and tragically.

All of the Finches seem to be under the spell of this master narrative and fall victim to the dangers entailed by teleological narrativization. Dawn apparently realizes this at some point, hence her decision to leave the house and family history behind. Edith returns later, melancholically obsessed with the exploration of her past like a classic gothic heroine (Kirkland 2020), and she gains similar insights to her mother. Speaking of the Finches, she concludes: "We believed so much in the family curse, we made it real." This clearly indicates her belief that the Finches became collectively absorbed by the doomed narrativization that had become sedimented as the family's structuring reality.

Edith, however, does not vilify the family matriarch or condemn stories in general. After leaving the Finch house, she spends some years with her mother, Dawn, who finally succumbs to an unnamed illness. Later, after investigating the house, Edith possibly dies in childbirth, but neither Dawn's nor Edith's deaths are discussed within the family's narrative framing. That is, they are just events listed in a family chronicle without allusions to a curse or a supernaturally induced doom. In her last words, Edith emphasizes how the brevity of life makes it impossible to fully grasp its meaning or even to thoroughly understand a mysterious family history. She says: "If we lived forever, maybe we'd have time to understand things, but as it is I think the best thing we can do is try to open our eyes and appreciate how strange and brief all of this is." This is surely an anticlimactic ending, as the Finch family mystery is never resolved and all that Edith offers is that we should apparently give up on trying to make sense of life or family history in terms of narrativization and finding structuring answers, turning instead to simply experiencing and appreciating existence.

But it should also be noted that Edith does not reject narrativization per se, given that she next says to her son: "This is where your story begins." Implicitly then, while stories have sense-making uses for human beings, they can be negotiated and reclaimed over against what earlier creators and readers have attempted to implant. This also marks Edith's evolution from a gothic heroine obsessed with death, fate and brooding about dark family history to an existentialist who rejects that any master narratives or semiotic structures hold defining power over us. Now she thinks it is up to us individually to make sense of life. Her final advice to her son is: "I want you to be amazed that any of us ever had a chance to be here at all."

Cognitively, then, the game articulates a state of dissonance (Kiss and Willemsen 2017, 65–104), as the pervasive ambiguities remain unresolved. Stories are presented as cognitive tools that are impossible to abandon, even though they can be toxic and dangerous, and there is barely any resolution with respect to how to approach them beyond trying to tell our own stories. This, however, cannot do away with all the risks of narrativization. In addition, the narrative gaps remain open and the central mysteries are left unsolved. Edith suggests we should stop our puzzle-solving preoccupations and just experience and appreciate life, but that advice only comes after her realization that she could not solve the overall puzzle of the family mystery. That is, only through the crucible of facing up to the family stories does she arrive at the conclusion that it is better not to allow such stories to gain so much traction that they come to seem determining of a family's self-perception. By extension, such a conclusion could be applied to those "families" exemplified by communities, nations or any other grouping that perceives its future in terms of a limiting narrative. Nevertheless, while Edith and Dawn had spent some years living without talking about the family's past, in the end Edith returned to try to solve the puzzle and to parlay them into stories to pass on to her son.

The central question of the game encapsulated in the title becomes then more and more ambiguous towards the end. What is it that remains of Edith? Is it her son? The family stories she decided to perpetuate? Her reclaiming of narrativizing? Her warning about narratives? Her insight into life in general? Moreover, the question extends to Edie, whose full name was also Edith. Are we to juxtapose what Edie and Edith left? Is the game's story a simple condemnation of Edith the elder's obsession with death, stories and a curse that brought demise on her family juxtaposed against Edith the younger's affirmation of liberation from constraining family tradition? The sheer amount of these unresolved ambiguities factors into potential cognitive dissonance among the players but also mirrors Edith's abandonment of puzzle-solving and of her quest to find out what the master narrative of her life is. As we finish the game's puzzles we also are left with the challenge of working out what it has all meant, whether we have simply uncovered a series of curious and visually arresting factual details of an unusual family's history, or whether there are wider conclusions to be drawn.

The game does not aim at producing this effect on a purely intellectual level but uses cognitive dissonance as part of a broader aim to work through certain emotional states. It is not just the declarative nature of

Edith's final message addressed to her son and to the player that suggests what lesson should be learned from the Finch family's stories, but it is rather the gaming enactment of all the visual narratives and how they are processed by the player that offers a kind of affective comprehension and attempts to trigger reflection in the player on an emotional level. I will elaborate on this in the following section.

Emotion

Although *What Remains of Edith Finch* seems to be primarily driven by the mystery solving and the attempts to understand family history that lead to a specific lesson, its chief machinery is located in the sensory, embodied and emotional aspects of the gaming experience. Just like Edith, the player is supposed to suspend cognitive pursuits and experience life, in the form of the game, prioritizing affective states such as being amazed at the very fact of human existence and the many unexpected ways it can end.

Of course discussions of how a player *should* feel about a particular game are fraught with difficulties and can be seen as negating the transgressive (Aarseth 2014, 180–188) and emancipatory (Farca 2016) qualities of interactivity, privileging an overreliance on an implied response that mimics non-interactive media. However, given how ambiguous and unusual the contents of the game are, the opposition between an implied and emancipated player collapses, as in *Edith Finch* the implied player is supposed to be emancipated by moving away from the basic gaming pleasures of beating a game or scoring points and turning to aesthetic appreciation and philosophical ruminations. In addition, trying to determine how a game is structured to elicit and guide certain emotional responses can only mean sketching the basic contours of such an implied experience and acknowledging that with every player or gameplay it can only be approximated. In other words, a type of analysis that is a modelling which does not exclude other responses or idiosyncrasies.

Finally, there already exists a growing body of research into how games are designed to elicit emotions that cuts across various approaches (Bednorz 2020, 108–112) from rhetorical and formalist game studies (Bogost 2008; Isbister 2016), philosophical ones (Tavinor 2010) and cognitive-neuroscientific ones (Perron and Schröter 2016). Some of this research overlaps with earlier work on stories and emotions in film or literature (Tan 1996; Plantinga 2009; Hogan 2018).

The emotional structure of *Edith Finch* articulates, I believe, a transformative and healing journey from the gothic preoccupation with death and a dark past to a life-affirming and renewed sense of wonder about existence itself. At first, we witness Edith brooding about the family curse in what seems like a haunted mansion of a family obsessed with death. But as soon as we begin to enact the stories behind their deaths and encounter their visual representations, they become the antitheses of gothic fiction. Most are metaphorical renditions of the Finches' final moments and are filled with supernatural occurrences and anti-mimetic representations of death. In fact, we never get to witness actual death, corpses, decay, funerals or mourning in the Finch stories, as they all end abruptly the very moment a family member is supposed to die.

These unrealistic, narrativized sequences that continually disrupt whatever the game establishes as its own rules of gameplay, visual aesthetics, mediality or interactions are instrumental in eliciting the emotional transformation in question. The process appears to involve working through negative emotions via defamiliarization of representations of death, but also via defamiliarization of the gameplay and interactivity, so as to encourage emotions of wonder and awe, rather than despair, melancholia or a sense of being trapped in a vicious cycle of the family curse. Defamiliarization here is understood along the lines of Viktor Shklovsky, who insisted that the chief role of art is to move beyond mere mimetic representation and challenge our perceptual habits by an inventive use of the creative resources of the particular art form being used. The purpose of art in this influential view is to make whatever has become fixed, established and habitual fresh and engaging again, to make whatever is familiar new and unfamiliar again, by challenging the habits of our perception through whatever means necessary. In Shklovsky's words: "Automatization eats things, clothes, furniture, your wife, and the fear of war. ... And so this thing we call art exists in order to restore the sensation of life, in order to make us feel things, in order to make a stone stony. ... the device of art is the 'estrangement' of things and the complication of the form, which increases the duration and complexity of perception" (Shklovsky 2015, 162). Although Shklovsky is talking about perception, it is clear that the aim of defamiliarization should lead to cognitive and affective change, that is not in simply appreciating the aesthetic affect of defamiliarization but in having our affective relation to things improved and enriched. In *Edith Finch*, it can be argued that defamiliarization works in such a fashion, gradually revealing a number of varied ontological layers of the world with which players interact before it reaches its ultimate goal of a more fundamental cognitive and affective transformation.

Moving from more fine-grained material objects to abstract ideas, the first level of defamiliarization involves dehabituating the perception of common objects and their medial characteristics: the texts of personal letters and diaries interweave with the mimetic world of the game and become superimposed over walls, floors or skies. Comic books come alive and photographs involve dialogue and continuously flowing narratives. Characters who disappear from a drawing disappear from real life as well. An in-game medical document triggers a generically different playable video game. Kites have the power to move objects on the ground, bathtub toys perform fairy-tale dances, a cannery becomes a fantasy palace, etc.

Defamiliarizing how players interact with common objects and media entails defamiliarization of the in-game spaces. As all stories take place either inside or in the vicinity of the house (the cannery being the farthest away, but still located on the same tiny island), the mimetic spaces that Edith traverses become unfamiliar, strange and tinged with a diverse array of affective charges evoking amazement that enrich and efface the original sensation of a gloomy gothic mansion. How they are perceived and responded to affectively accordingly changes dramatically. Defamiliarization of objects and spaces leads to a refreshed perception of the family biographies enacted in these spaces. Not only is more information about their deaths revealed, but they all acquire mysterious and even sublime and spiritual dimensions. As mentioned above, what could be seen as dark and dismaying cases of neglect, abuse or simply absurd accidents suddenly become the singular, lofty and awe-inspiring threads of a mysterious narrative.

Defamiliarization of the narratives of the Finches' deaths aims at evoking a refreshed perspective on life and death in more general terms. This works together with the suspension of the puzzle-solving pursuits with respect to the Finch curse and of attempts at comprehending the broader utility and significance of stories, as outlined in the previous section. The players, along with Edith and her son, are continuously exposed to the subversion of fixed, repetitive and formerly accepted notions about the depressing space of the house and how to interact with it, along with a subversion of corresponding notions about life and death. This encourages a process of cognitive and emotional transformation that works to reject the family masterplot and its obsession with death, moving rather towards the appreciation of everyday experiences that range from basic interactions with common objects and spaces to a more general affirmation of life as something awe-inspiring, even when it involves bizarre deaths and stupid accidents.

If defamiliarization is understood as a process of complicating perception that leads to dehabituation and a refreshed, more engaged perspective on whatever has become established, then strongly positive emotions such as wonder or awe may also be considered fitting candidates to describe its effects. Although wonder is a relatively vague state, some of its general characteristics can be inferred from diverse approaches to emotion studies. Shaun Gallagher et al.'s neurophenomenological studies of wonder define wonder as "a reflective experience motivated when one is unable to put things into a familiar conceptual framework–leading to open questions rather than conclusions" (Gallagher et al. 2015, 6). This surely implies destabilization of habituated meanings and a state of openness not unlike that encouraged by Edith. Gallagher thinks of wonder as a preliminary state that frequently leads to an experience of awe which he labels a "feeling when faced with something amazing, incomprehensible, or sublime" (Gallagher et al. 2015, 6). It is certainly true that even though wonder and awe are frequently grouped together and both involve a sense of surprise or amazement, wonder is seen as positively charged affectively, while awe is associated with a degree of fear or uneasiness at the perception of something sublime that tends to challenge our ability to comprehend and process it.

The connection between wonder and awe is even closer for Jesse Prinz, who sees the former as nothing less than "the most human emotion" (Prinz 2013) as well as the fundamental aesthetic emotion felt when experiencing art (Fingerhut and Prinz 2018). Prinz lists three key subemotional components and stages of experiencing wonder: "cognitive perplexity, perceptual engagement, and a sense of reverence" (Prinz 2013). First, we experience wonder when we encounter something sensually captivating, which is reflected in the flamboyant visual storytelling of *Edith Finch*. Second, wondrous things elude our established conceptual frameworks or beliefs, hence a sense of perplexity or surprise and the inability to solve the puzzle of Finch family history, accompanied by the game's highly unusual visual representations of death and the mementos linked to them. Finally, wonder involves a certain spiritual aspect, as we look up to wondrous things as giving us a sense of perspective about the complexity and richness of existence and the world. The fortunes of the members of the Finch family are so varied and strange that wonder is ironically an appropriate response, despite each of the family member's stories ending in their death.

A meaningful correspondence may thus be established among the above accounts of wonder and awe, the implied effects of the Finch family narratives and the lesson learned by Edith, and defamiliarization. That is, the emotional transformation that the game aims to bring about involves a transition from the negative and depressing emotions associated with lost family members, stories of a family curse and an obsession with death, towards questioning the overwhelming power of stories and moving on to an appreciation of everyday life, and an affirmation of human existence in general. This occurs in large measure on account of the visual storytelling that carries the largest responsibility for defamiliarizing interactions with the game objects, spaces and character biographies. A refreshed perspective on life and death is associated with attaining the closely related emotional states of wonder or awe, states that lift individual stories out of being defined by their end but rather by the attitudes to life and the imaginative actions of their protagonists as envisaged through the magical visual representations of everybody's stories.

Conclusion

What Remains of Edith Finch possesses a discernible and sophisticated emotional game design structured as a working through of negative emotions associated with multiple and mysterious deaths layered over by a family curse. The ultimate point is to attain a renewed state of awe and wonder where one appreciates everyday existence. The game encourages us to reach that state on a cognitive and affective level. With respect to the former, it attempts to curtail player's puzzle-solving operations and leave them in a state of cognitive dissonance involving the risks and benefits of storytelling. On an affective level, the game offers enactments of death scenarios that are highly unrealistic, attempting to elicit a sense of amazement through the defamiliarization brought about by the magical and mysterious visual possibilities offered by contemporary gameplay.

References

2017. *What Remains of Edith Finch*. US: Giant Sparrow.
Aarseth, Espen. 2014. I Fought the Law: Transgressive Play and the Implied Player. In *From Literature to Cultural Literacy*, ed. Naomi Segal and Daniela Koleva, 180–188. London: Palgrave Macmillan.

Abbott, H. Porter. 2008. *The Cambridge Introduction to Narrative*. Cambridge: Cambridge University Press.
Bednorz, Magdalena. 2020. Digital Experience of Love and Loss: Emotional Game Design in *Emily Is Away*. *Przegląd Kulturoznawczy* 1: 108–121.
Bogost, Ian. 2008. The Rhetoric of Video Games. In *The Ecology of Games: Connecting Youth, Games, and Learning*, ed. Katie Salen, 171–140. Cambridge: The MIT Press.
———. 2017. Video Games Are Better Without Stories. *The Atlantic*. April 25. https://www.theatlantic.com/technology/archive/2017/04/video-games-stories/524148/. Accessed 12 May 2023.
Bordwell, David. 1985. *Narration in the Fiction Film*, 48–62. Madison, WI: University of Wisconsin Press.
Bruner, Jerome. 1991. The Narrative Construction of Reality. *Critical Inquiry* 18 (1): 1–21.
Carroll, Noël. 2019. Movies, Narration and the Emotions. In *Philosophy and Film: Bridging Divides*, ed. Christina Rawls, Diana Neiva, and Steven Gouveia, 209–221. New York: Routledge.
Farca, Gerald. 2016. The Emancipated Player. In *Proceedings of 1st International Joint Conference of DiGRA and FDG*. http://www.digra.org/digital-library/publications/the-emancipated-player/. Accessed 1 Sept 2023.
Fingerhut, Joerg, and Jesse J. Prinz. 2018. Wonder, Appreciation, and the Value of Art. *Progress in Brain Research* 237: 107–128.
Gallagher, Shaun, Lauren Reinerman-Jones, Bruce Janz, Patricia Bockelman, and Jörg Trempler. 2015. *A Neurophenomenology of Awe and Wonder*. Basingstoke: Palgrave Macmillan.
Golden, Leon. 1976. The Clarification Theory of 'Katharsis'. *Hermes* 104 (4): 437–452.
Goldie, Peter. 2011. Life, Fiction, and Narrative. In *Narrative, Emotion, and Insight*, ed. Noël Carroll and John Gibson, 8–23. State Park: Penn State University.
Herman, David. 2003. Stories as a Tool for Thinking. In *Narrative Theory and the Cognitive Sciences*, ed. David Herman, 163–192. *Stanford*: Center for the Study of Language and Information.
Hogan, Patrick. 2018. *Literature and Emotion*. New York: Routledge.
Isbister, Katherine. 2016. *How Games Move Us: Emotion by Design*. Cambridge, MA: MIT Press.
Kirkland, Ewen. 2020. 'He Died a Lot': Gothic Gameplay in *What Remains of Edith Finch*. In *Death Culture & Leisure: Playing Dead*, ed. Matt Coward-Gibbs, 95–107. Bingley: Emerald Publishing.
Kiss, Miklós, and Steven Willemsen. 2017. *Impossible Puzzle Films: A Cognitive Approach to Contemporary Complex Cinema*. Edinburgh: Edinburgh University Press.

Perron, Bernard, and Felix Schröter. 2016. *Video Games and the Mind: Essays on Cognition, Affect and Emotion.* Jefferson, NC: McFarland.

Plantinga, Carl. 2009. *Moving Viewers.* Berkeley: University of California Press.

Prinz, Jesse. 2013. How Wonder Works. *Aeon.* https://aeon.co/essays/why-wonder-is-the-most-human-of-all-emotions. Accessed 12 May 2023.

Rajewsky, Irina O. 2005. Intermediality, Intertextuality, and Remediation: A Literary Perspectuve on Intermediality. *Intermedialites* 6: 43–64.

Shklovsky, Viktor. 2015 [1917]. Art, as Device. Alexandra Berlina (Tr. and Int.). *Poetics Today* 36 (3): 151–174.

Tan, Ed S. 1996. *Emotion and the Structure of Narrative Film: Film as an Emotion Machine.* Trans. B. Fasting. New York: Routledge.

Tavinor, Grant. 2010. *The Art of Videogames.* Chichester: Wiley-Blackwell.

CHAPTER 5

Look Behind You, Orpheus: Queer Archeology and Mythical Lesbians in Contemporary Film

Ana Bessa Carvalho

INTRODUCTION

One need not be a chamber–to be haunted.
  Emily Dickinson

In the 1996 film *The Watermelon Woman*, the filmmaker Cheryl Dunye, who appears both in front of and behind the camera, has recourse to ancient technology—VHS tapes—to look for a mythical being: a black lesbian. The ground-breaking film is fictional but it uses the language of documentaries to provide a portrait of Fae, a woman who, at the beginning of the twentieth century, was cast in the stereotypical role often given to black women: the maid. Dunye, through fake testimonies, counterfeit memories, and staged photographs brings Fae to life, while also providing a poignant view of the hardships of being a black lesbian in filmmaking.

A. B. Carvalho (✉)
University of Minho, Braga, Portugal
e-mail: anacarvalho@elach.uminho.pt

© The Author(s), under exclusive license to Springer Nature Switzerland AG 2024
D. Callahan (ed.), *Visual Storytelling in the 21st Century*,
https://doi.org/10.1007/978-3-031-65487-9_5

Although *The Watermelon Woman* is not one of the main case studies of this article, it seems relevant to evoke it briefly, not only due to its relevance as a part of the movement of New Queer Cinema, and how mythical a black lesbian filmmaker still is, but also for the look it casts over the past, in a cross-temporal dialogue that informs present experience, a concern that still marks much of current queer cultural objects, discourses, critical theory, and artistic creation. Moreover, Dunye's film gives voice—and a body—to what is often perceived as a ghostly presence, particularly in film:

> Why is it so difficult to see the lesbian—even when she is there, quite plainly, in front of us? In part because she has been "ghosted"—or made to seem invisible—by culture itself. It would be putting it mildly to say that the lesbian represents a threat to patriarchal protocol: Western civilization has for centuries been haunted by a fear of "women without men"—of women indifferent or resistant to male desire. (Castle 1993, 4–5)

It is exactly this look backwards created by Dunye that this article engages with, through a close reading of *Portrait of a Lady on Fire* (2019), directed by Céline Sciamma, in dialogue with *Ammonite*, directed by Francis Lee (2020), recurring to the tools provided by the critical framework of queer temporalities and queer haunting. It will be argued that these films are also a part of a current desire for queer and feminist approaches to narratives that are concerned with looking back at the past, directly engaging with it, and even altering it, reclaiming the existence of queer figures in a past which is erroneously thought to have been devoid of them.

Many of the cultural objects that have been produced over the last years seem to be fueled by this exact same desire, of which these films are only a part, having permeated several genres and rather distinct forms of representation. TV shows such as *Pose* (2018–2021), which echoes—and is rather derivative of—the ground-breaking documentary *Paris is Burning* (1990), have provided drag and ballroom culture with a renewed interest, showcasing a universe that Joseph Cassara has also brought back to life with the novel *The House of Impossible Beauties* (2018). Other visual objects such as the TV show *It's a Sin* (2021) or the films *Pride* (2014) and *120 Battements par Minute* (2017) also look back at the 1980s but move away from the tragic representations of HIV/AIDS that marked the immediate reaction to the epidemic, showing how, more than death, these times were also marked by resistance, activism, and the renewal of networks of support and care, as well as a redefinition of family.[1] While Sarah Schulman's *Let the Record Show* (2021) provides an intersectional account of ACT UP's activism that questions the claim that ACT UP's work was always and mainly carried out by white gay men, other more experimental works such as the graphic novel *Barbalien* (2021) look at the AIDS years from other angles, in this case through the eyes of a gay alien that has just landed on Earth. Even works of historical fiction that establish a queer, parallel timeline to the straight one that has been made official by history have been proliferating: from new retellings of a country's official accounts of history, and how they engage with queer history, as found in Almodóvar's *Parallel Mothers* (*Madres paralelas* 2021), to many biopics of individuals who, having been queer, are often remembered as straight, such as an unexpected romantic comedy that re-enacts Emily Dickinson's relationship with a woman, with the suggestive title *Wild Nights With Emily* (2018). It seems then safe to argue that queer objects are deeply engaged with the past, although it would also be reductive to claim that all they do is talk with the dead or to state conversely that non-queer objects are unconcerned with the past.

The films that make up the corpus of this article also want to engage with the past, and although very distinct when it comes to their artistic achievements and creative solutions, their similarities are also manifold. *Ammonite* and *Portrait of a Lady on Fire* both depict the relationships between two women, the latter in the early eighteenth century and the former in the late nineteenth. While *Portrait of a Lady on Fire* is a fictional account, although certainly many women were having affairs with each

---

[1] As Kate Weston writes, "[t]he number of PWAs [people with AIDS] without homes, family, or resources has grown year by year. When people told relatives and friends they had AIDS, kin ties were reevaluated, constituted, or alienated in the act, defined by who (if anyone) stepped forward to offer love, care, and financial assistance for the protracted and expensive battles with opportunistic infections that accompany this disease" (Weston 1991, 186). Moreover, "[s]ituated historically in a period of discourse on lesbian and gay kinship, AIDS has served as an impetus to establish and expand gay families. In certain cases blood relations joined with gay friends and relatives to assist the chronically ill or dying. Sometimes a family of friends was transformed into a group of caregivers with ties to one another as well as the person with AIDS. Community organizations began to offer counseling to persons with AIDS 'and their loved ones,' while progressive hospitals and hospices modified residence and visitation policies to embrace 'family as the client defines family.' Implicit in a phrase like 'loved ones' is an open-ended notion of kinship that respects the principles of choice and self-determination in defining kin, with love spanning the ideologically contrasting domains of biological family and families we create" (Weston 1991, 183).

other at the time, of the doomed relationship between a young painter and the subject of her paintings, *Ammonite* is a somewhat embellished biography of Mary Anning, a woman who has been defined as the first paleontologist, who, given her sex, saw her work being diminished by her male colleagues, who also prevented her from officially joining the Geological Society of London. As it will be argued, both films are haunted by the impossibility of lesbian relationships, the historical diminishing of women in scientific and artistic careers, and the will to tell stories of women who have been deemed invisible throughout history.

TRACING A GHOST

a ghost who proclaims, *Without this sheet, I would be invisible.*
Maggie Nelson, *The Argonauts*

Portrait of a Lady on Fire provides us with an intimate glimpse of the brief affair between Marianne, a young painter, and Heloise, a young woman who has recently come out of a convent and who will soon be forced to get married to a man. Heloise, who has never met her future husband, must have her portrait painted in order for him to see her face for the first time, at a time when social media did not exist. The act of creating her portrait works as a manner of entrapping Heloise and her husband will own not only her painting but also her body. If "[t]o photograph is to appropriate the thing photographed" (Sontag 2008, 4), to paint Heloise is a double act of appropriation that she tries to defy, in vain: first to be appropriated as the object of the painter's gaze and then, through marriage, to become her husband's propriety. Marianne and Heloise collaborate together in creating a painting that, once finished, will separate them, enhancing the tragic aspect of the film as well as the inability of changing the course of women who were meant to be wives and mothers. As Jackie Stacey writes:

> The looking that expresses their desires turns the task of one woman capturing the other's beauty on canvas for a man's pleasure into a painful paradox, with which each must reckon in their own way: if the painter satisfactorily completes the painting, she will be handing her lover over to a man for marriage; if the sitter acquiesces to her part, she will be facilitating her own unwanted fate ... once a satisfactory portrait has been completed, their love is destined to become a memory. (Stacey 2022, 280)

After Heloise refuses to sit for male artists, and therefore to be appropriated, Marianne, who earns a living by teaching young girls how to paint, is brought in as a companion maid to observe Heloise during the day and paint her by night. Eventually, Heloise finds out about Marianne's task and agrees to be painted, aware that the action will lead to her wedding. The women fall for each other, but are inevitably separated when Heloise is sent to her husband. The film provides a complex analysis of women's lives, and how they are informed by matters such as abortion, marriage, motherhood, patriarchal rule, mental illness, and the constraints for women with respect to a career in the Arts. It also dialogues directly with the myth of Orpheus, an intertextual narrative that is particularly productive for the analysis of the dialogue with the past that this film establishes, a detail that is also emphasized by the fact that the film is narrated as a long flashback, resulting in "a beautiful meditation on how the present ('at') becomes the past ('back'): how lived experience may be turned into images, although that risks replacing a dynamic living person with static pictures that degrade in replication; but ultimately must become memory alone" (Stevens 2020, 46).

Ammonite is simpler in its ambitions and aesthetic choices, perhaps missing the depth and spark found in the women of *Portrait of a Lady on Fire*. Charlotte, a woman who is sent by her husband to the healing beach of Lyme Regis to be cured of melancholia comes across Mary Anning, a paleontologist, with whom she starts digging for fossils while also unblocking what seems to be a repressed sexual desire toward women, perhaps one of the main causes for the myth of hysterical women. Charlotte eventually goes back to London but she invites Mary to live with her, but Mary refuses to do so, preferring her life as a woman of science rather than abandoning her career for a domestic life with Charlotte, again implying that even when unmarried, women can still be paralyzed by domesticity. Although it is known that Anning discovered the first plesiosaur, had an astounding ability to find and prepare fossils, and saw her findings sold to museums, the scientific community, and private collectors, much is unknown about her personal life. Unmarried and childless, Anning is reimagined in the film as a lesbian, although her sexual orientation, whether lesbian or heterosexual, was not formerly apparent. What is known is that Anning was working-class and a woman, two contexts that made it impossible for her to be taken seriously as a scientist, being instead perceived as a mere seller of fossils.

The ammonite, "an ancient marine shell, coiled around its secrets" (Shafak 2021, 289) is a particularly interesting type of fossil to look at, especially given this chapter's take on the relationship between past and present and the haunting effect of the former. As it grew, the animal that lived inside the shell would move into a larger chamber, closing the one behind it, never to be inhabited again, a chamber that would be filled with air and water to allow the animal to float and move. It "survived three mass extinctions and they weren't even good swimmers. But they had a fascinating ability to adapt, tenacity being their strong suit" (Shafak 2021, 409), in the same manner perhaps that "queers survive through the ability to invent or seize pleasurable relations between bodies ... across time" (Freeman 2005, 58). The body of the ammonite is a collection of haunted chambers that succeed each other, a past time and space that can never be visited again but that works as a propelling force for movement. Moreover, the animals that filled the chamber have been extinct for millions of years but their shells have been preserved, and are still found today in several locations, as a reminder that the past is always being dug up, unveiled, and brought back by these traces, these testimonial objects,[2] and the leftovers of animals who, although long gone, can still be perceived by what they left behind.

Both *Ammonite* and *Portrait of a Lady on Fire* overlap in several (queer) spaces. Images of women sketching each other, embroidering, or strolling along the coast can be found in both films, indicating similar aesthetic choices, while also tackling the difficulty that women met when it came to being recognized in their fields, whether science or the arts. Beyond the fact that these women are lesbians, both films also express concerns about the oppression felt by women over time when it comes to the intersection of sex, class, and education, in what seems to be a direct link with Linda Nochlin's reflection on how patriarchal institutions have always failed women:

---

[2] Marianne Hirsch's concept of the "testimonial object" seems a productive metaphor to think about how objects travel through time and space, carrying memory and narratives: "[s]uch 'testimonial objects' carry memory traces from the past, to be sure, but they also embody the very process of its transmission. They testify to the historical contexts and the daily qualities of the past moments in which they were produced and, also, to the ways in which material objects carry memory traces from one generation to the next" (Hirsch 2012, 178).

things as they are and as they have been, in the arts as in a hundred other areas, are stultifying, oppressive, and discouraging to all those, women among them, who did not have the good fortune to be born white, preferably middle class and, above all, male. The fault lies not in our stars, our hormones, our menstrual cycles, or our empty internal spaces, but in our institutions and our education … The miracle is, in fact, that given the overwhelming odds against women, or blacks, that so many of both have managed to achieve so much sheer excellence, in those bailiwicks of white masculine prerogative like science, politics, or the arts. (Nochlin 2018, 150)

Both films also look at how mental illness, depression, and even suicide often stem from repressed sex lives and women's conditioning brought by marriage and domesticity, particularly two centuries ago, which are portrayed in both films as entrapments. The fact that these women were lonely and, although married, had husbands who were often absent, is shown as leading them to find love and support in other women. Moreover, both films show how unmarried women had to work to earn a living, something that often translated into freedom and the ability to develop a craft and avoid unwanted marriages, offering a comment, in both Anning and Marianne's cases, of how being financially independent is the only way out of married life.

The films are so similar in their purpose and language that even their final scenes mirror each other. In *Portrait of a Lady on Fire*, Marianne exhibits a painting painted by her but submitted under the name of her father in order to be accepted by a museum. A man approaches Marianne, who is standing by her painting of Orpheus and Eurydice, to congratulate her on her father's skills. In *Ammonite*, Anning visits the British Museum, where she sees that a fossil she had collected is presented under a man's name. The fossils are now at the Natural History Museum, finally credited to her, but Anning is not alive to see this attempt at making amends for centuries and centuries of women's oppression.

Framing a Ghost

Girls, forget what you've read.
It happened like this—
I did everything in my power
to make him look back.
Carol Ann Duffy, "Eurydice"

As the title of this chapter proposes, the analysis of these films is anchored in the metaphors of the ghost and the fossil, with recourse to Carla Freccero's concept of queer haunting, as well as Heather Love's feeling backward, and how both expand the queer project beyond the time continuum. The figure of the ghost is also posited as central, featured in *Portrait of a Lady on Fire* through the myth of Orpheus, and works as a queer device for a dialogue with the past, considered multidirectionally. For Avery Gordon:

> Haunting raises specters, and it alters the experience of being in time, the way we separate the past, the present, and the future. These specters or ghosts appear when the trouble they represent and symptomize is no longer being contained or repressed or blocked from view. The ghost is not the invisible or some ineffable excess. The whole essence, if you can use that word, of a ghost is that it has a real presence and demands its due, your attention. Haunting and the appearance of spectres or ghosts is one way ... we are notified that what's been concealed is very much alive and present, interfering precisely with those always incomplete forms of containment and repression ceaselessly directed toward us. (Gordon 2008, xvi)

Although set in the past, both films offer a comment that remains relevant for contemporary audiences regarding the silencing of women, how old problems are still very much alive, and about the need to establish a broader sense of community, one that stretches backwards, as Sciamma's film

> envisions a social contract defined by a strong sense of community among women, no matter their age or class. It takes place in the late eighteenth century, but it also speaks to our own time, as many women continue to call for intersectional solidarity in their fight for equality. (Bittencourt 2020)

Heather Love also sustains the significance of this turn into the hurt of the past in order to face present struggles, claiming that "as long as homophobia continues to centrally structure queer life, we cannot afford to turn away from the past; instead, we have to risk the turn backward, even if it means opening ourselves to social and psychic realities we would rather forget" (Love 2007, 29) These queer temporalities deny the idea of a single timeline marked by sequential signs of progress, leaving space for a history that is marked by pride but also by shame, advancements, and setbacks, where the hard-won rights of women and LGBTQI+ individuals are often the first to be taken away in times of conflict, creating a timeline in which specters of past troubles re-appear. Looking at how our understanding of time is yet another device for the regulation of bodies, anchored in narratives of movement and change, Elizabeth Freeman writes on "an ethics of responsibility toward the other across time—toward the dead or toward that which was impossible in a given historical moment, each understood as calls for a different future to which we cannot but answer with imperfect and incomplete reparations" (Freeman 2010, 9–10), and both Sciamma and Lee's films seem to aim exactly at this reparation of the past.

In a "fluid approach" to *Portrait of a Lady on Fire*, Michèle Bacholle also hints at the ability of the film to offer contemporary audiences a moment for learning, a reparative reading, while establishing a cross-temporal dialogue, by claiming that the film must not be reduced to the lesbian or queer categories, nor be considered a period piece, for its themes, artistic dialogues, and aesthetic choices disrupt time, making it fluid in its attempt at "re-educating spectators" (Bacholle 2023, 148). The film works as a ghostly reminder of things yet to be repaired regarding "society's invisibilization and silencing of women across centuries" (Bacholle 2023, 148), either when it comes to their non-normative sexuality or to their precious but often forgotten contribution to the visual arts. This re-education is also carried out by Marianne, whose students are young girls, in an attempt to contradict the myth that there are no great female artists, as Marianne works as a mentor who intends to take women painters out of anonymity. *Portrait of a Lady on Fire* retrains the eye and the look, offering an alternative way to the male gaze, both in form and content, creating

> a meta-reflection of the place of the woman in cinema and art history by immersing its audience in the reconfiguration of the visual pleasures that were foundational to the birth of feminist cultural criticism. The academic attention to looking as desiring, at the heart of feminist work since its inception, becomes the central diegetic trope here, inviting a critical reflection on the history of the "male gaze" as the film holds us in the affective immediacy of female homoeroticism. (Stacey 2022, 281)

This look at the past is particularly clear in *Portrait of a Lady on Fire*, as the film is deeply engaged with the act of looking and being looked at; as bell hooks reminds us in her essay, not on male or female gazes but on the oppositional look, "[t]here is power in looking" (hooks 1992, 115), and

Sciamma knows that. When Heloise finally sits to be painted by Marianne she asks her: if Marianne looks at her, who does she look at, contradicting the male gaze in which women are always looked at but never look back? While performing this look at the past, the past also looks back, haunting us, in a double-directed gaze just as Heloise "looks back and turns the portrait painting into a collaboration" (Stacey 2022, 279).

Many reviews of the film claim it to be an example of a "female gaze." However, it can be argued that *Portrait of a Lady on Fire* is not interested in merely reverting the objectification of women in film but aims at a much more complex creation, a pleasure of looking in which the subject looks but is also looked at, while the object actively participates in that act of looking, offering a dismantling of a patriarchal gaze that is in and of itself not even interested in men at all (they barely appear on screen) or the mere inversion of what is an affectionless gaze upon a body. Warren Buckland writes on how the film refuses the mere inversion of the act of looking *at*—or looking *back*: "The film does not masculinize the female character—it avoids simply inverting gender roles (it does not place Marianne in the position of a male painter and appropriate the male gaze for her); instead, it deploys the gaze in a deliberate and reflexive manner, thematizes it, demonstrates its discursive procedures, and transforms it in order to express female desire" (Buckland 2020, 16). At the same time the film resists creating the lesbian through what Annamarie Jagose refers to as the self-licensing logic of sequence that always places homosexuality as secondary to heterosexuality's "natural" aspect, and lesbians as a product of sequence and the hierarchies that this logic establishes (Jagose 2002). The female look is not merely composed as negative or a lack; it is also an erotic look reclaiming an active role as sexual beings for women, and particularly lesbians, whose sexuality is often deemed inexistent as it is not dependent on the figure of the phallus. Such an intervention defies the image of "the castrated woman" (Mulvey 1999, 803) and reclaims the pleasure of looking. In Sciamma's film, women are agents and lovers and objectification is replaced by desire but also affect and a sense of sorority. Instead of merely challenging the male gaze, Sciamma, who claims the film to be "a manifesto on the female gaze" (qtd in James 2020) creates a longing gaze, a loving gaze, a type of scopophilia in which women take pleasure in looking at the object of their desire and the object of their painting, in a horizontal rather than a vertical line of vision. Even the patriarchal gaze is inflicted upon Heloise not by a man but by a woman, her mother, implying then that gazing at someone is a somewhat complex action in the service of an enforcement of power that, as it is difficult to dismantle, must be carefully articulated and perceived as a manifold (queer) act rather than as a mere inversion of the male gaze. And what to make of *Ammonite*, a film about lesbians directed by a man, but where the look into the past is not even backwards but downwards, underground—or, to use a metaphor familiar to the language of the myth of Eurydice, into the underworld?

Another moment of what Bacholle defines as the "re-education" that *Portrait of a Lady on Fire* offers its spectators can be seen when Marianne and Heloise read Ovid to/with Sophie, the young servant who will later have an abortion. Although slightly younger than Marianne and Heloise, Sophie could perhaps work as the object of a transgenerational dialogue, not only as she learns and discusses the classics with Marianne and Heloise but also when she draws on the knowledge of an older woman who will help her get rid of an unwanted child. The scene of the abortion is particularly striking, not only due to the fact that it features an event often hidden from film and other artistic creations but also in the subtle comment it provides on multiple temporalities.

While Sophie is lying down in front of the abortionist, who is removing the fetus from inside her, a baby lies next to her. Sophie looks warmly at the child, who looks back at Sophie. The comment that is offered can be seen either as a statement about how a fetus that can be aborted is not a child, distancing each from the other, or as an implication that, even though young Sophie may be having an abortion now, she may still find herself wanting to be a mother later. Either way, the intentions of Sciamma's strange and unexpected juxtaposition are obvious: abortion is not incompatible with caring or even motherhood, but it may rather express an inability to enter into these experiences at an earlier stage of life: "here, as elsewhere, the film oscillates between cycles of life and death that bring one into close proximity with the other" (Stacey 2022, 293).

After the abortion the three women collaborate again, just as Mary and Charlotte work together to dig up fossils in *Ammonite*, mimicking the abortion so that Marianne can crystalize the scene in painting; if it had been real, Marianne's painting could have been the very first pictorial representation of abortion in art history. "I do not believe there exists a *Workshop of the Backstreet Abortionist* in any museum in the world," claims Sciamma: her film, and the paintings it creates, questions exactly what matters can be turned into art and what supposedly must remain unrepresented (Sciamma quoted in Syme 2020).[3]

Sciamma's film contradicts the gaze of art history, of men over women, of men behind the camera, of a lover toward their object of desire, creating a cinematic language that resists appropriation, whether the appropriation of the body or of the representational codes of male-dominated arts, showing "how to find a language for desire between women in the context of its historical erasure; and how to conceptualize identifications and desires without reducing them to a social phenomenon" (Stacey 2022, 292). Even Marianne's first attempt at painting Heloise is criticized by the latter for lacking life, to which Marianne replies that she must follow rules and conventions of representation, those bequeathed by male artists and the ones that turn women into objects. Marianne's portrait of Heloise needs, however, to be painted not by convention but by desire, intimacy, and longing.

Through the myth of Orpheus, the spectrality of *Portrait of a Lady on Fire* becomes, paradoxically, more solid. While analyzing the myth of Orpheus and Eurydice, the women struggle to understand the reasons that led Orpheus to look back, to condemn his beloved to death. The film "queer(ie)d the myth in three ways: by questioning it through her characters, by challenging its commonly accepted interpretation, and by reconciling what appeared to be two conflicting, or at least diverging, interpretations" (Bacholle 2023, 153). The film finds its Orpheus in Marianne, who sees flashes of Heloise as a ghost even before losing her, the white sheet that cartoon ghosts wear replaced by a wedding dress, a metaphorical death *avant la lettre*, in which the loved one, like Eurydice, is already lost. In this process, "[e]ach such appearance is a spectre that interrupts the logic and flow of the narrative events" (Stacey 2022, 306), in the same manner that "haunting, ghostly apparition, reminds us that the past and the present are neither discrete nor sequential. The borderline between then and now wavers, wobbles, and does not hold still" (Freccero 2007, 196). Even the painting that Marianne has made of the myth offers an alternative narrative of the myth itself, opening up a third space of representation, once more giving preference to liminal, spectral spaces:

---

[3] This particular painting may not exist in museums but Paula Rego, Juanita McNeely, and Frida Kahlo painted scenes of abortion, even if the number of depictions of this act remains scarce.

Whereas the myth is more traditionally painted at the iconic moment of Orpheus "turning around" or after Eurydice has died, Marianne has chosen an interstitial moment, when Eurydice is in the midst of being snatched back down to the Underworld. With each figure reaching for the other, as the attendee notes, "They seem to be saying 'goodbye'." It is a heartbreaking moment, emphasizing shared but separate experience of loss. (Stevens 2020, 53)

Looking may very well be the main action of *Portrait of a Lady on Fire*, but only as a device to ensure the presence of the loved one, that they are still there, visible: the film, with its flashbacks, phantoms, and paintings on fire, is as much about loss and destruction as it is about creation. For Heather Love, this loss is also at the heart of the myth of Eurydice, and it is exactly that feeling that draws queer subjects to the myth, since "her specific attraction for queer subjects is an effect … of a historical experience of love as bound up with loss" in an act that is meant "to acknowledge the losses of both the past and the present" (Love 2007, 51). Heloise haunts Marianne as both women haunt the audience, reminding us that

> [t]he ghost is … pregnant with unfulfilled possibility, with the something to be done that the wavering present is demanding. This something to be done is not a return to the past but a reckoning with its repression in the present, a reckoning with that which we have lost but never had. (Gordon quoted in Freccero 2007, 196)

When Heloise asks Marianne to turn back and see her in her wedding dress, she becomes the agent of her own death, reducing herself to a memory. Scateni also supports the idea that Eurydice is ultimately an agent in her own death (just as Heloise's sister, who committed suicide in order to escape marriage), by referring to Carol Ann Duffy's feminist retellings of the lives of historical and mythical figures in *The World's Wife* (1996):

> The same reading of the myth can be found in a poem by Scottish author Carol Ann Duffy. In "Eurydice," both voice and agency are finally given to the woman, who recalls a life wasted trailing behind Orpheus's greatness. "Rest assured that I'd rather speak for myself … In fact, girls, I'd rather be dead," Eurydice says, and by titillating Orpheus's ego one last time, she makes him turn, finally freeing herself from his grasp. (Scateni 2020)

From here on, Marianne, who "chooses memory of their love over a doomed encounter" (Bacholle 2023, 153), can only have access to her loved one as an image, just as painting or photography condemn our dead to memory, in a movement similar to that which queer history imposes on the past: to look at it as memory, unreachable, but spectral and ghostly. For Love, the myth of Orpheus

> offers an apt emblem of the practice of queer history. The failed attempt to rescue Eurydice is a sign of the impossibility of the historical project per se: the dead do not come back from beyond the grave, and this fact constitutes the pathos of the historical project. But we might also read the Orphic lament as an effect of the particular losses suffered by queer historical subjects. (Love 2007, 50)

By the end of the film, Marianne sees Heloise for the last time but Heloise does not see her, just as Eurydice is also looked at but is unable to look back given that she is in the underworld. As Marianne's voice-off says, Heloise did not see her; the presence of the voice-off is another device of the "film's commitment to storytelling via the single character's memory" (Stevens 2020, 54), that of Marianne, who has only Heloise's memory to live with. However, through queer objects such as *Ammonite* and *Portrait of a Lady on Fire*, the past does look back, informing the present, and establishing a trans-temporal dialogue. Marianne has no other option but to turn back when told to do so, embracing the phantom pain of losing her lover, fully aware that the movement of turning backward means losing Heloise. Similarly, the queer historian must also look back in an emotional rescue of the queer figures of the past, aware of the loss and failure of such an action, since not to do so would be to betray the purpose of history:

> Orpheus's relation to Eurydice [is] an impossible relation: by turning back he betrays her, losing her forever in the lower depths; but the refusal to turn back would count as a betrayal as well. Such is the relation of the queer historian to the past: we cannot help wanting to save the figures from the past, but this mission is doomed to fail. In part, this is because the dead are gone for good; in part, because the queer past is even more remote, more deeply marked by power's claw; and in part because this rescue is an emotional rescue, and in that sense, we are sure to botch it. But, according to Blanchot, not to botch it would be a betrayal. Such a rescue effort can only take place under the shadow of loss and in the name of loss; success would constitute its failure. (Love 2007, 50–1)

As *Portrait of a Lady on Fire* suggests to its audience, there must be "a queer ethics of historical practice, a willingness to live with ghosts and to remember the most painful, the most impossible stories" (Love 2007, 43) given that "we cannot do justice to the difficulties of queer experience unless we develop a politics of the past" (Love 2007, 21). Heloise, as well as the long record of injustices done to queer bodies, still appear as ghosts, haunting us, lifeless and therefore unable to be killed.

Living with the Ghost

And when I am dead, come visit my bed/My fossil is bright in the sun.
Sufjan Stevens, "Beloved My John"

In *Ammonite*, Anning describes the work of digging for fossils as hard, often unproductive, without any finds; she could also be describing the effort of queer historians and critics who find themselves digging through the past, expecting to find spectral queer figures, as "[t]he past is in the present in the form of a haunting. This is what, among other things, we imagined for queer history, since it involves openness to the possibility of being haunted, even inhabited, by ghosts" (Freccero 2007, 194). Faced with the impossibility of traveling back in time, what remains is to bring back the past, respecting the memory of the dead, while reflecting on

> how past generations and events occupy the force fields of the present, how they claim us, and how they haunt, plague, and inspirit our imaginations and visions for the future ... each project—feminist, multicultural, and queer— also allows itself to be haunted in the context of an articulation of political aspirations in the present. (Wendy Brown 2001, quoted in Freccero 2007, 200)

In *Ammonite*, the spectator is told that Anning informs us not only of our past but also of our present, and the same can be said about the films here analyzed—and fossils and ghosts. Just as Anning and Charlotte dug up the sands of Lyme Regis to look for souvenirs of the past, queer historians and artists keep "mining the present for signs of undetonated energy from past revolutions" (Freeman 2010, xvi). The work of the paleontologist is time-consuming; it chips fingernails and one's hands become muddy and unclean. It is also a collaborative effort, one that ultimately allows us to have glimpses of a past that also inform us of our present. Queer paleontology is rather similar, particularly when Anning claims that she cannot promise that she will find anything while digging—but she will keep on dying and looking backwards, forwards, and even downwards.

It seems pertinent to rewind and go back to the wonderful object that is the VHS cassette, a fossil on its own, the object that allows Dunye, in *The Watermelon Woman*, to draw a line—a long strip of tape—from past to present and to a woman whose desires and experiences mirrored her own. The tape, like the ammonite, and maybe even this article, fold over themselves, reminding us that things often repeat themselves by succeeding each other in a more or less predictable manner, forming a pattern sown with the "threads in the fabric of collective grief" (Ahmed 2014, 157), as with the embroidering that Sophie and Charlotte bring to life. But as this past which does not want to stay dead was taken away from those who were often set aside by history, or made invisible, it is the job of queer cultural objects to reimagine the possibilities, not only of the queer future, or a "backward future" as Heather Love defines it, but also the queer past, given that sometimes, as Dunye claims in *The Watermelon Women*, one has to create one's own history. In this process it may be revealed that there is a person made of flesh under the white sheet of the ghost that keeps on haunting us, or that our fossils are actually made of hard, shiny plastic to be sold as souvenirs.

Think of your ghosts. Be kind: rewind.

References

Ahmed, Sara. 2014. *The Cultural Politics of Emotion*. Edinburgh: Edinburgh University Press.

Almodóvar, Pedro (Director). 2021. *Madres paralelas*. [Film]. El Deseo; Remotamente Films AIE

Bacholle, Michèle. 2023. For a Fluid Approach to Céline Sciamma's *Portrait of a Lady on Fire*. French Cultural Studies 34 (2): 147–160.

Bittencourt, Ela. 2020. *Portrait of a Lady on Fire*: Daring to See. The Criterion Collection. June 23. https://www.criterion.com/current/posts/6991-portrait-of-a-lady-on-fire-daring-to-see. Accessed 29 May 2022.

Brown, Wendy. 2001. *Politics out of History*. Princeton, NJ: Princeton University Press. Quoted in Freccero, Carla. 2007: 200.

Buckland, Warren. 2020. The Logic of the Cinematic in *Portrait of a Lady on Fire*. Quarterly Review of Film and Video 39 (2): 1–18.

Campillo, Robin (Director). 2017. *120 Battements par Minute*. [Film]. Les Films de Pierre; France 3 Cinema; Page 114; Memento Films; FD Production.

Cassara, Joseph. 2018. *The House of Impossible Beauties*. New York: HarperCollins Publishers.

Castle, Terry. 1993. *The Apparitional Lesbian: Female Homosexuality and Modern Culture*. New York: Columbia University Press.

Davies, Russell T., Peter Hoar, and Nicola Shindler (Executive Producers). 2021. *It's a Sin* [TV series]. Red Production Company.

Dunye, Cheryl (Director). 1996. *Watermelon Woman, The*. [Film]. First Run Features.

Freccero, Carla. 2007. Queer Spectrality: Haunting the Past. In *A Companion to Lesbian, Gay, Bisexual, Transgender, and Queer Studies*, ed. George Haggerty and Molly McGarry, 194–213. Malden, MA & Oxford: Blackwell.

Freeman, Elizabeth. 2005. Time Binds, or, Erotohistoriography. *Social Text* 23 (3–4): 57–68.

———. 2010. *Queer Temporalities, Queer Histories*. Durham, NC: Duke University Press.

Gordon, Avery F. 2008. *Ghostly Matters: Haunting and the Sociological Imagination*. Minneapolis: University of Minnesota Press.

Hirsch, Marianne. 2012. *The Generation of Postmemory: Writing and Visual Culture After the Holocaust*. New York: Columbia University Press.

hooks, bell. 1992. The Oppositional Gaze: Black Female Spectators. In *Black Looks: Race and Representation*, 115–131. Boston: South End Press.

Jagose, Annamarie. 2002. *Inconsequence: Lesbian Representation and the Logic of Sexual Sequence*. Ithaca, NY and London: Cornell University Press.

James, Emily St. 2020. *Portrait of a Lady on Fire* Director Céline Sciamma on Her Ravishing Romantic Masterpiece. *Vox*. February 19. https://www.vox.com/culture/2020/2/19/21137213/portrait-of-a-lady-on-fire-celine-sciamma-interview. Accessed 12 May 2022.

Lee, Francis (Director). 2020. *Ammonite*. [Film]. BBC Films; British Film Institute; See-Saw Films.

Lemire, Jeff, Tate Brombal, Gabriel Hernandez Walta, Jordi Bellaire, and Aditya Bidikar. 2021. *Barbalien: Red Planet*. Milwaukie, OR: Dark Horse.

Livingston, Jennie (Director). 1990. *Paris Is Burning*. [Film]. Academy Entertainment; Off White Productions.

Love, Heather. 2007. *Feeling Backward: Loss and the Politics of Queer History*. Cambridge, MA: Harvard University Press.

Mulvey, Laura. 1999 [1975]. Visual Pleasure and Narrative Cinema. In *Film Theory and Criticism: Introductory Readings*, ed. Leo Braudy and Marshall Cohen, 6th ed., 837–848. New York: Oxford University Press.

Murphy, Ryan, Brad Falchuk, Nina Jacobson, Janet Mock, and Brad Simpson (Executive Producers). *Pose*. [TV Series]. 2018–2021, 3 seasons. Color Force; Brad Falchuk Teley-vision; Ryan Murphy Television; Fox 21 Television Studios; FX Productions.

Nochlin, Linda. 2018 [1971]. Why Have There Been No Great Women Artists? In *Women, Art, and Power and Other Essays*, 145–178. New York: Routledge.

Olnek, Madeleine (Director). 2018. *Wild Nights with Emily*. [Film]. P2 Films; UnLTD Productions; Salem Street Entertainment; Embrem Entertainment.

Scateni, Ren. 2020. How *Portrait of a Lady on Fire* Celebrates the Female Gaze. BFI. February 26. https://www.bfi.org.uk/features/portrait-lady-fire-female-gaze. Accessed 29 Mar 2023.

Schulman, Sarah. 2021. *Let the Record Show: A Political History of ACT UP New York, 1987–1993*. New York: Farrar, Straus and Giroux.

Sciamma, Céline (Director). 2019. *Portrait de la jeune fille en feu* [*Portrait of a Lady on Fire*]. [Film]. Lilies Films, Arte, Hold Up Films.

Shafak, Elif. 2021. *The Island of the Missing Trees*. New York: Bloomsbury.

Sontag, Susan. 2008 [1978] *On Photography*. London: Penguin Books.

Stacey, Jackie. 2022. Lesbian Cinema Without Lesbians: Portraits, Lovers, Siblings. *Screen* 63 (3): 279–308.

Stevens, Benjamin. 2020. "Not the Lover's Choice, But the Poet's": Classical Receptions in *Portrait of a lady on fire*. *Frontière.s* 2: 45–58.

Syme, Rachel. 2020. 'Portrait of a Lady on Fire' Is More Than a 'Manifesto on the Female Gaze'. *The New Yorker*. March 4. https://www.newyorker.com/culture/cultural-comment/portrait-of-a-lady-on-fire-is-more-than-a-manifesto-on-the-female-gaze. Accessed 18 Jan 2022.

Weston, Kate. 1991. *Families We Choose: Lesbians, Gays, Kinship*. New York: Columbia University Press.

CHAPTER 6

"All These Things into Position": Intermedial Storytelling via Radiohead's "Street Spirit," the Novels of Ben Okri, and Feminist Dystopia

Alena Zhylinskaya

Introduction: From *The Handmaid's Tale* to Postcolonial Intermediality

In 2017, the streaming service Hulu released a dystopian series *The Handmaid's Tale* (created by Bruce Miller) based on the 1985 novel of the same name by well-known Canadian author Margaret Atwood. Since adaptation is an interconnected process in which both media are being "mutually adapted to each other" (Elliott 2020, 271), the continuity among *The Handmaid's Tale* and other media forms serves as an exemplification of one current development in the realm of storytelling in which resonances across media provide part of the pleasures of audiences.

A. Zhylinskaya (✉)
Belarussian State University, Minsk, Belarus
e-mail: alenazhylinskaya@gmail.com

© The Author(s), under exclusive license to Springer Nature Switzerland AG 2024
D. Callahan (ed.), *Visual Storytelling in the 21st Century*,
https://doi.org/10.1007/978-3-031-65487-9_6

Pleasure, however, is in short supply in Atwood's book, or in the relatively faithful first season of the television show. The main character, named Offred (played by Elisabeth Moss), lives in a patriarchal and militaristic state, "The Republic of Gilead." After having overthrown the US government, Gilead imposes quasi-religious ideas aimed at controlling women and increasing birth rates. The totalitarian state replaces women's identities and priorities with differentiated social roles such as that of Handmaids, Marthas, Wives, and Aunts, in which the Handmaids represent the most unprivileged group, deprived of basic human rights, education, personal choices, and reproductive freedom. Zahra Sadeghi and Narges Mirzapour point out the similarities between the women's position in Gilead society and that of colonized subjects everywhere. In the latter condition, women are held captive, silenced, marginalized, and alienated from themselves: "What happens to the handmaids, or the women in Gilead generally—being forbidden from writing or reading a book, having no opportunity for gathering or communicating with each other, being deprived of the freedom to choose their clothes, and the custom of naming people after their owners—is very similar to what happens to the Black people during colonialism" (sic; Sadeghi and Mirzapour 2020, 11). Further elaborating this point, Adam Briedik labels Atwood's novel as a "postcolonial feminist dystopia" (Briedik 2021). Offred's experience embodies a "double colonization" by both the patriarchal society and the privileged classes of women who have aligned themselves with the hegemonic discourses of patriarchy: "She is victimized by the North American postcolonial patriarchal society of the 20th century and oppressed by the domineering classes of women, who struggle for power in the battle between the sexes—struggles based on Foucauldian differentials of knowledge and power similarly as postcolonial fiction" (Briedik 2021, 63). Functioning the same way as an imperial power center, Gilead monopolizes the production and distribution of knowledge and universalizes patriarchal ideology. From the position of authority, the regime dictates women's place in society and denies their subjectivity while turning them into objects of colonization who cannot speak for themselves. Just like the colonized, Offred resists the oppression by telling her story. As Dennis Walder points out, the ability of the colonized to tell their story empowers them to retrieve history, and "by retrieving their history to regain identity" (Walder 1998, 7).

In the novel's last chapter "Historical Notes," it is revealed that Handmaid Offred did not write her story down. Instead, she recorded it on thirty tapes, organized randomly. The scholars of the future transcribed the tapes and rearranged them in some sort of order. Among other things, each tape contained popular songs that covered the Handmaid's testimony:

> There were some thirty tapes in the collection altogether, with varying proportions of music to spoken word. In general, each tape begins with two or three songs, as camouflage no doubt: then the music is broken off and the speaking voice takes over. ... The labels on the cassettes were authentic period labels, dating, of course, from some time before the inception of the Early Gilead era, as all such secular music was banned under the regime. (Atwood 1985, 461)

Thus, the primary form of the tale is, in fact, a voiceover narration upon music cassettes. The 2017 Hulu TV adaptation implements the figure of a female narrator as well as the off-camera commentary which runs through the majority of the scenes. Understandably, since a modern TV series is an audiovisual medium, the show incorporates a soundtrack—a mix of the original score composed by Adam Taylor and popular songs of different genres. As a result, the visual storytelling techniques of the TV series translate the original form of Handmaid's story arguably even more accurately than the literary ones. While transmedia adaptation is usually considered a continuation of the diegesis of the initial medium (Wells-Lassagne 2017, 92), this case study calls into question what exactly should be labeled as an adaptation or as a discrete media form in itself. Is it productive to perceive the written narrative of *The Handmaid's Tale* as an adaptation of the audio tapes? Or should we consider the soundtrack and the voiceover narration of the TV show to be an original part of the source tale on music cassettes?

In addition, the success of Hulu's series gave rise to a number of *Handmaid's Tale* TV tie-in editions with Elisabeth Moss on the cover (2017 Vintage and Emblem Edition paperbacks), while the shot of Margaret Atwood directing the first episode appears on the cover of the collection of essays *Adapting Margaret Atwood: The Handmaid's Tale and Beyond* (Wells-Lassagne and McMahon 2021). These cases not only indicate the dissolving boundaries between literary and cinematic media but also subvert the hierarchy between the original literary source and the audiovisual (cinematic) copy. Within this perspective, the present chapter argues for the existence of a certain hybrid medium of *The Handmaid's Tale* where Atwood's novel, Miller's series, and the show's soundtrack become equal signifiers.

Regarding the process of adaptation, it should be noted that adaptations "tend to invoke not only their source texts but also a host of further cultural and textual layers" (Straumann 2015, 262), including those generated by means of a soundtrack. As explained by Kevin J. Donnelly, "multipurpose music" that recontextualizes stock, licensed pop, and rock songs to use them on screen circulates as a "prime cultural logic" (Donnelly 2005, 148). The soundtrack functions as a form of an intertext that alludes to a variety of cultural phenomena, art, literature, and social movements, while the reiteration of the same music pieces accentuates "how similar and repetitive screen action and narrative situations can be" (Donnelly 2005, 122). However, apart from the narrative and structural functions, emotional impact, and creation of the atmosphere, music "also tends to take on a life or identity of its own, like the discourse that frames the story" (Goldmark et al. 2007, 3). The discursive potential of a soundtrack opens up new avenues for research, since a single song choice can generate a new framework of meanings, thereby enabling increased and nuanced transcultural and intermedial communication.

Leaving Taylor's original score aside, this chapter focuses entirely on the selection of popular music in *The Handmaid's Tale* and its impact on the storytelling. In particular, it discusses the reiteration of the same song in various scenes, the transparent boundary between the diegetic and non-diegetic, and the transmedia communication between Atwood's novel and the television adaptation. In this, something becomes apparent that should always have been obvious: visual storytelling in filmed media is also auditory storytelling, and not merely through character dialogue. It can be seen, for example, that special emphasis has been placed on the song choice in the third episode of season four (entitled "The Crossing"). The episode features Radiohead's track "Street Spirit" (aka "Fade Out") which in turn was inspired by the 1991 Booker Prize-winning novel *The Famished Road*, written by Ben Okri. The purpose of the present study is accordingly to reveal how this song choice connects Margaret Atwood's feminist dystopia with Ben Okri's postcolonial novel.

Both intermedial and postcolonial studies take an interest in hierarchical structures and power dynamics that constitute cultural knowledge. Birgit Neumann highlights the political aspect of intermediality in the following way:

> The concept of intermediality points to the constitutive and dynamic role of media in construing forms of sociality and perpetuating cultural knowledge,

including concepts of identification, alterity and power, in colonial and postcolonial times. As such, it invites us to question the overarching political structures in which different medial practices and self-representation become possible. (Neumann 2015, 512)

Neumann stresses here the vital characteristics of intermediality such as the connectivity of different cultures as well as the connectivity of media. By crossing cultural boundaries, intermediality explores "in-between" spaces similar to postcolonial studies. According to Neumann, the combination of the two approaches to postcolonial intermediality could be "a powerful means of revealing the contact zones, exchanges and passages between what were once considered separated and homogenous entities" (Neumann 2015, 527). The "transgression of boundaries" (Wolf 2015, 460) and "investigation of how meaning is generated by cross-medial references" (Rippl 2015, 9) make the concept of intermediality comparable to the idea of hybridity, foregrounded in postcolonial discourse since Homi Bhabha's influential essays of the 1980s and 1990s, collected in *The Location of Culture* (1994).

According to Leela Gandhi, the term "hybridity" refers to the "mutual contagion and subtle intimacies between coloniser and colonised" (Gandhi 1998, 129). She notes that the discourse of hybridity originates from the works of Frantz Fanon, who was one of the first to consider colonial oppression as "a catalyst for the accelerated mutation of colonised societies" (Gandhi 1998, 130). Fanon insisted on the mutual transformation of the consciousness of the colonizer and the colonized, while identifying cultural instability as an opposition to the national myth of cultural purity. Homi Bhabha further developed the discussion of hybridity and substantiated the influential concept of the "third space" (Bhabha 1994, 37) also referred to as "in-between spaces" (Bhabha 1994, 1) or an "interstitial space" (Bhabha 1994, 3). The mutual contact between opposed or differentiated cultural systems results in the creation of a new hybrid or "the third place." As explored by Bhabha, this space of hybridity is an intermediary between clearly defined oppositions, such as the East–West dichotomy, Us–Them, Center–Periphery, not to mention I–The Other. Nowadays, the discourse of hybridity incorporates the questions of borderline identities as well as the interconnectedness of cultural and aesthetic paradigms and forms of representation. Madina Tlostanova notes the increasing interest in the concept of hybridity across various research fields that study modern culture, identity, and "otherness" such as postcolonialism, postmodernism, feminist, gender, and queer theories (Tlostanova 2012).

The Soundtrack of *The Handmaid's Tale*: Three Cases

"You Don't Own Me" by Lesley Gore (S01:E01 "Offred" and S04:E10 "The Wilderness")

At the beginning of the pilot episode ("Offred"), the main character describes the status quo of a new reality. Women are forced to take the patronymic names of their rapists. "My name is Offred [of Fred]. I had another name but it is forbidden now. So many things are forbidden now" (S01:E01). Patronymic names emphasize women's position as properties of their "Commanders," the honorable men of the Republic of Gilead. The fact that "Offred" cannot reveal her real name even in an interior monologue shows the extreme level of suppression of any signs of individuality. However, the character undergoes the first major development of the plot by the end of the episode. While conforming to the regime on the outside, she commits her first act of rebellion on the inside—she reclaims her name. In the final scene, she says: "Because I intend to survive. ... My name is June" (S01:E01). The episode ends with a closing song, "You Don't Own Me" performed by Lesley Gore. Since its release in 1963, this musical composition has been strongly associated with women's empowerment and has been used as a feminist anthem, both in the 1960s and during the #MeToo movement in the 2010s (Ulaby 2019). Gore sings from the point of view of a girl who does not want to be seen as her boyfriend's property. The female protagonist declares that her freedom cannot be limited by the normative idea of an obedient and submissive "ideal girl":

> You don't own me
> Don't try to change me in any way
> You don't own me
> Don't tie me down 'cause I'd never stay
> I don't tell you what to say
> I don't tell you what to do
> So just let me be myself
> That's all I ask of you
> (Gore 1963, 7)

In *The Handmaid's Tale*, this song captures a shift in the main character's state of mind. Not only does it symbolize hope but acts as a promise of June's future resistance. It marks her intention to stay true to herself and regain her identity.

The single is featured for the second time in the final episode of season four ("The Wilderness"). Despite June's testimony about sexual, physical, and psychological abuse, Fred Waterford escapes punishment and is released after the trial. Failed by the law and justice system, June and other former Handmaids feel powerless and decide to take justice into their own hands. They arrange the abduction of the Commander and eventually execute him. The scene of June's revenge, where she hunts her abuser in the forest as if he is prey, is accompanied again by "You Don't Own Me." The reiteration of the song connects the first and the final stages of June's transformation, highlighting the profound discontinuity between the character's original situation and the outcome of her story at this stage. It leaves the viewer questioning whether June actually breaks free or loses herself in vengeance. Is she restoring her identity by taking control and finding satisfaction in violent retribution or is she getting further away from her old self? "June Osborne you knew doesn't exist anymore. Gilead changed her. I've changed her," Waterford states previously in the show (S03:E12 "Sacrifice"). And even after his death, there is no closure for June just yet, as the questions of freedom, control, and identity reconstruction remain open. Analysis of the scenes (S01:E01 and S04:E10) reveals that the story of June's oppression has not been heard by the justice system. The inability of the legal system to hear and validate June's experience plays an important part in the process of the character's alienation from herself. By implication, to what extent do we own ourselves if our stories are not witnessed and endorsed by the systems set up to arbitrate on justice in our society?

"Heaven Is a Place on Earth" by Belinda Carlisle (S03:E09 "Heroic" and S04:E03 "The Crossing")

Another example of the integration of music and image in the Hulu adaptation of *The Handmaid's Tale* is episode nine of season three, entitled "Heroic." In this episode, June's mental state is challenged by solitary confinement in hospital. While being forced to spend weeks on her knees praying for a dying Handmaid, June struggles with intrusive thoughts, hallucinations, and homicidal and suicidal ideas. The sound of a heart monitor reminds her of the snippets of the late 1980s hit song, "Heaven Is a Place on Earth," performed by Belinda Carlisle.

"Do you hear it?" says June via voiceover narration.
"I didn't at first. Not for a few weeks."
"Don't you hear it?"
Then she starts to mumble the lyrics of the song matching the beat of the heart monitor.
"Ooh, baby, do you know what that's worth?
Ooh, Heaven is a place on Earth."
"Right?"
"They say in Heaven, love comes first
We'll make Heaven a place on Earth
Ooh, Heaven is a place on Earth."
"Don't you hear it?"
"You will."
(Carlisle 1987, 1)

As June sings the lyrics, acapella singing can be heard in the background. The music reappears several times throughout the episode, sometimes coming from June, sometimes foregrounding June's voice. June's borderline state between sanity and madness is mirrored by the music's borderline location between diegetic and non-diegetic positions. June's singing becomes the source music along with the song's echo in the background, as it allows an added avenue into the character's point of view. However, the song also plays during the opening sequence which makes it initially non-diegetic, coming outside of the story's "reality." Robynn J. Stilwell calls this boundary between the story on screen and cinematic means of storytelling a "fantastical gap," a liminal space that captures "the sense of unreality that always obtains as we leap from one solid edge toward another at some unknown distance and some uncertain stability" (Stilwell 2007, 187). When the song keeps coming from different directions, shifting between diegetic and non-diegetic, it destabilizes "the reality" of the world on screen. Is the soundtrack recognized by the character as a narrative technique? Or does the character's subjective perspective control the narrative, all the means of the storytelling including the soundtrack? In this case, all of the songs featured in the series should be recontextualized as diegetic, constituting the means that June chooses to reconstruct what happened to her. In the context of the episode, the way the soundtrack crosses boundaries allows the viewer to experience disorientation and subtly lose touch with reality, similar to what happens to June in the story albeit on a different narrative level.

The lyrics of the song "Heaven Is a Place on Earth" are heard yet again in season four episode three entitled "The Crossing." Similar to the scene described in the preceding paragraphs, June is locked and tortured in prison. She mutters the same lines as before, and the singing functions as a flashback to the previous season. Furthermore, it completes the story arc, given that in "Heroic" June conceived the idea of saving children from Gilead, while in "The Crossing" she faces the consequences of her action.

Starting again as source music, the singing continues throughout the sequence of various scenes featuring different locations and characters. Stilwell points out that this moving boundary between being diegetic and non-diegetic is a place of transformation, "The border region—the fantastical gap—is a transformative space, a superposition, a transition between stable states" (Stilwell 2007, 200). In this sense, the show uses the soundtrack as a narrative tool to cross cinematic borders. It emphasizes the character's borderline position, since June also exists in a liminal space as a marginalized subject. Further on in the episode, this liminality is highlighted by another song choice: "Fade Out" (aka "Street Spirit") performed by Radiohead.

"Street Spirit" (aka "Fade Out") by Radiohead (S04:E03 "The Crossing")

In the third episode of season four, June faces the aftermath of a successful rescue (or a kidnap according to the Gilead law) of fifty children and their transfer to Canada. The red van transports rebellious Handmaids to the Colonies but makes a required stop at a railway crossing. Immediately, June sees an opportunity to escape. The four-minute scene of the escape features "Street Spirit" (aka "Fade Out"), a prominent 1990s single performed by Radiohead.

The first verse of the song underscores the intensity of a sequence of actions inside the van: June makes eye contact with other Handmaids in the car bringing the possibility of an escape to their attention. After making sure that everyone understands her intentions and is mobilized, June attacks Aunt Lydia. However, the soundtrack's lyrics contain apocalyptic imagery that does not allow any hope:

> Rows of houses, all bearing down on me
> I can feel their blue hands touching me
> All these things into position
> All these things we'll one day swallow whole
> And fade out again and fade out
> (Radiohead 1995, 12)

The second verse is playing while June is contemplating killing Aunt Lydia. The lyric describes what can be interpreted as a failure of communication that occurs in depersonalized systems. It calls for humanity associated with the image of a "world child" (Radiohead 1995, 12). In the context of the scene, "the machine" that "will not communicate" (Radiohead 1995, 12) reminds the audience of the Republic of Gilead itself and of how the repressive system changes people. The viewer sees June willing to do what it takes to break free, even if that means walking on the edge of humanity. Surprisingly enough, Aunt Lydia happens to be the one to summon up the Handmaid's humanity by using her real name. Under the threat of death, Aunt Lydia says, "June … June, don't do it" (S04:E03).

All of the six Handmaids make a run for the level crossing. Taking the lead, June and Janine gain some distance from the rest of the group and turn out to be the only ones who manage to cross the railway before the train arrives. In the meantime, two of the girls get shot by the guardian and two others get hit by the train. The third verse of "Street Spirit" foreshadows the tragic ending with its ominous lyrics:

> I can feel death, can see its beady eyes
> All these things into position
> All these things we'll one day swallow whole
> Fade out again
> Fade out again
> (Radiohead 1995, 12)

While the heartbroken Handmaids, June and Janine, escape from the guards, the scene ends with contrasting lyrics in the background: "Immerse your soul in love" (Radiohead 1995). This episode is the directorial debut of the leading actress Elisabeth Moss who was also responsible for choosing Radiohead's "Street Spirit" for the show's most prominent and devastating escape scene. Another essential point to keep in mind while analyzing this particular song choice is the background of the track. According to Thom Yorke, the main vocalist and songwriter of the band, "Street Spirit" was heavily influenced by the 1991 Booker Prize-winning novel *The Famished Road* written by Ben Okri (Draper 2004, 16). This leads to yet another layer of analysis in the unpacking of the intermedial relations among the various texts summoned here, by way of a brief examination of *The Famished Road*'s main themes and motifs.

The Crossing: Storytelling, Borderline Identities, and Images of Transition

The Famished Road (1991) is a postcolonial novel by Nigerian author Ben Okri. It is the first novel in the trilogy about a boy named Azaro, the Spirit Child. The story of Azaro is continued in two sequels, *Songs of Enchantment* (1993) and *Infinite Riches* (1998). In his trilogy, Okri describes a formerly colonized society right after Independence. An abstract African country (since Nigeria is never named directly) is torn by inner political conflicts. The author mentions armed clashes and bloodshed that may refer to the terrible civil war in Nigeria during 1967–1970. But the story's main focus is on the ghetto settlement where Azaro lives with his family. The settlement exists in a hybrid reality of magical rituals, political campaigns, superstitious beliefs, and technological progress.

On another level of duality, the cosmic model of Okri's world suggests the existence of two dimensions, the World of the Living and the World of the Spirits. Spirits can live among humans, take anthropomorphic, animal, or hybrid forms, and interact with villagers while remaining unrecognized. The only one who can distinguish spirits from humans is the main character and the narrator, Azaro, the Abiku child. According to Yoruba belief, Abiku is a spirit-child "who dies and is reborn several times into the same family" (Mobolade 1973, 62). Thus, Azaro belongs neither to the World of the Living nor to the World of the Spirits. He remains forever in between. And due to his borderline existence, he can observe the intercommunication of the worlds and travel through multiple realities. However, there is another entity in the novel, similarly positioned between worlds, whose voice breaks into the narrative throughout the story—the African community. Okri depicts a formerly colonial society that seeks to "imagine" itself as a nation and is searching for its own voice. Therefore, the author draws parallels between a wandering spirit-child and a politically unstable country that has barely gained independence and whose identity formation is not yet complete. The resemblance is suggested in the following lines, "Our country is an abiku country. Like the spirit child, it keeps coming and going. One day it will decide to remain. It will become strong" (Okri 1991, 478). The ambiguous position of an object and a subject of identification, the state of transition, and the existence between temporalities bind the images of Abiku and the "the unborn nation" (Okri 1991, 393) together.

As the summary above outlines, the main theme of *The Famished Road* is the search for the identity of a postcolonial society that reflects on the trauma of colonization and tries to find its own voice. Similar themes are present in *The Handmaid's Tale*, even if not apparent at first sight. Both stories touch upon oppressive systems that divide the world through binary oppositions. In the case of *The Famished Road*, the opposition is based on race or ethnicity, and in *The Handmaid's Tale* on gender. Groups that are marginalized are deprived of subjectivity and individuality and struggle to find their own voice. Accordingly, storytelling becomes a crucial element of both *The Famished Road* trilogy and *The Handmaid's Tale* in both the novel and television adaptation.

The dichotomies of the individual and collective, the first-person singular and the first-person plural modes of storytelling are other important elements in both tales. In *The Famished Road* cycle, the collective "we" is actualized in the context of experiencing and overcoming the shared trauma of colonization where the community is an object of humiliation and oppression, including during periods of solidarity. As an example, during a major political rally, the colonial authorities mock people's expectations of democratic elections. The bulk of the population feel like they have neither the right to vote nor the ability to speak: "We, the crowd, were the ghosts of history We were the empty bodies on whose behalf the politicians and soldiers rule; ... the mere spectators of phenomena, the victims of speeches. We were meant only to listen, never to speak. ... Assent was all we were good for" (Okri 1998, 263). Here, "We" represents not only the oppressed and silenced, but also those who, on account of being in that position, strive to take control over the narrative. Hence, Azaro, as a narrator, becomes the medium through which the community gains the ability to tell their own story. "This is the song of a circling spirit. This is a story for all of us" (Okri 1993, 3) states the heterogeneous voice of the narrator, who represents a syncretism of individual and collective consciousness.

In the case of *The Handmaid's Tale*, the first-person singular narration is the character's tool of resistance against the oppressive regime that unifies, erases any complexity, and restricts people's individuality. In the voiceover narration of season two episode eleven, June states: "I keep on going with this limping and mutilated story because I want you to hear it. ... I tell. Therefore, you are" (S02:E11 "Holy"). The military state imposes a collective mentality on women by depriving them of privacy, requiring them to wear mandatory uniforms, walk in pairs, and participate in collective rituals. Nevertheless, the usage of "we" is not limited to describing the Handmaid's mechanical function in a new society. It also refers to their collective identity as oppressed subjects, the marginalized group that opposes and even confronts the regime. In the second episode of season one June finds out that there is a network of the Handmaids who are fighting against Gilead. In disbelief, she says: "There is an 'us'?" and answers herself: "Now there has to be an 'us.' Because, now, there is a 'them'" (S01:E02 "Birth Day"). By the end of season one, June realizes that the Handmaid's identity can also empower her and other Handmaids to rebel against the Gilead regime collectively. She states: "They should have never given us uniforms if they didn't want us to be an army" (S01:E10 "Night"). It is apparent that "we" in *The Handmaid's Tale* contains the contrasting meanings of an enforced identity that is alienating women from their inner selves, but is also binding them together and providing them a sense of community.

While *The Famished Road* and *The Handmaid's Tale* approach the opposition of the individual and collective from different perspectives, they both portray the quest for subjectivity and the ability to tell their own stories by oppressed and marginalized groups. By telling their story, colonized subjects gain control over their story, at least to themselves. By owning the narrative, they have the potential to acquire (or rather reconstruct) their identity. In this light, it is no coincidence that the episode featuring Radiohead's "Street Spirit" is entitled "The Crossing." Not only does the title articulate the intermedial communication taking place through the choice of song but it also emphasizes the motif of liminality that is characteristic of both *The Famished Road* cycle and *The Handmaid's Tale* in both versions.

As mentioned above, *The Famished Road*'s main character is the spirit-child who travels between the multiple realities of the Living, the Spirits, the Ancestors, etc. But as a part of a postcolonial community, Azaro is also located at the intersection of different cultures: the culture of the former empire and the indigenous cultures of the former colony. The liminal position between cultures is reflected in the image of the main character. The boy is named "Azaro" in honor of the biblical hero Lazarus. This name symbolizes the child's miraculous return to the World of the Living after a form of existence in the death-like state. The image of Azaro embodies the mythological motif of death and resurrection, which simultaneously correlates with the biblical story of Lazarus and the belief of Abiku from Yoruba mythology.

In *The Handmaid's Tale* series, the protagonist's identity is split between that of Handmaid "Offred," prescribed by the regime, and the autonomous identity of "June." The acquired identity of "Offred" is inherently linked to Gilead, as it only can be described in relation to the regime, whether as its victim, its property, or even its rebel. In contrast, "June" articulates autonomy since it refers to the character's identity as a free American woman, a mother, a wife, a college student, and a friend. Moreover, "June" denotes the possibility of choosing a range of identity scripts and making independent decisions about her own life. The detachment of the "June" identity from the signifying center of colonial power presents a threat to Gilead. The regime accordingly attempts to alienate the character from her "June" identity. In episode four of season two, Aunt Lydia says to the pregnant Handmaid, "You see, June will be chained in this room until she gives birth. And then June will be … executed. Offred has an opportunity" (S02:E04 "Other Women"). In response, June accepts "Offred" as a survival mechanism for now, but continues to devise other ways to challenge the power of the oppressive regime and its imposition of the oppressed subject role. On the one hand, she is able to manipulate the Commander and his wife, overpowering them with her will. On the other hand, she channels her rebellion to other Handmaids. In this process, she also exists at the crossroads of different timelines, as she dissociates from the present and escapes into the memories of her past before Gilead. Her identity is located between "Offred" and "June". The character is always looking for ways to reconstruct her self-identity, adapt, and adjust. The Handmaid becomes both the victim and the hero, the object and the subject of identification.

Finally, the visual images of transition pervade the escape scene featuring "Street Spirit." The Handmaids break out of the claustrophobic van, bursting out of its doors. They then run down the roadway to the rail crossing while the train is getting closer and threatening to block their escape. The scene contains a series of long panoramic shots that put into perspective the road, the crossing, and the tiny figures of the running Handmaids. The image of the road is prevalent in this scene, alluding to *The Famished Road* by Ben Okri as a major influence behind "Street Spirit". The road is a transitional place from what is known as "home" to "alien" and vice versa. It is a hybrid "third" space, a border zone, which is always "hungry for great transformations" (Okri 1991, 180), waiting for things that are only coming into being, such as Abiku, the unborn nation, national self-identification, or identity reconstruction.

Conclusion: Storytelling, Borderline Identities, and Images of Transition

The fact that the soundtrack plays a crucial role in the narratives of *The Handmaid's Tale*, both Atwood's novel and Hulu's serial adaptation further resonates with the revelation at the end of the novel that the Handmaid's story is a novelized translation of a series of audiocassettes. From this point of view, the novel itself becomes a transmedial adaptation of a source tale in the same way the TV show does. Moreover, the TV series adapts the main character's voiceover narration and ties it in with the carefully chosen soundtrack. As a result, the boundaries between the source tale and adaptation fade away, creating the hybrid medium of *The Handmaid's Tale*, which includes Atwood's novel, Hulu's TV series, and its soundtrack.

This cross-media and cross-cultural communication is extended to significant choices of accompanying tracks in the series. The reiteration of the single "You Don't Own Me" by Lesley Gore not only becomes a leitmotif for June's deeply traumatic experience, but also references unfinished feminist projects, highlighting the continuation of gender-based violence and women's struggle for equality. It specifically evokes the hopes of the period of second-wave feminism, given the date of Gore's hit (ironically written by two men). The usage of this musical composition is not mere background but serves to contribute to and enrich the discussion of identity loss in oppressive systems, commenting on the means of its restoration through defiant assertion, while implicitly indicating that the battles entered into in the 1960s and 1970s have by no means been won by women.

The second song discussed here, "Heaven Is a Place on Earth" by Belinda Carlisle, sheds light on the soundtrack's location between diegetic and non-diegetic borders. Moreover, it allows June's character to cross narrative boundaries in an attempt to control her story by controlling the means of storytelling. Overall, it can be summarized that the way the single "Heaven Is a Place on Earth" is integrated into the episodes blurs the distinction between the diegetic and non-diegetic and suggests that the soundtrack belongs to the storyworld, being chosen by June as a part of her reconstruction of the events. Additionally, it underlines the borderline position of the main character.

Finally, Radiohead's "Street Spirit" provides intermedial communication among Ben Okri's postcolonial novel, Margaret Atwood's feminist dystopia, and its 2017 Hulu TV adaptation. The comparison of the three media reveals not only common themes but also a related use of storytelling techniques while addressing the problem of the individual-collective dichotomy. Both main characters—June and Azaro—acquire the functions of mediators, navigating between "I" and "We," the object and the subject of identification, challenging narrative and cinematic boundaries. As colonized subjects, the characters are searching for the means to tell their story and control the narrative about themselves in order to regain an identity and agency.

"All these things into position" (Radiohead 1995, 12) are things in constant transition, existing at the crossroads. In Okri's evocative words these are: "Things that are not ready, not willing to be born or to become, things for which adequate preparations have not been made to sustain their momentous births, things that are not resolved, things bound up with failure and with fear of being, they all keep recurring, keep coming back, and in themselves partake of the spirit-child's condition" (Okri 1991, 487). Radiohead's line does not in fact suggest that things have found their rightful position, given that the next line points to an as yet unreached future reality: "All these things we'll one day swallow whole" (Radiohead 1995, 12). Both a hope and an awareness of roads still to travel, the triangulation of Radiohead, Okri, Atwood and the series exists as an evocative exemplar of contemporary intermedial storytelling, a development athwart the elitist inwardness with literary allusions that characterized the encounter with canonical texts in the past. As a cultural strategy, it enacts the drive for a more democratic freedom present as theme in both Atwood's and Okri's books, connecting texts that speak about oppressive systems and marginalized subjects while recontextualizing *The Handmaid's Tale* as part of postcolonial as well as feminist discourse.

References

Atwood, Margaret. 2016 [1985]. *The Handmaid's Tale*. London: Vintage.
Bhabha, Homi K. 1994. *The Location of Culture*. London: Routledge.
Briedik, Adam. 2021. A Postcolonial Feminist Dystopia: Margaret Atwood's *The Handmaid's Tale*. Ars Aeterna 13 (1): 57–67.
Carlisle, Belinda. 1987. Heaven is a Place on Earth. In *Heaven on Earth*, ed. Rick Nowels and Ellen Shipley, 1. Virgin Records Ltd. US: MCA Records.

Donnelly, K.J. 2005. *The Spectre of Sound: Music in Film and Television*. London: The British Film Institute.

Draper, Brian. 2004. Chipping Away–Brian Draper Talks to Thom Yorke. *Third Way* 27 (10): 16–21.

Elliott, Kamilla. 2020. *Theorizing Adaptation*. New York: Oxford University Press.

Gandhi, Leela. 1998. *Postcolonial Theory: A Critical Introduction*. Edinburgh: Edinburgh University Press.

Goldmark, Daniel, Lawrence Kramer, and Richard Leppert. 2007. Introduction. Phonoplay: Recasting Film Music. In *Beyond the Soundtrack: Representing Music in Cinema*, ed. Daniel Goldmark, Lawrence Kramer, and Richard Leppert, 1–9. Berkeley: University of California Press.

Gore, Lesley. 1963. You Don't Own Me. In *Lesley Gore Sings of Mixed-Up Hearts*, ed. John Madera and David White, 7. Canada: Mercury Records.

Miller, Bruce (Created by). 2017–present, 4 seasons. *Handmaid's Tale, The* [TV Series]. Daniel Wilson Productions; Littlefield Company; White Oak Pictures; MGM Television.

Mobolade, Timothy. 1973. The Concept of Abiku. *African Arts* 7 (1): 62–64.

Neumann, Birgit. 2015. Intermedial Negotiations: Postcolonial Literatures. In *Handbook of Intermediality: Literature–Image–Sound–Music*, ed. Gabriele Rippl, 512–529. Berlin and Boston: De Gruyter.

Okri, Ben. 1991. *The Famished Road*. London: Vintage.

———. 1993. *Songs of Enchantment*. London: Vintage.

———. 1998. *Infinite Riches*. London: Phoenix.

Radiohead. 1995. Street Spirit (Fade Out). In *The Bends*, ed. Jonny Greenwood O'Brien, Colin Greenwood, Philip Selway, and Thom Yorke, 12. UK: EMI Records Ltd. Parlophone.

Rippl, Gabriele. 2015. Introduction. In *Handbook of Intermediality: Literature–Image–Sound–Music*, ed. Gabriele Rippl, 1–31. Berlin and Boston: De Gruyter.

Sadeghi, Zahra, and Narges Mirzapour. 2020. Women of Gilead as Colonized Subjects in Margaret Atwood's Novel: A Study of Postcolonial and Feminist Aspects of *The Handmaid's Tale*. *Cogent: Arts & Humanities* 7 (1). https://doi.org/10.1080/23311983.2020.1785177. Accessed 17 May 2023.

Stilwell, Robynn J. 2007. The Fantastical Gap Between Diegetic and Nondiegetic. In *Beyond the Soundtrack: Representing Music in Cinema*, ed. Daniel Goldmark, Lawrence Kramer, and Richard Leppert, 184–202. Berkeley: University of California Press.

Straumann, Barbara. 2015. Adaptation–Remediation–Transmediality. In *Handbook of Intermediality: Literature–Image–Sound–Music*, ed. Gabriele Rippl, 249–267. Berlin and Boston: De Gruyter.

Tlostanova, Madina. 2012. Постколониальная теория, деколониальный выбор и освобождение эстезиса [Postcolonial theory, decolonial choice, and the liberation of aesthesis]. *Человек и культура* 1: 1–64. https://nbpublish.com/library_read_article.php?id=141. Accessed 14 May 2023.

Ulaby, Neda. 2019. 'You Don't Own Me,' a Feminist Anthem with Civil Rights Roots, Is All About Empathy. *American Anthem: The Complete Series* 42. https://www.npr.org/2019/06/26/735819094/lesley-gore-you-dont-own-me-american-anthem?t=1654003625165. Accessed 15 Feb 2023.

Walder, Dennis. 1998. Introducing the Post-Colonial. In *Post-colonial literatures in English: history, language, theory*, 1–22. Oxford; Malden, Mass.: Blackwell Publishers.

Wells-Lassagne, Shannon. 2017. Crossing over: Television Adaptation, Between Universality and Specificity. In *Television and Serial Adaptation*, 88–122. New York and London: Taylor & Francis.

Wells-Lassagne, Shannon, and Fiona McMahon. 2021. *Adapting Margaret Atwood: The Handmaid's Tale and Beyond*. Cham: Palgrave Macmillan.

Wolf, Werner. 2015. Literature and Music: Theory. In *Handbook of Intermediality: Literature–Image–Sound–Music*, ed. Gabriele Rippl, 459–474. Berlin and Boston: De Gruyter.

CHAPTER 7

What's the Story? How Hybrid Comics Against Gender Violence Rework Narrative and Support Artivism

Nicoletta Mandolini

INTRODUCTION

Comics and graphic narratives have been generally classified as a multimodal medium whose expressive functions are guaranteed by the interplay of words and images (see Jacobs 2013; Pinar 2014; Cohn et al. 2017). Notwithstanding this common assumption, some scholars have labeled comics as a predominantly visual medium. Among these is the Belgian comics semiotician Thierry Groensteen, who points out that in graphic narratives the verbal dimension, despite not being merely accessory, can be considered subordinated to the visual, which is in charge of executing the narrative purpose of comics. In Groensteen's words:

> the apparent irreducibility of the image and the story is dialectically resolved through the play of successive images and through their coexistence, through their diegetic connections, and through their panoptic display, in

---

N. Mandolini (✉)
CECS - University of Minho, Braga, Portugal
e-mail: Nicoletta.mandolini@ics.uminho.pt

© The Author(s), under exclusive license to Springer Nature Switzerland AG 2024
D. Callahan (ed.), *Visual Storytelling in the 21st Century*,
https://doi.org/10.1007/978-3-031-65487-9_7

which we have recognized the foundation of the medium. As we can see, it is through this collaboration between the arthrology and the spatio-topia that the sequential image is seen to be plainly narrative, without necessarily needing any verbal help. (Groensteen 2007, 9)

What this tells us is that the definition of comics as a visual medium remains deeply connected to the medium's narrative potential. In other words, if we follow Groensteen, one of the main semiotic strategies employed in comics, namely, the manifestation of time as space (spatio-topia) resulting from the articulation of images representing different time-frames in a sequence, grid, or set of scattered panels (arthrology), is what makes the storytelling practice in comics possible. Given this spatial (sequential or tabular) organization and its ability to represent polichrony or time-movement, comics can be considered, together with film, as one of the visual media with the highest level of narrativity or capacity to tell a story (Pratt 2009; Kukkonen 2011). Other visual media that generally work with still pictures standing by themselves, such as painting or photography, are typically described by narratologists as low in narrativity, based on the gradual or scalar conceptualization of narrativity that dominates contemporary narratology (Thön 2017, 258). Marie-Laure Ryan, for instance, states that "pictures, left by themselves, lack the ability to articulate specific propositions and to explicate causal relationships," which results in an "illustrative narrativity" that, despite being worth analyzing by transmedial narratologists, she defines as a "rather weak and subordinated mode" (Ryan 2004, 139). In this sense, the "modern comic strip" should be considered as "vastly superior in narrative versatility ... to the most eloquent of narrative paintings" (Ryan 2004, 143).

Comics and graphic narratives, moreover, are an extremely porous medium, whose exposure to intermedial and transmedial exchanges or hybridizations, as well as their propensity to adapt to distribution through different platforms, have historically determined frequent evolutions and formal changes (Rippl and Etter 2013; Di Paola 2019). These transformations include, for example, comics' development into the recent graphic novel format, the growth of the phenomenon of digital comics, and the advent of abstract comics. Such transformations clearly modify comics' narrative capacity, whether increasing, diminishing, or complicating it. In the case of graphic novels, for example, the reference to the literary genre of the novel boosts (at least at the superficial level of definition) comics' narrative potential. This is suggested by the fact that another controversial

7 WHAT'S THE STORY? HOW HYBRID COMICS AGAINST GENDER VIOLENCE...

but frequently mentioned principle that classical narratologists have used to assess degrees of narrativity, that of unity, is formally achieved by surpassing the fragmented mode of comic strips or magazines and entering that of the (often self-contained) book (Wolf 2004, 88–89).[1] Contrastingly, digital comics project the narrative potential of comics in the area of interactivity, immersivity, and reader participation (Dittmar 2012; Kirkhoff 2013), thus radically re-working some of the elements that classical narratology associates with narratives, such as the presence of a clear author. Abstract comics, on the other hand, generally work with a significantly lower level of narrativity, given their foregrounded relation to abstract painting and abstraction in general, which, as Jan Baetens points out, relies on a decreased degree of narrativity (Baetens 2011, 95).

Departing from these general observations, this chapter proposes the analysis of a corpus of comics-based but hybrid products employed in the context of Italian feminist activism against gender-based violence. These products are part of transmedial and multiplatform projects that blend comics with other media or modes such as street-art, collage, sticker art, and illustration. The hypothesis is that this combination results in the disruption of the linearity of traditional sequence-based comics narrative and in the activation of a method that, despite lowering the level of narrativity that pertains to more traditional forms of graphic narratives, serves the needs of feminist movements to build an open and highly participatory type of visual storytelling. The analysis will critically engage with existing studies and reflections developed within the field of narratology and transmedial narratology (Elleström 2018; Ryan 2004, 2014; Thön 2017; Wolf 2017; Walker 2004a, 2004b) in order to assess the eccentric narrative dimension of assorted comics-based products and discuss the implications that these practices have for feminist activism.

The two cases of comics-based artivistic practices, both produced by Italian feminist groups that employ comics as a tool to encourage participative responses to their activities, are the *Luchadoras* project promoted by

---

[1] This can be said even in the case of graphic novels that collect works previously published as serial comics, a common strategy, especially in the first decades of the success of graphic novels, the 1980s and 1990s. In these cases, an interest in reaching a thematic unity is generally showcased by the editorial project of bringing the works together in a single (or sometimes double) book. The "plasticity" that, according to Charles Hatfield (2005, 5), characterizes the graphic novel label, and that has also contributed to scholarly inability to reach a coherent and generally accepted definition of the term, nevertheless does not compromise the idea of narrative unity that graphic novels embody.

the Roman collective and women's shelter *Lucha y Siesta* (https://luchaysiesta.org/) as part of a broader campaign to protect the building where the group works so as to prevent the risk of eviction, and the *Matrioske parlanti* [Speaking Matryoshkas] project, an artivistic idea launched by the feminist network *Non una di meno* [Not one woman less] (https://nonunadimeno.wordpress.com/) aimed at denouncing gendered discrimination and violence. Artivistic practices, namely, the employment of artistic tools and methods to reach broad or specific activist goals (Serafini 2018), have been connected to feminist activism, movements, and instances since (and before) they were recognized as a specific political method of intervention. As indicated by Mary Jo Aagerstoun and Elissa Auther, "feminist artists have pursued activism around a wide range of issues pertaining to race, gender, and sexuality and their intersections with social, political and cultural forms of oppression." In the process "[t]hey have utilized a rich variety of media and approaches, including performance, installation, organized public disruption, guerrilla postering, billboards, video, radical forms of pedagogy, and other creative uses of public space that emphasize collaboration and coalition-building" (Aagerstoun and Auther 2007, vii). Despite not being widely explored by scholarly research, comics-based artivism is one of the forms that feminist artivism has taken in order to tackle issues such as gender violence, lack of reproductive justice, ecofeminism, and structural gender-related inequalities (Lund 2018, 44–47; Gandolfo and Turnes 2020; Munt and Richards 2020; Mandolini 2023, 4; Nordenstam and Wictorin 2023). In the Italian context, artivistic practices employed by feminist movements or collectives and availing themselves of the comics medium are a reality, especially in the area of gender-based violence prevention, which is the most vibrant among feminist groups that populate the country (Mandolini 2023). This is not a coincidence, given the relevance that gender-based violence and femicide have had in Italian public discourse since the beginning of the new millennium and, in particular, since 2012, the year that saw feminist debates on lethal sexist abuse entering the area of mainstream communication (Mandolini 2021, 2–5). Since then, superficial changes have been introduced, both in terms of legislative and media approaches toward the matter (Pittaro 2014; Giomi 2019; Mandolini 2020). However, significant issues remained, including the problematic coverage that journalism and television provided of gender violence victims, who are often silenced and/or stereotyped, and perpetrators, whose frequent portrayal as deviant subjects implicitly denies the systemic nature of the phenomenon (Gius and Lalli 2014; Giomi 2015, 2019; Mandolini 2020; Formato 2023). It is precisely as a consequence of these persisting matters that Italian feminist activists have continued to insist on the hot topic of gender violence and have made the effort to create campaigns where artistic practices serve as tools for denouncing patriarchal abuse and, simultaneously, for sketching alternative victim-centered narratives within this practice.

THE *LUCHADORAS* PROJECT: THE MERITS OF LOW NARRATIVITY

The first of the two cases to be analyzed is the *Luchadoras* project, which was started in 2019 by the Roman group *Lucha y Siesta*. Since 2008, the collective *Lucha y Siesta* have been carrying out activities in a (previously) occupied building where they have organized a women's shelter and a feminist cultural center. Following a notice issued by the City Council of Rome, which wanted to sell the building, which officially belonged to one of their agencies, the capital's public transport agency ATAC, the women of *Lucha y Siesta* began a series of campaigns aimed at avoiding the eviction and supporting a crowdfunding project with which the activists attempted to collect money to sustain their work. This crowdfunding project, not by coincidence, was titled *Lucha alla città* [Fight to the City], the same name as the committee composed by local people and activists that Lucha y Siesta had previously created in order to widen the spectrum of its struggle and present the occupied space as a common good that belongs to the entire city, given the essential cultural and social services it provides.

Among the campaigns organized to support the *Lucha alla città* project, the *Luchadoras* campaign, which was thought up by the comics artist, and Lucha y Siesta friend, Rita Petruccioli. The campaign consisted in a call for action that Petruccioli launched online (mostly on the social media Instagram) using the hashtag #DrawThisInYourStyle, and directed to other comics artists and illustrators interested in reproducing in their own style the image of a *luchadora*, a woman in the Mexican form of wrestling known as *Lucha Libre*. The decision to turn the image of a *luchadora* into an iconic figure to be multiplied and re-interpreted, which clearly follows the same mythopoetic practice that characterizes one of the most important genres of Western comics, the superhero genre (Bahlmann 2016), is based on a double alignment of the *luchadora* symbol with the ethos of

Lucha y Siesta. Not only does the *luchadora* evoke the name of the collective and the network of transnational relationships with Mexican feminist groups that brought *Lucha y Siesta*'s activists to adopt a Spanish name,[2] it also challenges the dominant image of women and gender violence survivors/victims as passive objects of abuse, thus contributing to the re-symbolization of the category as composed by active subjects who fight for the life and dignity that *Lucha y Siesta* have always promoted. Petruccioli's call was endorsed by hundreds of creatives, who created and illustrated a squad of racially, bodily and stylistically diversified female superheroes ready to symbolically defend Lucha y Siesta from the eviction, or they donated a drawing specifically created for the occasion to support the cause in the crowdfunding campaign. Among these famous artists from the Italian comics scene could be found such figures as Zerocalcare, Sio, Cristina Portolano, Leo Ortolani, Zuzu, Silvia Ziche, and Altan. The drawings circulated widely online, to the point of becoming iconic of the collective's struggle, and many of them were later printed and attached to the walls of Rome by activists belonging to the collective (Fig. 7.1).

In the context of this chapter, I will offer a brief analysis of the urban or local operation carried out by *Lucha y Siesta*, as opposed to the virtual aspect of the *Luchadoras* campaign.[3] This is because the street intervention through which the inhabitants of the neighborhood surrounding Lucha y Siesta were introduced to the *luchadoras* is that which better displays the hybridization of the comics medium by mingling it with other media or modes such as street art, illustration, sticker art and collage. However, before outlining the specific narrative dynamics that the hybridization of the comics medium implies, as well as the advantages that this contamination discloses for the practice of visual storytelling on the topic of

---

[2] On Lucha y Siesta's transnational network see Mandolini, 2023, 14. Another reason that led the activists to the choice of the name Lucha y Siesta is the fact that the building where the collective carries out their activity is located in Via Lucio Sestio [Lucio Sestio steet], which provides a form of linguistic assonance, even if it does not mean *Lucha* or *Siesta* in Italian, and another implicit link with the local community within which Lucha y Siesta works.

[3] The virtual campaign consisted in the dissemination of the received images of *luchadoras* as part of a series of collective digital collages posted on social media like Instagram and Facebook. A spin-off campaign generated by the *luchadoras* figures is that of Lucha 2.0 (https://www.facebook.com/lucha.ysiesta/photos/2720095031602235?locale=es_LA), where the images of two or more *luchadoras* were juxtaposed and enriched by speech balloons in order to create dialogues able to convey an explicit narrative around the project. These juxtaposed images were disseminated through social media and through Lucha y Siesta's website.

7 WHAT'S THE STORY? HOW HYBRID COMICS AGAINST GENDER VIOLENCE... 115

Fig. 7.1 *Luchadoras* on the walls of Rome. Source: Lucha y Siesta's Facebook page: https://www.facebook.com/lucha.ysiesta/photos/2556500114628395?locale=es_LA

gender-based violence, it is necessary to clarify the approach that guides my understanding of a controversial concept such as that of medium and, more in particular, of the comics medium. Here, the comics medium is considered in its totality, which comprises both the cultural and thematic tendencies of the comics industry (such as the comics-related genre of the superhero), its formal or semiotic characteristics (such as sequentiality, the previously discussed tendencies toward narrativity, or image-word combination) and its propensity to avail itself of specific technologies or platforms (generally, the paper format of the book). This approach draws on Marie-Laure Ryan's idea of medium as a categorization that encompasses three aspects: the semiotic substance, the technical dimension, and the cultural dimension (Ryan 2014, 29).

In light of this, it is possible to state that in the *Luchadoras* intervention, comics are still present in the essential reference to the superhero genre on which the *luchadora* figure clearly draws, as well as in the participation of many comics artists (including the creator, Rita Petruccioli) in the project. However, comics lose most of their formal characteristics as they transmigrate from the book/paper platform, which is generally associated with the tradition of the medium,[4] onto the city walls. One of the most evident alterations to be noticed in the *Luchadoras* operation is the lack of a sequential dimension fostered by the combination of illustration, an artistic practice that differs from comics because it generally works with single/standalone images, and with collage, a practice that relies on juxtaposition rather than sequentiality (Raaberg 1998, 154). Moreover, the multimodal semiotic mode that generally characterizes comics[5] is lost in the *Luchadoras* collage, where no speech balloon or caption (apart from scattered inclusions of the names "Lucha y Siesta" or "Lucha alla città") is present. In other words, the *luchadoras* affixed on the walls of Rome are a set of silent and coherent illustrations of a superhero-like character juxtaposed in a tabular or linear manner. These radical changes do have a consequence when it comes to the narrative capacities (or level of narrativity) of the discussed works.

In the *Luchadoras* operation, narrative is considerably lowered, if compared to the narrative capacity of traditional comics. This is because of the absence of an explicit polychrony or time-movement, which is one of the narrative characteristics guaranteed by comics sequentiality. Instead of providing the viewer with a sequence of images conveying a story that unfolds in time, the *Luchadoras* project consists of the juxtaposition of images (the aforementioned illustrations that resulted from the #DrawThisInYourStyle call) without any temporal connection between each other. Polychrony, or the ability to display actions unfolding in time, is one of the narremes that classical narratologists identified as constitutive of a narrative (e.g., Labov 1972, 359–60; Prince 1973, 31; Ricoeur 1980, 169; Onega and García Landa 1996, 5; Sternberg 1996, 109). This is partially true even in the case of transmedial narratologists who, despite

---

[4] Notwithstanding the unarguable association of modern comics with the book/paper platform, the porosity and adaptability of the medium have stimulated evolutions, such as those of digital comics and street comics.

[5] The existence of what scholars have labeled as "silent comics," namely, comics where the verbal dimension is absent, prevents us from saying that multimodality is a universal characteristic when it comes to graphic narratives. On this see Postema (2016).

not denying in its totality the narrative value of products where time-movement is absent or implicit (we will see how later on), do insist on the "creation of a temporal dimension" (Ryan 2004, 8–9) and on the presence of "characters which exist in a chronotopos" (Wolf 2017, 262) when providing their definitions of narrative objects.

Despite this clear disruption of traditional narrative patterns and notwithstanding the absence of crucial narremes, in the *Luchadoras* project narrative is constantly evoked. The reiteration of the *luchadora* character, which is reproduced with different features that nevertheless highlight some clear common traits (the *luchadoras* are all female fighters wearing the same type of mask), is a marker of cohesion that, following Kai Mikkonen's reflection on the role played by character repetition in comics narratology, can be interpreted as a sign of narrative continuity (Mikkonen 2017, 90–92). This applies, in particular, to the superhero icon, which is explicitly referenced by the *Luchadoras* project, and is generally associated by readers or viewers with an existing narrative or with what the transmedial narratologist Lars Elleström calls "recognised story," which is to say stories that result "from earlier encounters with narratives or events in the world" (Elleström 2018, 38). But in the case of Lucha y Siesta, the story is somehow encrypted, given that it is not widely known or recognized. For this reason, passers-by who come across the *Luchadoras* collages in the streets of Rome cannot but ask themselves what those sets of illustrations stand for, for they are clearly not random images or flyers. This effect becomes reinforced if people also happen to see the collages in other parts of the neighborhood or city, a presence that clearly fosters an idea of continuity. Facilitated by the incidental presence of captions where the name of the collective (*Lucha y Siesta*) or that of the crowdfunding campaign (*Lucha alla città*) are stated, the viewer has the possibility of carrying out an online search that will easily reveal the story of *Lucha y Siesta* and of its attempt to denounce the eviction notice issued by the City Council. By accessing the collective's website (https://luchaysiesta.org/) and social media pages, or the numerous newspaper articles that report the statements and declarations released by *Lucha y Siesta* to launch their campaigns (e.g., Crisafi 2019; "Se toccano Lucha y Siesta" 2019; Valtorta 2019; "Lucha y Siesta" 2020), the viewer will discover the narrative that the group has crafted, based on its positioned experience and beliefs, in order to sustain its struggle. This narrative represents *Lucha y Siesta* as a collective good, as a space owned by the local community and managed by a group of women who, for over a decade, have hosted and supported women who have survived patriarchal violence in an urban area (that of Rome) and in a country (Italy) where institutional help against gendered abuse is scarce, and public women shelters are insufficient to meet the demand or chronically underfunded (Guerra 2019; GREVIO 2020, 49–50). This narrative is precisely what is evoked by the transmedial symbolic apparatus that *Lucha y Siesta* created around the *luchadora* icon, distributed on the walls of Rome in the comics-related format discussed here, which was also used by activists as a mask during demonstrations or events, and projected as a luminous signal on the monuments of Rome at night.

As this brief discussion demonstrates, the encrypted narrative that describes *Lucha y Siesta*'s story can only be accessed by means of the active participation of the viewer, who is responsible for carrying out the search, following the awakening of a sense of curiosity stimulated by the *Luchadoras* collages randomly encountered in the streets of Rome. In other words, the narrative dimension of the artivistic operation is dependent on the recipients' ability and will to search for clues that allow them to interpret the pictures as part of a story, the story of *Lucha y Siesta* and its struggle against the eviction that can be accessed by gathering the many hints disseminated by the collective at a transmedial and multiplatform level both in the urban landscape and in the online world. Narratologists who have engaged with the trend of transmedial narratology, analyzing levels of narrativity in different media and genres, have paid attention to eccentric and hidden narratives like the one proposed by *Lucha y Siesta*. Werner Wolf discusses the issue of single pictorial images that display no clear sense of time and ended up assigning to these products an "indirect" type of narrativity, which is to say a narrativity that the viewer accesses by means of references to an existing storyworld or to a pre-text (Wolf 2017, 256–257). According to Wolf, this often happens, for example, with pictorial images representing mythological or religious scenes, where the absence of time-movement and other narremes is compensated for by an allusion to a myth or religious tale that might remain implicit or possibly explicitly referenced by the work's title (Wolf 2017, 256–257). That is, these images do not possess a direct narrative dimension (they are not narrative in themselves), but their (low) narrative potential is characterized as open and vague, given their thorough dependency on the viewer's active elicitation (Wolf 2017, 271).

Similarly, Marie-Laure Ryan has considered single/standing alone pictures such as those juxtaposed in the *Luchadoras* collages as bearers of an illustrative type of narrativity that, notwithstanding its limitations in terms of storytelling articulation, do possess a strong evocative capacity (Ryan 2004, 139). By referring to Gotthold Ephram Lessing's idea of the "pregnant moment," which is to say a cogent moment in a broader narrative trajectory that pictorial images display, Ryan states that single images activate crucial symbolic connections with the general transmedially conveyed story, thus presenting "the spectator with an array of narrative possibilities" (Ryan 2004, 140). These considerations, which apply to the *luchadoras* case given the highly iconic value that the images of the female fighters have in relation to the narrative on gender violence promoted by *Lucha y Siesta*, do, once again, re-direct our analysis to a viewer-oriented approach that takes into account the role of the recipient in establishing relations and directing the open symbolic potentials that pertain to the images.

The example of *Lucha y Siesta*, where the indirect narrative is used as a trigger to push viewers and passers-by to actively search for the story that the images reference, allows us to re-assess the value that indirect narratives can have in the context of politically and socially relevant artistic operations. In the case of the *Luchadoras* collages, the artivistic initiative, by encrypting the narrative dimension, clearly limits the quantity of interactions with and accesses to *Lucha y Siesta*'s story. A creative product with direct narrativity would potentially have been more effective in conveying the story and the message to a wider audience. However, the strategy of the indirect narrative significantly fosters a qualitatively relevant and more active experience in the audience. Those who activate the process of narrative discovery by accessing the online content where the story of the collective is displayed definitely have more chance to also make contact with other initiatives organized by the group and maybe think of anything from actively taking part in some of them to supporting their viewpoints and activities in conversation and daily life. Apart from this practical side, the stimulation of a participatory role in the viewer symbolically matches the idea of community and collective building that *Lucha y Siesta* aimed at promoting with the *Lucha alla città*'s crowdfunding campaign. In this way, the narrative, as well as *Lucha y Siesta*'s project, can be thought of as a common good that belongs to everybody.

Matrioske Parlanti: Comics Between Intersectionality and Distributed Narrative

The second artivistic project I will look at is called *Matrioske parlanti* (talking Matrioskas), authored by *Non una di meno*, which can be considered the most successful and influential feminist initiative in the Italian context nowadays. *Non una di meno* was created in 2016 as a network aimed at gathering feminist collectives spread across the peninsula and, since its successful irruption in the public scene with the organization of a series of campaigns and demonstrations on 25 November 2016 and on 8 March 2017, it multiplied into a series of smaller and local groups that either complemented an existing feminist scene or compensated for its absence. As the group's name suggests, *Non una di meno* is deeply related to the Argentinian movement against gender violence and femicide *Ni una menos*, which was selected as primary model by the Italian activists, given their interest in articulating a feminist agenda aimed at challenging patriarchal abuse in all its numerous declinations.[6] *Non una di meno* is characterized by an explicit intersectional approach to feminism, which is to say a tendency to take into account the intersection of different discriminatory practices that affect subjects and communities within and beyond the gender paradigm. These practices include racist and ethnic discrimination, exclusions based on sexual orientation, classism, ableism, or ageism.[7] Following the same inclusive propensity, the group is openly transinclusive, thus welcoming transsexual, transgender, and non-binary individuals. In this sense, the struggle against gender violence is seen by *Non una di meno* as a transversal struggle where women are only one of the identity categories involved.

The *Matrioske parlanti* project originated as a specific artivistic action thought up by one of the collectives belonging to the network of *Non una di meno*, "Freedom for birth," an association from Rome whose efforts are dedicated to the denunciation and prevention of obstetric violence. Originally, the project had the objective of raising awareness of the frequent and often subtle abuse carried out on women or persons with a womb who avail themselves of gynecological and obstetric services in Italy.

---

[6] On *Ni una menos*, see Cabral and Acacio (2016), Palmeiro (2019). On the relationships between *Ni una menos* and *Non una di meno* see Salvatori (2022).
[7] On intersectional feminism see Crenshaw (1989), Carastathis (2016), and Chaddock and Hinderliter (2020).

It consisted of the distribution of a series of diverse (both in terms of racial and gender connotations) matrioskas—the matrioska being the symbol of *Non una di meno*—which carried a speech balloon as part of their bellies. The speech balloon was filled with words, either by the activists who wrote general statements on the different manifestations of obstetric violence or by women who came across the matrioskas and wanted to contribute writing their personal experiences of abuse. This symbol, with different and often personalized political denunciations, circulated online, was carried as banner during demonstrations and was affixed on the walls of different Italian cities between 2017 and 2018. On occasion of the international feminist strike to which *Non una di meno* subscribed on 8 March 2018, activists in different parts of the peninsula re-proposed the action of the talking matrioska to advertise the event. In Bologna, the local branch of *Non una di meno* organized a massive distribution on the city walls that followed a workshop during which feminist activists and supporters crafted the matrioskas and either filled their speech balloon with political demands and statements or left it blank so as to allow passers-by to participate in the initiative.[8] In this reproposition of the original project, the speech balloon was moved (from the belly to outside the matrioska's body) and it was used by activists who participated in the collective laboratory to address a broader topic: that of gender discrimination and violence. The hashtag #Lotto Marzo (a word pun where the date of Women's Day, 8 March (eight being "otto" in Italian), is associated with the idea of struggle, which is "lotta" in Italian), a *Non una di meno* stamp as well as the time and location of the demonstration were added at the bottom of the speech balloon and the matrioskas were attached in different parts of the city, especially close to crucial spots where people gather (creches and schools, hospitals, trade union offices, etc.).

If compared to the *Luchadoras* operation, the narrative here is less encrypted, given that the speech balloon always includes references to the organization's name and related event (the strike), thus facilitating viewers' searches significantly. However, the indirect dimension of the narrative, at least if we consider Wolf's definition, is maintained in the *Matrioske parlanti* project. The big overreaching narrative, which in this case is that

[8] This action is documented by a video that *Non una di meno* Bologna made available through YouTube: https://www.youtube.com/watch?v=3NUY5UOwFeY [Accessed 3 March 2023]. The video is part of the transmedial narrative that accompanies the actions undertaken on the occasion of the feminist strike of the 8 March 2018.

of the struggle against patriarchal violence undergone by *Non una di meno* and its supporters on the occasion of the strike, is not directly included in the image, because the speech balloons only contain fragmented descriptions of the current situation that women and gender non-conforming subjects experience in Italy and which require contextualization in order to be understood as part of a story. Examples are political claims such as "Sciopero perché voglio consultori liberi, laici e gratuiti" [I strike because I want free and secular gynecological clinics] or "Sciopero perché a pari lavoro pari salario" [I strike because I want equal pay for the same work], as well as personalized feminist statements such as "Sciopero perché la pacca sul culo non è parte del contratto" [I strike because a smack on my ass is not part of the contract] and "Sciopero perché voglio il reddito di autodeterminazione" [I strike because I want an income that will allow me to self-determine].

This fragmentation is further complicated by the dissemination of the matrioskas in different parts of the city, which testifies to the disruption of an important (and already mentioned) principle of narrative cohesion: unity.[9] Viewers' access to the story is conditioned by their ability to put together fragments that are scattered in space and time. This refers not only to the matrioskas affixed on other walls but also to the matrioskas that on the day of the demonstration associated with the strike were carried by activists. In other words, *Non una di meno*'s matrioskas artivistic operation can be labeled as a "distributed narrative." Distributed narrative is an expression introduced by Jill Walker (2004a, 2004b) to describe contemporary narratives that imply a distribution in time and space. Distributed narratives, according to Walker, also frequently imply a distribution of authorship (Walker 2004a, 96–97), as is the case of the matrioskas, whose speech balloons were filled in by different people, possibly including the viewer herself in the case of the speech balloons that activists decided to leave blank. It was also the case if viewers decided to reproduce the easily reproducible image of the talking matrioska, which was also made available online on *Non una di meno*'s website (Fig. 7.2), and bring it with them to the demonstration of 8 March.

---

[9] According to Henry Jenkins, disruption of unity is one of the major characteristics of transmedial narrative operations produced in the era of so-called convergence culture, where content flows "across multiple media platforms" and where this "circulation of media content—across different media systems, competing media economies, and national borders—depends heavily on consumers' active participation" (Jenkins 2006, 3).

Fig. 7.2 Matrioskas made available online by *Non una di meno*. Source: *Non una di meno*'s website: https://nonunadimeno.wordpress.com/2017/03/04/matrioske-parlanti-senza-sfondo/

Examples of distributed narratives mentioned by Walker include web-based types of narrative such as those of weblogs, where links to other texts function as connections that the reader needs to activate (Walker 2004a, 100–101). But a more cogent example of distributed narrative in terms of visual storytelling is that of sticker art with which, not by coincidence, the Talking Matrioskas project has a lot in common. As we are reminded by Walker, sticker art provides viewers with a series of repeated images scattered across the walls of a city or cities (Walker 2004a, 104). When encountered more than once, they allow the viewer to establish connections through visual memory and, when no or scarce reference to the associated project is present, activate a sense of curiosity that might lead to an online search that will reveal the overreaching narrative. In light of this, Walker stresses the importance of repetition as a practice that fosters narrativity in sticker art (Walker 2004a, 104–015). Iteration is, as already seen in the case of the *Luchadoras* project, that which grants consistency and supports the process of the construction of images into icons or symbols that epitomize the narrative proposed by the collective. The repetition of analogous figures that can be recognized by the viewer as related is a crucial component even in the case of the matrioskas, given their distribution in different parts of the city and the common cartooning style that characterizes their otherwise different bodily features. And it is precisely this coexistence of difference and unity—the same displayed by the assorted squad of *luchadoras*—that further sustains the intersectional feminist narrative against gender violence of *Non una di meno*. Intersectional feminism, namely, that branch of feminism that aims at bringing together a multitude of different identities (women, non-binary and trans persons, other members of the LGBTQ+ community, racialized subjects, differently abled persons, etc.) under the common fight against patriarchal discrimination, is clearly referenced by the set of matrioskas, which is variegated in terms of race, gender, and ability.[10] In other words, in the case of *Non una di meno*'s operation, content and form productively overlap, if it is true that unity is also the result of a re-composition process that viewers are encharged with completing by mentally assembling the fragmented images and information that they gathered. And it is precisely this switch toward an active and preponderant role of the reader/viewer that is particularly useful in the idea of distributed narrative. In fact, as Walker states, when narratives are distributed in terms of space, time, and authorship, their re-composition into a meaningful (but always open and differentiated) whole cannot but happen through the vigorous engagement of the receiver:

> Distributed narratives break down the aesthetics of unity we have followed for millennia. They take this disunity a step further than the bricolage of postmodernism, by collapsing the unity of form as well as that of content and concept. Yet perhaps they also point to a new kind of unity: a unity where the time and space of the narrative are the same as the time and space of the reader. (Walker 2004b, 11)

Conclusion

Italian feminist collectives active in the field of gender-based violence prevention and in the broader area of activist struggle against gendered discrimination avail themselves of artivistic practices where references to the comics medium play a crucial role. However, in the case of the feminist collectives analyzed—*Lucha y Siesta* and *Non una di meno*—most of the formal characteristics of comics are diluted or get lost in the process of hybridization with other media and artistic practices (street art, collage, illustration, sticker art) to which the medium is subjected in the context of artivistic campaigns where the communicative urgency disrupts media

---

[10] On intersectional feminism as a political current that articulates the principle of unity in difference see Gunnarsson (2017).

boundaries. These alterations, including the interruption of comics' sequentiality and the breaking of the principle of unity, have an impact on the narrativity conveyed by such artivistic projects, a narrativity that is substantially diminished. But this loss does not come as a negative event, being complemented by the artivists' decision to challenge the viewers with fragmented and distributed pieces of narrative or "pregnant images" that need to be brought together and linked to the transmedial overreaching narrative proposed by the feminist groups in order to be read as part of a story. This testifies to the highly participatory and open dimension of the artivistic operation, an aspect that proves essential in the context of political activism, where the aim of its creators is to encourage people to participate in mobilizations connected to the issues referenced. This is particularly effective in the case of feminist activism against gender violence and discrimination, a phenomenon that, in public mainstream discourse, is often represented as being annihilating for victims who are, consequently, silenced or portrayed as passive entities. Allowing participants to either communicate their stances and experiences of violence (as in the case of the Talking matrioskas project) or to have a preponderant role in the construction of the narrative (as in the case of *Lucha y Siesta*'s campaign) is a way to practically confront the aforementioned representational pattern and substitute it with an active re-subjectification of oppressed categories (victims/survivors of gender violence certainly, but women and non heterocisnormative subjects more broadly).

In light of this, comics-based narratives like those promoted by *Non una di meno* or *Lucha y Siesta* can further push narratology and transmedial narratology toward the systematic study of open and participative visual storytelling in which traditional narremes might be absent but the strong engagement of the viewer activates strongly participatory dynamics. These are essential in contexts of political activism or campaigning and encourage us to re-consider narrativity as a broad concept that needs to be addressed in a variety of manners in order for us to grasp its complexity and usefulness.

Acknowledgments This work is financed by Portugal National Funds through the Foundation for Science and Technology (UIDB/00736/2020).

References

Aagerstoun, Mary Jo, and Elissa Auther. 2007. Considering Feminist Activism Art. *NWSA Journal* 19 (1): vii–xiv.

Baetens, Jan. 2011. Abstraction in Comics. *SubStance* 40 (1): 94–113.

Bahlmann, Andrew R. 2016. *The Mythology of the Superhero*. Jefferson, NC: McFarland.

Cabral, Paz, and Juan Antonio Acacio. 2016. La violencia de género como problema público. Las movilizaciones por 'Ni una menos' en la Argentina. *Question* 1 (51): 170–187.

Carastathis, Anna. 2016. *Intersectionality: Origins, Contestations, Horizons*. Lincoln and London: University of Nebraska Press.

Chaddock, Noelle, and Beth Hinderliter. 2020. Introduction. In *Antagonizing White Feminism: Intersectionality's Critique of Women's Studies and the Academy*, ed. Noelle Chaddock and Beth Hinderliter, xi–xxiv. Lanham, MD: Lexington Books.

Cohn, Neil, Ryan Taylor, and Kaitlin Pederson. 2017. A Picture Is Worth More Words Over Time. Multimodality and Narrative Structure Across Eight Decades of American Superhero Comics. *Multimodal Communication* 6 (1): 19–37.

Crenshaw, Kimberlé. 1989. Demarginalizing the Intersection of Race and Sex: A Black Feminist Critique of Antidiscrimination Doctrine, Feminist Theory and Antiracist Policy. *University of Chicago Legal Forum*: 139–167.

Crisafi, Livia. 2019. Più libri più liberi, 'Le luchadoras': il fumetto può essere intrattenimento ma anche arma di difesa. *La Repubblica.it*. December 6. https://video.repubblica.it/dossier/piu-libri-piu-liberi-2019/piu-libri-piu-liberi-le-luchadoras-il-fumetto-puo-essere-intrattenimento-ma-anche-arma-di-difesa/349657/350234 Accessed 3 Mar 2023.

Di Paola, Lorenzo. 2019. *L'inafferrabile medium. Una cartografia delle teorie del fumetto dagli anni Venti ad oggi*. Naples: Polidoro.

Dittmar, Jakob. 2012. Digital Comics. *SJoCA Scandinavian Journal of Comic Art* 2 (1): 82–91.

Elleström, Lars. 2018. *Transmedial Narration. Narratives and Stories in Different Media*. New York: Palgrave.

Formato, Federica. 2023. Femminicidio in Italian Televised News: The Case Study of La Vita in Diretta. In *Routledge Companion on Gender, Media and Violence*, ed. Karen Boyle and Susan Berridge, 75–83. London: Routledge.

Gandolfo, Amedeo, and Pablo Turnes. 2020. Chicks Attack! Making Feminist Comics in Latin America. *Feminist Encounters* 4 (1): 1–22.

Giomi, Elisa. 2015. Tag femminicidio. La violenza letale contro le donne nella stampa italiana. *Problemi dell'informazione* 40 (3): 549–574.

———. 2019. La rappresentazione della violenza di genere nei media. Frame, cause e soluzioni del problema nei programmi RAI. *Studi sulla questione criminale* 14 (1–2): 223–248.

Gius, Chiara, and Pina Lalli. 2014. 'I Loved Her So Much, But I Killed Her'. Romantic Love as a Representational Frame for Intimate Partner Femicide in Three Italian Newspapers. *ESSACCHESS. Journal of Communication Studies* 7 (2): 1–14.

GREVIO (Group of Experts on Action against Violence against Women and Domestic Violence). 2020. *Baseline Evaluation Report. Italy*. Council of Europe. https://rm.coe.int/grevio-report-italy-first-baseline-evaluation/168099724e. Accessed 3 Mar 2023.

Groensteen, Thierry. 2007. *The System of Comics*. Trans. B. Beaty and N. Nguyen. Jackson: University Press of Mississippi.

Guerra, Jennifer. 2019. Ogni due giorni una donna viene uccisa. Ma la politica chiude i centri antiviolenza. *TheVision.it*. July 26. https://thevision.com/attualita/femminicidio-centri-antiviolenza/. Accessed 3 Mar 2023.

Gunnarsson, Lena. 2017. Why We Keep Separating the 'Inseparable': Dialecticizing Intersectionality. *European Journal of Women Studies* 24 (2): 114–127.

Hatfield, Charles. 2005. *Alternative Comics: An Emerging Literature*. Jackson: University Press of Mississippi.

Jacobs, Dale. 2013. *Graphic Encounters. Comics and the Sponsorship of Multimodal Literacy*. New York: Bloomsbury.

Jenkins, Henry. 2006. *Convergence Culture. Where Old and New Media Collide*. New York and London: New York University Press.

Kirkhoff, Jeffrey S.J. 2013. It's Just Not the Same as Print (And It Shouldn't Be): Re-thinking the Possibilities of Digital Comics. *Technoculture* 3.

Kukkonen, Karin. 2011. Comics as a Test Case for Transmedial Narratology. *SubStance* 40 (1): 34–52.

Labov, William. 1972. The Transformation of Experience in Narrative Syntax. In *Language in the Inner City: Studies in the Black English Vernacular*, vol. 3, 354–396. Philadelphia: University of Pennsylvania Press.

"Lucha y Siesta: iniziativa incomprensibile da Raggi, ennesima improvvisazione?" 2020. *RomaDailyNews.it*. January 29. https://www.romadailynews.it/politica/lucha-y-siesta-iniziativa-incomprensibile-da-raggi-ennesima-improvvisazione-0440585/. Accessed 3 Mar 2023.

Lund, Martin. 2018. Comics Activism. A (Partial) Introduction. *SJoCA. Scandinavian Journal of Comic Art* 3 (2): 39–54.

Mandolini, Nicoletta. 2020. Femminicidio, prima e dopo. Un'analisi qualitativa della copertura giornalistica dei casi Stefania Noce (2011) e Sara Di Pietrantonio (2016). *Problemi dell'informazione* 45 (2): 247–277.

———. 2021. *Representations of Lethal Gender-Based Violence in Italy between Journalism and Literature. Femminicidio Narratives*. London: Routledge.

———. 2023. Wonder Feminisms: Comics-Based Artivism Against Gender Violence in Italy, Intersectionality and Transnationalism. *Journal of Graphic Novels and Comics* 14 (4): 535–555. https://doi.org/10.1080/21504857.2022.2135551. Accessed 3 Mar 2023.

Mikkonen, Kai. 2017. *The Narratology of Comic Art*. New York: Routledge.

Munt, Sally, and Rose Richards. 2020. Feminist Comics in an International Frame. *Feminist Encounters* 4 (1): 1–8.

Nordenstam, Anna, and Margareta Wallin Wictorin. 2023. Climate Activism: Contemporary Swedish Feminist Comics. *Journal of Graphic Novels and Comics* 14 (5): 735–747. https://doi.org/10.1080/21504857.2022.2075413. Accessed 3 Mar 2023.

Onega, Susana, and José Angel García Landa. 1996. Introduction. In *Narratology: An Introduction*, ed. Susana Onega and José Angel García Landa, 1–44. New York: Routledge.

Palmeiro, Cecilia. 2019. Ni una menos: las lenguas locas del grito colectivo a la marea global. *Cuadernos de literatura* 23 (46): 177–195.

Pinar, Maria Jesus. 2014. Comic Books. In *Interactions, Images and Texts. A Reader in Multimodality*, ed. Sigrid Norris and Carmen Daniela Maier, 357–370. De Gruyter: Mouton.

Pittaro, Paolo. 2014. La legge sul femminicidio: le disposizioni penali di una complessa normativa. *Famiglia e diritto* 7: 715–725.

Postema, Barbara. 2016. Silent Comics. In *The Routledge Companion to Comics*, ed. Frank Bramlett, Roy Cook, and Aaron Meskin, 201–208. London: Routledge.

Pratt, Henry J. 2009. Narrative in Comics. *The Journal of Aesthetics and Art Criticism* 69: 107–117.

Prince, Gerard. 1973. *A Grammar of Stories*. The Hague: Mouton.

Raaberg, Gwen. 1998. Beyond Fragmentation: Collage as Feminist Strategy. *Mosaic: An Interdisciplinary Critical Journal* 31 (3): 153–171.

Ricoeur, Paul. 1980. Narrative Time. *Critical Inquiry* 7 (1): 169–190.

Rippl, Gabriele, and Lukas Etter. 2013. Intermediality, Transmediality, and Graphic Narrative. In *From Comic Strips to Graphic Novels. Contributions to the Theory and History of Graphic Narrative*, ed. Daniel Stein and Jan-Noël Thön, 191–217. Berlin and Boston: De Gruyter.

Ryan, Marie-Laure. 2004. Still Pictures. In *Narrative Across Media. The Languages of Storytelling*, ed. Marie-Laure Ryan, 139–144. Lincoln and London: University of Nebraska Press.

———. 2014. Story/World/Media. Turning the Instruments of a Media-Conscious Narratology. In *Storyworlds Across Media. Toward a Media-Conscious Narratology*, ed. Marie-Laure Ryan and Jan-Noël Thön, 25–29. Lincoln and London: University of Nebraska Press.

Salvatori, Lidia. 2022. The Deep River of Feminism: From Ni una menos to Non una di meno. *Critical Times* 5 (1): 241–248.

"Se toccano Lucha y Siesta, toccano tutte." 2019. *DinamoPress.it*. November 13. https://www.dinamopress.it/news/toccano-lucha-y-siesta-toccano-tutte/. Accessed 3 Mar 2023.

Serafini, Paula. 2018. *Performance Action: The Politics of Art Activism*. New York: Routledge.

Sternberg, Meir. 1996. What Is Exposition? An Essay in Temporal Delimitation. In *Narratology: An Introduction*, ed. Susana Onega and José Angel García Landa, 103–114. New York: Routledge.

Thön, Jan-Noël. 2017. Transmedial Narratology Revisited: On the Intersubjective Construction of Storyworlds and the Problem of Representational Correspondance in Films, Comics and Video Games. *Narrative* 25 (3): 286–320.

Valtorta, Luca. 2019. Quando il fumetto diventa un'arma. *Repubblica.it*. December 6. https://www.repubblica.it/dossier/cultura/piu-libri-piu-liberi-2019/2019/12/06/news/il_fumetto_come_arma-242747309/. Accessed 3 Mar 2023.

Walker, Jill. 2004a. Distributed Narrative: Telling Stories Across Networks. *Internet Research Annual* 3: 91–104.

———. 2004b. Distributed Narrative: Telling Stories Across Networks. *AoIR 5.0, Brighton*. https://jilltxt.net/txt/Walker-AoIR-3500words.pdf. Accessed 3 Mar 2023.

Wolf, Werner. 2004. 'Cross the Border–Close the Gap': Towards an Intermedial Narratology. *European Journal of English Studies* 8 (1): 81–103.

———. 2017. Transmedial Narratology: Theoretical Foundations and Some Applications (Fiction, Single Pictures, Instrumental Music). *Narrative* 25 (3): 256–285.

CHAPTER 8

Voices of Graffiti in Urban Settings: Symbolic Contestation and Political Narratives

Patrícia Oliveira, Carlos Vargas, and Cristina Montalvão Sarmento

INTRODUCTION

Graffiti is one of the most powerful and immediate expressions of symbolic contestation in urban settings. The 2008–9 financial crisis in Europe and austerity measures, particularly in Portugal (2012–4), gave voice to renewed public protests in varying registers, including broadly cultural responses and focused political arguments. Public spaces in urban settings

---

P. Oliveira (✉)
Observatório Político, Lisbon, Portugal
e-mail: patriciaoliveira@observatoriopolitico.pt

C. Vargas
Department of History, Nova University of Lisbon, Lisbon, Portugal
e-mail: cmvargas@fcsh.unl.pt

C. M. Sarmento
Institute of Social and Political Sciences, University of Lisbon (ISCSP-ULisboa), Lisbon, Portugal
e-mail: msarmento@iscsp.ulisboa.pt

© The Author(s), under exclusive license to Springer Nature Switzerland AG 2024
D. Callahan (ed.), *Visual Storytelling in the 21st Century*,
https://doi.org/10.1007/978-3-031-65487-9_8

were appropriated as a legitimate space for the visual manifestation of democratic protest, and the evidence of this cultural and political practice could be found increasingly in Lisbon between July 2012 and April 2014, constituting the visual voice of a historical and political moment of dissent.

The political and social development of communities combines the domain of techniques or accepted procedures with the domain of imagination and creativity, with the latter constituting sources of vitality for the maintenance of collective identity. Political manifestations through graffiti have proven to be increasingly significant and relevant as sources for an interpretative and comprehensive analysis of the praxis and consequences of politics, particularly in the fields of political theory, political culture, and visual politics. Unsurprisingly, perspectives drawn from political science lie behind the consideration of the dynamics of protest through the visual instrument of graffiti. This chapter accordingly aims to analyze the political dimensions of graffiti embedded not only as a cultural practice but mostly as a political urban location for symbolic contestation.

First, we argue that graffiti is a powerful expression of symbolic contestation and of political narratives in urban settings. Second, we will also discuss conceptual dimensions related to informing, influencing, and challenging communities based upon visible messages. Last, but not least, we consider graffiti as visual representations of voices for potential political change. Recently, protest publics have been considered to be one of the principal global trends with respect to demands for transition and the contestation of existing orders. Within the logics of protest, graffiti and the power of visual writing in public exist as a disruptive political gesture that merits analysis in terms of its contribution to the debates that it focuses on.

CONCEPTUAL DIMENSIONS

Graffiti and *street art* are not exactly the same thing, although naturally they possess similarities. Moreover, an analysis of what is understood as graffiti and street art is itself politically strategic. Without its roots in graffiti, nevertheless, street art could not have started to develop an autonomous path. This path drew on the context of the first steps of New York graffiti in the 1970s, rich with communicative and protest potential, as a means to claim space for its concerns and as an element of hip-hop culture; and it also drew on the late European context in the 1990s, more philosophical and avowedly political, even if partly executed in imitation of what had originated in the United States, in conjunction with moments of locally referential artistic and spontaneous creation on the walls of cities. These two contexts were essential in the creation of another, new and influential artistic movement on a global scale, so-called street art (Bischoff 2000; Waclawek 2011).

Street art is created in public places and is generally unsanctioned, spanning a wide range of media and created by those wishing to communicate directly with the general public, free from the supposed constraints of the formal art world (Underdogs 2017). All such works are found in the urban public space, and the term street art has generally encompassed two institutionally differing but visually related aspects, the institutional and the non-institutional. Its objective is to communicate directly with the public, making use for its purposes of visual and linguistic wit and playfulness, political pungency, aesthetic experimentation, and technical inventiveness, all of which the public do not have to search out in a separate space but which are encountered in the streets in the course of one's daily activities, making up a sort of open-air exhibition space without the formalities of galleries, museums, official sanction, or similar institutional environments (Neves 2015).

This art, accessible to everyone, with free admission and unlimited hours, is normally considered as ephemeral art. Temporary by nature and strongly guided by a set of unofficial rules of execution, both street art and graffiti see the city space as an infinite canvas in constant renewal. For this reason, in Portugal, there have been few institutional initiatives for its preservation. Its duration depends entirely on external forces and public reaction. At the same time, graffiti is also inevitably linked to gang culture and vandalism, given its association with marking territory through tags (Dogheria 2015), which "are usually based on letters of the alphabet and are considered the signature of a graffiti writer" as opposed to "murals" which are "more complex artworks" (Chamberlain 2022, 23).

Graffiti has no rules, is performed spontaneously, and is usually illegal. It aims to spread throughout the city and, the more visible it is, the greater its impact and importance are considered to be. On walls, train carriages, or hard-to-access surfaces, the important thing is the visibility, quantity, and frequency of these signatures as a way of marking territory between *crews* of writers (Chalfant & Cooper 1984). Over time the alphabetic characters associated with graffiti evolved, acquiring an iconography with more complex themes. In this process, they have moved closer to the art world, transforming themselves in some cases into extremely elaborate signatures which some have called "masterpieces," or simply "pieces," a process which reached its peak in the 1980s (Dogheria 2015).

As graffiti grew as a culture, new techniques were explored, and new symbols and abstract pieces appeared. In this movement, changes took place in the cultural and aesthetic contexts of graffiti, as well as in the dimensions and scale in which it was performed, in the relationship between legal and illegal, and also in the style and techniques used (spray, stickers, stencils, or posters). The results have blurred the line between what was considered to be an act of vandalism and criminality in the past and what may come to be considered an aesthetically valuable addition to the visual landscape of the city, increasingly appreciated by a wide range of audiences.

Confronting graffiti and urban art with conventional visual arts (gallery art), it became clear that these two universes, at least from a conceptual point of view, refer to different space-time logics (Ehrlich & Ehrlich 2007). Graffiti and urban art live intensely in space, both as a strategy and as a practice, with the street being the place par excellence for the production and exhibition of such works. In this case, the creative act dialogues intensely with the physical surrounds and the territory, and these become, in turn, integral parts of the work (GAU (Gallery of Urban Art) n.d.; Neves 2015).

Such street expressions contribute decisively to the social construction of urban settings within the city, in the sense attributed by Low (2014), while gallery art is marked by spatial fragmentation, in which the spaces have a narrowly functional role, serving to accommodate certain practices understood as appropriate to studio or gallery objectives and identities. From an operational and symbolic point of view, the nature of such interior spaces is very different to that of spaces which have been designed for other functions, without considering their potential for appropriation in the service of political agendas via unsanctioned visual alteration.

What art is and what it is for have been considered very differently in recent history. It has been many years since works of art were seen merely as an aesthetic expression (Tiburi 2017b), and the concern with what art is has become one more site of social contestation (Tiburi 2017a) or, as Rancière suggests, an issue deeply intertwined with doing visual politics (Rancière 2009). Nevertheless, the visuality of art, including street art and graffiti, cannot be irrelevant in the public's processing of its attempts at intervention with respect to the narratives through which powerful agents try to enforce their versions of reality. The experience of street art and graffiti as art, and therefore as participating in valorized cultural categories, may be critical, allowing it to expand its reach to social and economic issues much more effectively than if it were simply considered an ugly and anti-social eyesore.

Graffiti as Visual Narratives

As a contemporary expression, graffiti is part of so-called urban cultures, although the debate about its worth in view of the prestige of elite cultural values and practices pushes it toward "subcultures," "marginal cultures," or perhaps "youth culture." The explanation of these categories is dependent on different starting points and cultural and even legal approaches, which tells us something of the heterogeneous nature of graffiti. In particular, legal frameworks establish the criteria of legality and normalization, or of disobedience and transgression of the performative act of graffiti. This does not mean that the preference for such an approach to graffiti necessarily leads to the exclusion of others, since the criterion of legality can, in some cases, coexist in a multifaceted way with different protagonists, ethnic groups, age groups, and urban settings.

Graffiti can be said to aim to help in building a creative and urban identity in the face of the limited avenues to power and prestige for certain sectors of society. Contemporary art, in general, as Sullivan (2006) notes, deliberately seeks to expand its individual role to fit any communicative model. Urban art exemplifies this attempt at enduring public visibility, particularly through street art, bearing in mind that street art encompasses not only graffiti but also murals, stickering, guerrilla art, flash mobs, and public performances. These practices attempt to influence viewers through expressing perspectives on social, political, cultural, and economic issues via a strident visibility in locations that cannot be ignored. The visual intensity and public venue of graffiti as a protest art form searches to provoke public response and not simply to be admired for its technical virtuosity.

Thus, graffiti can be understood as an instrument to create awareness regarding a social issue, to mobilize for collective action as an "art of protest of what a revolution looks like" (Nichols 2021). It can also, of course, generate objection and resistance, but in either case it has acted upon the world. The motivation of such an "art of protest" tends to be clearly acknowledged by viewers as coming from a place of resistance, whatever the viewers' relation to the issues being commented upon (Fig. 8.1).

Fig. 8.1 "While art entertains, money acts." Ginjal Street, Cacilhas, Portugal. June 15, 2013. Photograph by Pedro Fidalgo

In this sense, we may consider graffiti (from both the perspective of whoever creates it and whoever sees it) as a performative urban activism, rather than individual self-expression. On the one hand, the impact of graffiti and its would-be messages seeks to act within the short-term temporality that characterizes political demands. Graffiti depends on the political cycles and principal topics discussed in the public sphere. Twenty-four hours a day the visual narratives of graffiti are offered to every spectator walking past, promoting multiple individual interactions between the walking citizen and the political concerns of the graffiti's maker(s).

On the other hand, this individual experience becomes collective when a community of citizens is mobilized and recognizes the need for change in society. Thus, this interactive process of giving public visibility, political meaning, and therefore attempting to influence action is neither more nor less than a form of *artivism* (Nichols 2021, 20). With respect to graffiti, *artivism* can be accepted as a type of activism combining the creative power of visual, performative, and experiential art.

Graffiti, whether considered in the inscription of the word or the image, symbolizes the expression of change in the everyday life on urban settings. In its initial instance, the performative act of graffiti is invisible. In fact, the act of engraving and scratching the graffiti's message is usually practiced rapidly and clandestinely, away from the gaze of local residents. Consequently, graffiti emerges in urban settings unpredictably and not necessarily ascribed to a named author and originally contaminated by this potentially clandestine initial gesture.

These characteristics allow us to distinguish protest graffiti from the graffiti visited in street art circuits and sites. The disruptive gesture of protest graffiti carries with it a powerful communicational dimension that addresses the indiscriminate urban masses, which are by nature circumstantial. Thus, protest graffiti meets all the conditions necessary to break the routines of urban life (Fig. 8.2).

Fig. 8.2 "Hold on, hold on." Deutsche Bank. 100 Pascoal de Melo Street, Lisbon, Portugal. March 31, 2013. Photograph by Pedro Fidalgo

The nature of graffiti is susceptible to the spontaneous act and is rooted in the conditions of its creation: the transgressive immediacy and the condition of its ephemeral existence. The implications of graffiti demonstrate their centrality to the construction of urban settings and mostly to the expression of political contents associated with the denouncing of social conditions, with the demand for political rights, and with protest dynamics.

Thus, the visual narrative is constructed from that initial and disruptive gesture of the writer's action (of the graffiti artist him or herself), of inscribing a visual message (word or image) and its unexpected perception and interpretation with collective consequences and goals. In this sense, graffiti has an exploratory dimension with respect to its urban settings, revealing itself to be more multidimensional than expected.

Urban Setting Narratives

The city is the preeminent space of encounter and confrontation with the social issues in which graffiti is inscribed. Graffiti contributes to the recognition of place, of an urban context that does not necessarily need to be named, but which is recognized through identification—through the coexistence between and among individual and collective identities, housing and urbanism, tourist flows, economic dynamics, and financial impacts, simulacra of authenticity and the expectations inflected by all of these. It is accordingly in urban contexts that graffiti contributes to the recognition of place as a setting (Campo 2007; Ferro 2016; Jein 2016).

Moreover, the city is also the place of influence, capture, and inscription. Geographical and historical contexts have been impacted by the social and cultural processes of globalization, including through symbolic contestation at both global and local levels. The city place mobilizes through being a location for action, the projection of messages, and the focus of social networks and makes available local canvases for multiple visual assets, supporting debates at the local level and sometimes reaching the global public sphere. As graffiti becomes eminently political, its political dimensions, embedded not only as a cultural practice but also as a political urban setting for contestation, have the potential to intervene in encouraging communities toward a democratic political process involving negotiation and reasoned deliberation.

Usually, the street is a place that does not filter people. The city with its multiple material variants, and a wide diversity of scales, is a huge and permanent billboard that allows all those who circulate in it to appreciate and absorb all the messages on display, without there being any mechanism that sorts or hierarchizes its spectators-in-movement. There is no set time for the exhibition of any specific work to be visited, so the piece can remain for many years in that location and continue to be appreciated by different generations of audiences (Sanchis 2010; Alves 2014). In addition, it is an art that has the power to create special connections with its audience due to the habits and routines that are created, by remaining in place for several generations, when it is not destroyed by external factors. The fact that you can value the memory of a work of street art over time, through different moments in the life of the individual and the city, is also a structuring factor. Such memories are generated by a community that identifies itself and its city in part with what is visible on its walls.

Another of the benefits mentioned in the execution of street art pieces is the experience that it may provide, both to the artist and the spectator, who end up exchanging understandings in the place of execution, becoming closer to each other, even complicit with each other, in ways that are rarely possible with art situated in formal gallery spaces (Bengsten 2013). The variation in size is one further factor that differentiates street art and graffiti from other forms of two-dimensional art, given that in some cases the walls of entire buildings, including those that are many stories high, may be painted over from top to bottom.

The clandestine and peripheral dimension of street art and graffiti, in particular, often associated with acts of vandalism closer to anarchic urban movements, has been appropriated by political movements more involved in the transformation of the social, labor, and political conditions of certain communities. In this way, such artistic manifestations have gained a certain instrumental expression within discourses of political protest and activism, registered on the large empty walls on the streets of the run-down peripheries in which many of those communities live. Represented through those manifestations of urban art in public outdoor space, the cultural distinctiveness of these communities gained, perhaps for the first time, a degree of visibility in the public sphere that seemed to correspond to the dimension of the political tensions resulting from an apparently unchanging peripheral political condition (Fig. 8.3).

However, cities and the communities that inhabit them are intrinsically dynamic. The degraded territories that the economic process (temporarily) disregards offer, in turn, generous opportunities for artistic intervention, permeated or not with openly political messages. The inherent visibility and associations with creative dynamism that these urban

Fig. 8.3 "Low wages, Unemployment, Precariousness, Theft of the Christmas allowance, Increase in gas, Increase in VAT, Sacrifices, Increase in work hours, General strike, Participate!, It's for everyone." Sete Rios Train Station, Lisbon, Portugal. June 16, 2013. Photograph by Pedro Fidalgo

interventions bring to those territories contribute, often swiftly, to the valorization of the land, to real estate speculation, and, inevitably, to the attention of the markets. Brick Lane in London may serve as a typical example of this process. Expelled from once-peripheral territory, or domesticated within that territory, and yet ambiguously welcomed by certain social and economic actors, urban art does not stand still or accept its cooptation, but continues to seek new opportunities and places to inscribe its messages.

These cultural and political practices, which as seen above oscillate between anarchic dimensions and more or less engaged activism, gained particular expression in the United States, particularly in New York, and especially in certain areas of Manhattan, the Bronx, and Brooklyn. With an effervescent circuit of art galleries, it did not take long for street art and graffiti, among other manifestations of urban art, to move from the streets to the galleries, already in the early 1970s, thus reaching market values that quickly approached the market values of works produced within canonical production networks. This trajectory led to galleries showing graffiti in Europe as well, so that, unsurprisingly in this context, crews of writers were created in Portugal, alongside individual street artists, and began to show a desire to bring this art form from the street into interior spaces (GAU (Gallery of Urban Art) n.d.).

Visual Writers and Voices of the Crisis

Since the financial crisis of 2008, governments, municipalities, developers, and, ultimately, more informal communities have had to rapidly adapt to a new more uncertain reality (Carmona et al. 2019). Some argue that the period has marked a new and distinctive era with its own political economy, governance, and societal norms. For others, the period is simply a continuation, perhaps even a deepening, of the neo-liberal project—a project that has frequently been underestimated as regards its capacity for transformative and adaptive change, and which continues to thrive and evolve.

As shown by Sarmento et al. (2019), the link between social network mobilization and its role in public protest is manifest in several other cases that have emerged in recent years. The 2010 wave that shook the Arab world (Algeria, Libya, Bahrain, Jordan, Morocco, and Yemen) was the first such wave of related cases. Later, similar mobilizing tactics appeared in Europe, particularly in Southern European countries. In May 2011, for example, thousands of protesters came together in Spain to demand political, economic, and social change. The Spanish demands and protest models could also be seen in Portugal. The apparent roots of such emergent protest practices appear to be linked to a mimetic crisis process that affected several countries. The 2008–9 financial crisis in Europe and its accompanying austerity measures stimulated renewed public protest, sometimes more directly political and other times more loosely cultural.

In Portugal, the contestation was felt later in a particular context. In March 2011, and in order to mitigate the growing weight of interest on the Portuguese public debt, the Government negotiated the entry of the Troika in Portugal—the name given to the joint representation of the European Commission, the European Central Bank, and the International Monetary Fund put together for the purpose—in order to obtain financial assistance, with Socialist Party Prime Minister José Sócrates presenting the official request on April 6 of that year (Reis 2020; Rodrigues and Silva 2015; Frasquilho 2013) (Fig. 8.4).

On May 5, 2011, the Troika publicly presented the Memorandum of Understanding on Economic Policy Conditions, also known as the Troika Plan, which involved an injection into the Portuguese economy of a total amount of 78 billion euros over 2012–4. Three years later, on May 4, 2014, Social Democratic Party Prime Minister Pedro Passos Coelho, leading the Government (2011–5) that had succeeded that of José Sócrates, announced the conclusion of that particular process of external financial intervention (Karazouni et al. 2013).

During that period, the country underwent a vast set of public reforms, strong financial control, and a reduction in state expenditure, with the implementation of a set of austerity measures (Blyth 2013; Caldas 2012)

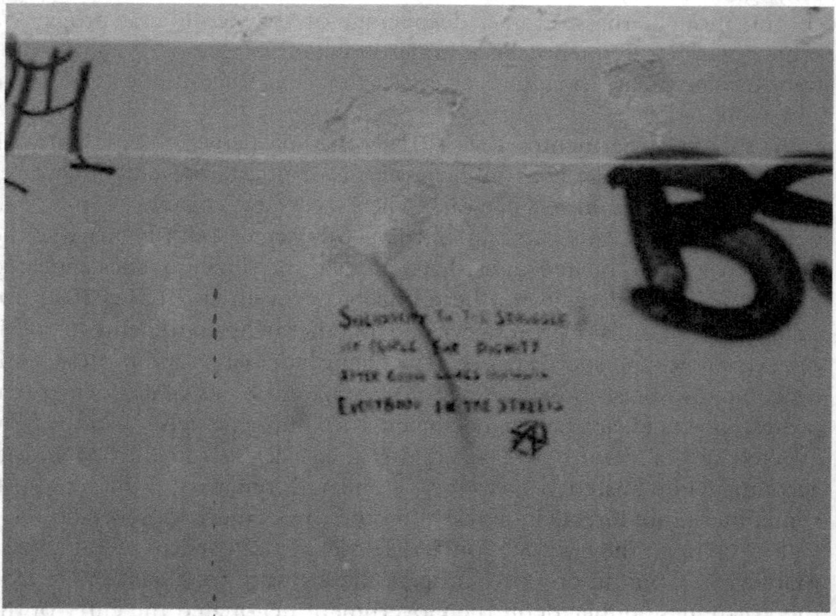

Fig. 8.4 "Solidarity to the struggle of people for dignity. After Greece comes Portugal. Everybody onto the Streets." 154 Luz Soriano Street, Lisbon, Portugal. October 4, 2012. Photograph by Pedro Fidalgo

that led to an acute social crisis and widespread discontent among the Portuguese population (Caldas and Almeida 2016; Pedroso 2014). Social protest was taken to the streets, led by political parties and trade unions, but also via organic social movements in which social networks played a decisive role (Beiguelman 2012) (Fig. 8.5).

It is in this context of social contestation of the austerity measures then in force that a significant production of graffiti associated with political protest, and appealing to insubmission and revolt, began to appear in many streets of Lisbon (Sequeira 2015; Torre & Ferro 2016; Sarmento et al. 2019), in the face of the cost of living, changes in the labor market (Carvalho and Carvalho 2015) and the housing market (Drago 2021; Xerez et al. 2018), and many other measures identified as burdensome by opposition parties, trade unions, and various sectors of civil society (Abreu et al. 2013).

Fig. 8.5 "Sold to the Troika." University City. Old Canteen main entrance, Lisbon, Portugal. June 13, 2013. Photograph by Pedro Fidalgo

Method, Assembly, and the Use of Images

Methodologically, we focus on a comprehensive set of graffiti photographs taken in the city of Lisbon, between July 2012 and April 2014 (unfortunately, most of them no longer exist), simultaneously as a record, a collection, and a catalogue of the historical and political momentum of dissent. It is in this context of intense visual transformation of the city streets that a colleague Pedro Fidalgo decided to photograph many of these graffiti, systematically covering an area of the city which he delimited as being that with the greatest concentration and diversity of images. Aware of the political and historical importance of the moment the country was going through, and of how many of the graffiti seemed to illustrate many of the dimensions of popular discontent in Portugal but also the difficult circumstances experienced in other Southern European countries, particularly Greece, Pedro Fidalgo decided to initiate a systematic campaign of the photographic registration of artistic and political interventions of protest in a pre-determined set of Lisbon streets.

Photography takes on, in this work, the role of collection, registration, and digital memory, by capturing and later recovering the graffiti image, associating it with discursive meanings and narrative dimensions. The description of graffiti involves an approach that connects the practice to a local and, simultaneously, global urban context. Graffiti clearly considers part of its role to be that of an instrument of protest, in a strategy of visibility and presence in view of a global crisis in which technocrats leave little space for alternative narratives.

In addition to graffiti associated with the current political situation of the moment, Pedro Fidalgo also decided to include graffiti related to other themes, for example, that of a philosophical, poetic, informative, or even obscene character produced concurrently or that had survived from previous periods, to allow the main theme to be contextualized and analyzed within a wider reality. According to Fidalgo:

> in this collection, we did not consider the capturing of graffiti similar to others previously photographed, as this would exponentially increase the work to be carried out, leading only to the visually monotonous gathering of a multiplicity of images that would only allow the analysis of the quantification and distribution of their typology. However, whenever the existence of similar graffiti was found, but which differed from each other due, for example, to the use of a different color, these were included in the survey. Also, during this survey, concerns of a visual nature were considered, with each

image having been recorded considering its scale, support, and physical setting, in order to obtain photographs with high aesthetic quality. (Fidalgo 2022)

As an archival methodology, and considering the possibility that these records could be studied later, Fidalgo created a table with six columns, the first of which was intended to numerically and sequentially reference each image, the second to put the photographs in miniature so as to have an idea of the type of content being described, the third column was reserved for the digital reference number of the image, created automatically by the camera when recording, the next column was to indicate the date the photograph was taken, and the fifth column was reserved for the identification of the place where each image was taken. The last column was used for observations, among which the transcription, for the most part, of the text contained in the graffiti, often difficult to read or interpret, or particular aspects considered relevant at the time. In the numbering of the records, whenever it was found that there were several photographs relating to the same graffiti, due, for example, to different aspects that it presented or the complexity of its elaboration, it was decided to give each of these images the same number, adding a sequential letter of the alphabet in order to differentiate them. With the conclusion of the fieldwork, Pedro Fidalgo counted a total number of 810 graffiti (Fidalgo 2022). In connection with the latter, grounded in the methodology established for this collection, the registered graffiti were mapped, analyzed, and their spatial distribution clarified, making it possible to define such aspects as thematic typologies, diversity of supports, and execution techniques, or to generate readings of individual pieces or of groups of related pieces. In this way, multiple contexts were made apparent through which the potential of the collection could be considered.

The principal reading we propose is that in which a historical moment encouraged the dissemination of widespread frustration by mean of the possibilities of inscribing alternative stories through multiple graffiti, even if temporarily, and that this moment can continue to enjoy an afterlife via the mediation and support of photography (Elkins 2007; Clarke 1997). As it does in other instances, photography operates as a mechanism to register the transformations that have occurred in urban settings, as a mechanism to approach the historical process, as an alternative source of information, as well as a support document without which analysis would be extremely difficult (Barber and Peniston-Bird 2010; Burke 2001). Seen from the other end of the process, given that images function as a prime access condition for a reading of the world and the social movements that permeate it, such readings become more effective when we are aware of the inscription of these images in the cultural, social, and political contexts that generated them (Rose 2016). As it is unmanageable to show the entire collection, we have shown throughout this chapter a small but representative number of images containing visual protest narratives.

Looking Ahead

The contemporary condition of art, particularly urban art, is in itself transitory. Simultaneously, this same condition has been established through a tense relationship between the concept of tradition and an innate desire for modernity, a concept which is always already outdated. In this sense, the dimension of history coexists with a continuous present that will become history, a circumstance that urban art, in particular, reveals so well. It is, in fact, a present full of cultural, political, and social tensions not yet settled and in permanent negotiation in the public sphere.

Art is a reality inseparable from historical conditions, and the cultural life of a society is naturally determined by multiple factors that constitute its political, economic, and social life. Post-Marxism had to confront the non-inevitability of social change, with a plurality of actors being involved in what change occurs, including the hegemonic mechanisms of mass communication, while trying to explain the emergence of new narratives such as feminism (Criado Perez 2020; Braidotti 2022), black and postcolonial feminism (Mirza and Joseph 2012), gay culture (Woods 2017; Martel 2017), ecology and class inequalities (Frey et al. 2019), ecology and imperialism (Crosby 2015), orientalism and imperialism (Said 1994, 2003 [1978]), culture and conflicts that are not class conflicts (Lane and Wagschal 2012), inclusion and diversity (Brown 2017), post-colonialism (Gandhi 1998; Lazarus 2004), decolonialism (Mignolo and Walsh 2018), the new geographies (Lowe and Lloyd 1997), the crisis of democracy and populism (Aikin and Talisse 2020; Przeworski 2019; Norris and Inglehart 2019), and post-democracy (Crouch 2020) (Fig. 8.6).

This is a non-exhaustive list of possible innovations that indicates the many directions in which additional research could go. Further, these numerous approaches deal with one or more aspects of values-oriented narratives and the prospects for understanding ongoing societal transformations, and deconstructing power, according to their different

Fig. 8.6 "Hail Markets, who art in heaven. Speculate with us consumers. From now until the hour of our death. Ah mother." 146 Luz Soriano Street, Lisbon, Portugal. October 12, 2012. Photograph by Pedro Fidalgo

frameworks. Faced with the pulverization of narratives and values in contemporary society, as well as with social life implying permanent negotiation among equals, the need arose to construct discourses that would detect and defuse the tensions resulting from this process. Such discourses would be the mobilizers no longer of one class in opposition to another, but of diverse groups mobilizing against unjust conditions imposed by the power of dominant groups, conditions present in multiple hegemonic discourses (Laclau and Mouffe 2014).

Since Winston Churchill argued that we should "never let a good crisis go to waste," the Occupy movement as a transnational and urban attitude of political activism became central in the process to support alternative visions to those of dominant politics, debating local strategies to respond to the crisis and to participate beyond the traditional mechanisms of representative democracy. Given the Occupy movement's focus on habitation and the use of the built environment in more socially responsible ways, public spaces in urban settings became marked in many streets by street art and graffiti as an output of protest democracy related to the protest narratives of the Occupy movement.

Graffiti is intrinsically then an instrument of protest, articulating ideas, practices, places, and symbols. The recognition of the protest act through graffiti denounces the organization of power relations in the space of social life and the manner in which different urban identities express their ideologies and political demands. In this way, graffiti provokes the reinforcement of urban identities (Simões 2013; Sequeira 2015; Ferro 2016) simultaneously with attempting to intervene upon local and global consciences in general.

Street art also widens perspectives on contemporary polymorphic political discourse, which can no longer be reduced to verbal and formal strategies. If all arts broadly conceived encourage us to consider what it is that promotes the values we approve of, enhancing our moral compass and self-knowledge (Nussbaum 1990; Koopman and Hakemulder 2015), then Democracy itself becomes the ultimate object of discussion when political campaigns use social media and citizens and residents express themselves emotionally through protests (linking disgust with disagreement), activism (linking hope and public action), and via emotions more generally (linking emotional reaction to political communication). Street art not only dovetails with all of these informal sites and practices but provides perhaps the most democratic venue of all, given that the inherently visual stories it tells will be encountered whether you align yourself with their ideological preferences or not.

Acknowledgments The authors express their gratitude to Pedro Fidalgo, the photographer and researcher responsible for the exhaustive and systematic photographic survey, who kindly provided access to his material. The photographic documentary archive by Pedro Fidalgo served as a starting point for the scaling of the political analysis—that of symbolic contestation and political narrative—without which access to and retrieving of memory would be highly compromised.

References

Abreu, Alexandre, et al. 2013. *A crise, a Troika e as Alternativas Urgentes.* Lisbon: Tinta da China.

Aikin, Scott F., and Robert B. Talisse. 2020. *Political Argument in a Polarized Age: Reason and Democratic Life.* Cambridge: Polity Press.

Alves, Alice N. 2014. Emerging Issues of Street Art Valuation as Cultural Heritage. In *Lisbon Street Art & Urban Creativity: 2014 International Conference*, ed. Pedro Soares Neves and Daniela V. de Freitas Simões, 21–27. Lisbon: Urban Creativity.

Barber, Sarah, and Corinna M. Peniston-Bird, eds. 2010. *History Beyond the Text: A Student's Guide to Approaching Alternative Sources*. London: Routledge.

Beiguelman, Giselle. 2012. Espaços de subordinação e contestação nas redes sociais. *Revista USP [Brazil]*. 92: 20–31.

Bengsten, Peter. 2013. Beyond the Public Art Machine: A Critical Examination of Street Art as Public Art. *Journal of Art History* 82 (2): 63–80.

Bischoff, Gautier. 2000. *Kapital: Un an de graffiti à Paris*. Paris: Éditions Alternatives.

Blyth, Mark. 2013. *Austerity: The History of a Dangerous Idea*. Oxford: Oxford University Press.

Braidotti, Rosi. 2022. *Posthuman Feminism*. Cambridge: Polity Press.

Brown, Jennifer. 2017. *Inclusion: Diversity, the New Workplace & the Will to Change*. Hartford, CT: Publish Your Purpose Press.

Burke, Peter. 2001. *Eyewitnessing: The Uses of Images as Historical Evidence*. London: Reaktion Books.

Caldas, José Castro. 2012. The Consequences of Austerity Policies in Portugal. *Friedrich Ebert Foundation*. http://library.fes.de/pdf-files/id-moe/09311.pdf. Accessed 14 Nov 2022.

Caldas, José Castro, and João Ramos de Almeida. 2016. Narrativas da crise no jornalismo económico. *Cadernos do Observatório* 7. https://hdl.handle.net/10316/41131. Accessed 17 May 2023.

Campo, Ricardo. 2007. *Pintando a cidade. Uma abordagem antropológica ao graffiti urbano*. PhD thesis. Lisbon: Open University. http://hdl.handle.net/10400.2/765. Accessed 28 Feb 2023.

Carmona, Matthew, et al. 2019. Public Space in an Age of Austerity. *Urban Design International* 24: 241–259.

Carvalho, Sónia, and Messias Carvalho. 2015. Memorando de Entendimento sobre as Condicionalidades da Política Económica e a reforma laboral: causa e consequência? *Revista Jurídica da Universidade de Santiago* 2: 493–522.

Chalfant, Henry, and Martha Cooper. 1984. *Subway Art*. London: Thames and Hudson.

Chamberlain, Rebecca. 2022. Aesthetics of Graffiti: Comparison to Text-Based and Pictorial Artforms. *Empirical Studies of the Arts* 40 (1): 21–36.

Clarke, Graham. 1997. *The Photograph*. New York: Oxford University Press.

Criado Perez, Caroline. 2020. *Invisible Women: Exposing Data Bias in a World Designed for Men*. London: Vintage.

Crosby, Alfred W. 2015. *Ecological Imperialism: The Biological Expansion of Europe (900–1900)*. Cambridge: Cambridge University Press.

Crouch, Colin. 2020. *Post-Democracy After the Crises*. Cambridge: Polity Press.
Dogheria, Duccio. 2015. *Street Art 2: Graffiti Stars, Street Art: Técnica e Protagonistas*. Trans. A.M. García Iglesias. Lisbon: Levoir.
Drago, Ana. 2021. *Habitação entre crises: Partição das classes médias, políticas de habitação acessível e o impacto da pandemia em Portugal*. Cadernos do Observatório 15. Coimbra, Portugal: Centro de Estudos Sociais.
Ehrlich, Dimitri and Gregor Ehrlich. 2007. Graffiti in Its Own Words. *New York Magazine*. June 22. http://nymag.com/guides/summer/17406/. Accessed 28 Feb 2023.
Elkins, James, ed. 2007. *Photography Theory*. London: Routledge.
Ferro, Lígia. 2016. *Da Rua para o Mundo: Etnografia urbana comparada do graffiti e do parkour*. Lisboa: Imprensa de Ciências Sociais.
Fidalgo, Pedro. 2022. *Graffiti in Lisbon During the Troika (2011-2014)*. Interview with Pedro Fidalgo. November 13. Our translation.
Frasquilho, Miguel. 2013. *As raízes do mal, a Troika e o futuro*. Lisbon: Bnomics.
Frey, R. Scott, Paul K. Gellert, and Harry F. Dahms, eds. 2019. *Ecologically Unequal Exchange: Environmental Injustice in Comparative and Historical Perspective*. Basingstoke: Palgrave Macmillan.
Gandhi, Leela. 1998. *Postcolonial Theory: A Critical Introduction*. Edinburgh: Edinburgh University Press.
GAU (Gallery of Urban Art). n.d. http://gau.cm-lisboa.pt/gau.html. Accessed 28 Feb 2023.
Jein, Gillian. 2016. Suburbia, Interrupted: Street Art and the Politics of Place in the Paris banlieues. In *Cities Interrupted: Visual Culture and Urban Space*, ed. Shirley Jordan and Christoph Lindner, 87–104. London: Bloomsbury.
Karazoumi, Eirini, et al., eds. 2013. *A Strategy for Southern Europe. Special Report SR017*. London: London School of Economics.
Koopman, Eva, and Frank Hakemulder. 2015. Effects of Literature on Empathy and Self-Reflection: A Theoretical-Empirical Framework. *Journal of Literary Theory*. 9 (1): 79–111.
Laclau, Ernesto, and Chantal Mouffe. 2014. *Hegemony and Socialist Strategy: Towards a Radical Democratic Politics*. London: Verso.
Lane, Jan-Erik, and Uwe Wagschal. 2012. *Culture and Politics*. London: Routledge.
Lazarus, Neil, ed. 2004. *The Cambridge Companion to Postcolonial Literary Studies*. Cambridge: Cambridge University Press.
Low, Setha, Manissa Macleave Maharawal, and Dimitris Dalakoglou. 2014. Public Space Reasserts Its Political Role. *Oculus: A Publication of American Institute of Architecture, New York Chapter* 76 (3): 24–25.
Lowe, Lisa, and David Loyd, eds. 1997. *The Politics of Culture in the Shadow of Capital*. Durham, NC: Duke University Press.

Martel, Frédéric. 2017. *Global Gay: La longue marche des homosexuels*. Paris: Flammarion.
Mignolo, Walter, and Catherine Walsh. 2018. *On Decoloniality: Concepts, Analytics, Praxis*. Durham, NC: Duke University Press.
Mirza, Heidi Safia, and Cynthia Joseph, eds. 2012. *Black and Postcolonial Feminisms in New Times: Researching Educational Inequalities*. London: Routledge.
Neves, Pedro S. 2015. Significado de Arte Urbana, Lisboa 2008-2014. *Convocarte: Revista de Ciências da Arte* 1: 121–134. http://hdl.handle.net/10451/27730. Accessed 28 Feb 2023.
Nichols, De. 2021. *Art of Protest: What a Revolution Looks Like*. London: Big Picture Press.
Norris, Pippa, and Ronald Inglehart. 2019. *Backlash: Trump, Brexit, and Authoritarian Populism*. Cambridge: Cambridge University Press.
Nussbaum, Martha. 1990. *Love's Knowledge*. New York: Oxford University Press.
Pedroso, Paulo. 2014. Portugal and the Global Crisis: The impact of austerity on the economy, the social model, and the performance of the state. *Friedrich Ebert Foundation.*. https://library.fes.de/pdf-files/id/10722-20220207.pdf. Accessed 14 Nov 2022.
Przeworski, Adam. 2019. *Crises of Democracy*. Cambridge: Cambridge University Press.
Rancière, Jacques. 2009. *A partilha do sensível*, 34. Trans. M.C. Netto. São Paulo: Editora.
Reis, Luís. 2020. *Da Troika à Geringonça*. Lisbon: Guerra e Paz.
Rodrigues, Maria de Lurdes, and Pedro Adão e Silva. 2015. *Governar com a Troika: Políticas públicas em tempo de austeridade*. Coimbra, Portugal: Almedina.
Rose, Gillian. 2016. *Visual Methodologies. An Introduction to Researching with Visual Materials*. London: Sage.
———. 1994. *Culture and Imperialism*. New York: Vintage Books.
Said, Edward. 2003 [1978]. *Orientalism*. London: Penguin.
Sanchis, Javier Abarca. 2010. *El postgraffiti, su escenario y sus raíces: graffiti, punk, skate y contrapublicidad*. PhD thesis. Complutense University of Madrid. http://eprints.ucm.es/id/eprint/11419/. Accessed 28 Feb 2023.
Sarmento, Cristina Montalvão, Patrícia Oliveira, and Patrícia Tomás. 2019. Retracing Protest Publics in Portugal: A Generation in Trouble. In *Protest Publics: Towards a New Concept of Mass Civic Action*, ed. Nina Belyaeva, Victor Albert, and Dmitry G. Zaytsev, 83–100. Cham, Switzerland: Springer.
Sequeira, Ágata. 2015. *A cidade é o habitat da arte: Street art e a construção de espaço público em Lisboa*. PhD thesis. University Institute of Lisbon. http://hdl.handle.net/10071/11538. Accessed 28 Feb 2023.
Simões, Marta C. 2013. *Graffiti e street art em Portugal*. Masters thesis. University of Lisbon. http://hdl.handle.net/10451/12225. Accessed 28 Feb 2023.

Sullivan, Karen. 2006. How Does Art 'Speak,' and What Does It 'Say'?: Conceptual Metaphor Theory as a Tool for Understanding the Artistic Process. In *Thought Tools for a New Generation: Essays on Thought, Ideas and the Power of Expression*, ed. David E. Boyes and Frances B. Cogan, 81–89. Eugene, Oregon: Robert D. Clark Honors College/University of Oregon.

Tiburi, Márcia. 2017a. Arte e Autoritarismo. *CULT [São Paulo]* 230: 12–13.

———. 2017b. A negação de todos os poderes. *CULT [São Paulo]* 230: 28–31.

Torre, Elena, and Lígia Ferro. 2016. O Porto sentido pelo graffiti: As representações sociais de peças de graffiti pelos habitantes da cidade do Porto. *Revista de Ciências Sociais [Fortaleza, Brazil]* 47 (1): 123–147.

Underdogs. 2017. *Art Map* [pamphlet].

Waclawek, Anna. 2011. *Graffiti and Street Art*. London: Thames & Hudson Ltd.

Woods, Gregory. 2017. *Homintern: How Gay Culture Liberated the Modern World*. New Haven, CT: Yale University Press.

Xerez, Romana, Pedro G. Rodrigues, and Francielli Dalprá. 2018. A política de habitação em Portugal de 2002 a 2017: Programas, políticas públicas implementadas e instituições envolvidas. In *Habitação: Cem anos de políticas em Portugal 1918-2018*, ed. Ricardo Costa Agarez, 465–511. Lisbon: Institute of Housing and Urban Renewal.

CHAPTER 9

Bourne-Again Bond: Retooling the Spy Story in the New Millennium

Anthony Barker

INTRODUCTION

The fantasy spy movie has been a staple of film production since the heyday of the Cold War in the 1960s. But it has also come under pressure internally from other forms of representation in film culture and externally from radical shifts in world geopolitics. What has been at stake over the last sixty years is a negotiation over the perceived credibility and relevance of the genre's plots and postures deriving from this secretive world. The cliché of a lone hero struggling to save the world from various megalomaniacs and malefactors, which was invented to defuse out-and-out villainy from the détente-era Soviet Union (then a potentially welcome member of the New World order), has come to look extremely shop-worn. Other more plausible plots have obtruded themselves on the genre, like threats to the earth's ecological balance, but most notably they have been narratives of special or dark ops generated by our own security services.

A. Barker (✉)
University of Aveiro, Aveiro, Portugal
e-mail: abarker@ua.pt

© The Author(s), under exclusive license to Springer Nature Switzerland AG 2024
D. Callahan (ed.), *Visual Storytelling in the 21st Century*,
https://doi.org/10.1007/978-3-031-65487-9_9

The movie franchise that straddles most of the Cold War period is the *James Bond* film series. Navy Intelligence operative Ian Fleming wrote and published the original Bond novel, *Casino Royale*, in 1953, and the first Bond film *Dr No* appeared in 1962 after Fleming had published a further nine Bond novels. Dying in 1964 (a month before the release of the third film *Goldfinger*), having completed twelve novels and two short-story collections, Fleming left the field free to movie adaptors. Subsequent films tend just to use the titles (*Casino Royale* is an anomalous case in various ways). Thereafter, the Bond franchise retained its popularity at the box office for over forty years, experiencing various transformations in budget and personnel while trying to adhere to the successful 1960s formula of licensed violence, glamour and sexual entitlement projected by the original Bond protagonist Sean Connery. There were problems and false starts and predictable criticisms of the formula, but it remained resolutely a favourite with the public.

The issues of credibility and relevance, mentioned earlier, came to a head in the new Millennium. *GoldenEye* (1994) had been the first Bond movie to be made after the collapse of the Soviet Union, introducing a new and slick Bond in Pierce Brosnan and a new female M in actress Judy Dench. Because of these novelties, Martin Campbell's sure direction and the genuflection to female agency in a less polarized world, the formula seemed to survive intact. It did, however, mean fewer gadgets, toned-down cynical one-liners, and less sex on demand. The crisis, however, which was never a purely box-office affair, came with *Die Another Day* (2002). The plot of world domination harked back to the overblown narratives of the Roger Moore era, the verbal quips were misfiring, the attitude to women became once again equivocal (not helped by a dire theme song and cameo by Madonna) and the film's special and computer-generated effects were clearly being bested by other productions (most notably the first two *Mission Impossible* films). On top of this, the three *Austin Powers* movies (1997, 1999 and 2002) openly mocked the spy film. Although the parody was extremely broad, taking in other film and television originals and centring its ridicule on the self-delighted aesthetics of the 1960s, it does manage to skewer some of the plot and character absurdities of the Bond formula seen in the contemporaneous *Die Another Day*.

The need for a reboot seems therefore to have been in the air. The most commonly cited source for the pressure to revamp the Bond franchise was the success of the film *The Bourne Identity*, which was released in 2002, four months before *Die Another Day*. Here was another type of spy drama, adapted from the novels of Robert Ludlum. Ludlum, by virtue of being American and familiar with the workings of the CIA, brought the spy story to a new level of relevance in terms of global power. Fleming's Bond was the product of the post-war age of British decolonization and clearly had the purpose of cheering Britons up about their declining role in the world. But, on many occasions, even the plucky Bond cannot achieve his aims without American assistance. The USA is the understated factor in Bond movies, both the real power that made pretending to police the world possible and the finance and the cinema-going market that made Bond films prosper. Film Bond weathered the period of American self-criticism around Vietnam and Watergate, perhaps because they were not directly about American institutions, but the return of American self-confidence in the 1980s created the conditions for Ludlum's Jason Bourne and Tom Clancy's Jack Ryan to appear. These fictional heroes came complete with a national context one could believe in.

Rebooting in the new Millennium was also an attractive option for other reasons. There had been an exponential growth in fantasy cinema since the release of *Star Wars* in 1977, driven by all-conquering computer-assisted imaging, which had dynamized animation and action genres and is perhaps best epitomized by the success of the *Lord of the Rings* trilogy (2001–3). Effects teams were to be found all over the most mundane of movies as well as the most spectacular. In order to be different, rebooting entailed taking the action back to the gritty and the grounded. To be sure, the special effects teams were still there, the dollars were still up upon the screen, but the characters and the acting had to be less two-dimensional, the plots a lot more believable. The best-known case of squaring this particular circle is Christopher Nolan's re-interpretation of the Batman franchise in *Batman Begins* (2005), an attempt to erase the costume camp of the 1990s and, as the title suggests, to start again. The three Ludlum novels that were adapted for the cinema were literary products of the Reagan years, but influenced by the counter-culture's bad memories of espionage and dirty tricks, such as the Iran/Contra scandal. The trilogy was re-issued in one volume (2003) and, critically, the films were made after 9/11, when the war on terror sanctioned all manner of secret activity. In addition, the George W. Bush administration and the deceit around the reasons for invading Iraq in 2003 created a new climate of political dissent. *The Bourne Identity* brought counter-intelligence back to street level, but it also isolated its protagonist from the institutions that had created him. He could be the embattled private individual again, instead of the agency man.

INTRAMEDIAL ESPIONAGE

The first *Bourne* film was largely the invention of director Doug Liman (who acquired the rights from Ludlum) and writer Tony Gilroy. Ludlum died in 2000 and his fiction provided little more than the title and the bare bones of the Bourne film narrative. Liman's father had been the Senate's chief counsel in the Iran–Contra investigation, so Liman was intimately acquainted with the dark deeds done in the name of national security (he also went on to direct *Fair Game* [2010] about the outing of CIA agent Valerie Plame by Bush's White House). The script of *Identity* was hugely changed from the novel, but it retained the perception that self-serving over-reachers could penetrate the CIA's hierarchy and that it could easily be convinced that its own operative (Bourne) was a traitor. Although Ludlum deploys a super-villain in the adapted historical figure of Carlos the Jackal in his *The Bourne Identity* (1980), the seed of the idea that the agency could easily turn on its own agents is there. The figure of the enemy within rather than the enemy without generated more credible plots and a more central sympathetic character. Since American spy fiction tends to have a strong right-wing orientation, Liman's political sensibility informs the *Bourne* film franchise with a particular counter-culture scepticism. This was partly what the *Bourne* films gave to the Bond franchise, a less assured sense of their mission. How exactly and in what tones and forms this took shape needs further detailed investigation. Actual synergies between the two franchises were largely behind-the-camera technical ones; only Albert Finney performs in both, in *The Bourne Ultimatum* (2007), minimally in *The Bourne Legacy* (2012) and in *Skyfall* (2012).

There is, however, one clarification that should be made. Just as the Bond films have their anomalous *Never Say Never Again* (1983), which is a curious unlicensed remake of the fourth Bond film, *Thunderball* (1965), whose origin lies in an issue of contested film rights and whose only claim to consideration is that it had lured Sean Connery back to play the role after he had said "Never Again" (hence the film's ironic copyright-dodging title), the *Bourne* film cycle has *The Bourne Legacy*, starring Jeremy Renner as the main protagonist, Aaron Cross. Bond films may require a Bond in them, but at least they do not have his name in their title. The franchise owners of *Bourne* could not entice Matt Damon (or favoured director

Paul Greengrass) back for a fourth film, so they branched out with a parallel plot using the same house style and a script that references Bourne's name liberally. As *Legacy* is written and directed by Tony Gilroy, the co-creator of the first film in the series, and made by the same production team, for the purposes of this chapter I am considering it integral to the *Bourne* series. The processes of influence and cross-influence, which are my subject, accordingly operate between the five *Bourne* films (2002–2016) and the five Daniel Craig/Bond films (2006–2021). But for practical purposes, it is necessary to get the chronology clear: the first two *Bourne* films were released two years before the first Craig Bond film, and the influential *Bourne* trilogy, with its largely stable plot elements, was complete before the second Craig film was released in 2008.

The great good fortune of the Bond reboot lay in the availability of Fleming's first novel *Casino Royale* (1953) for film adaptation. Ian Fleming sold the film rights in 1955, and they were resold in 1960 to Charles K. Feldman, before the Saltzman/Broccoli/Eon Bond films, released through United Artists, had established themselves as a successful franchise. Eon adapted the remaining novels out of chronological order, omitting the one novel to which they did not possess the rights. Feldman eventually produced *Casino Royale*, released by Columbia Pictures in 1967, as a spy spoof film comedy (in some ways, *Austin Powers avant la lettre*); it did limited business and had minimal impact on the runaway success of the main Bond franchise. In 1999, MGM/UA obtained the film rights from Sony/Columbia in a partial trade for the rights of *Spider-Man*. Thereafter, Eon/MGM/UA could complete their set of Fleming adaptations and, in an important sense, re-launch the franchise.

Following *Die Another Day*, Eon dropped Pierce Brosnan and began the search for a new Bond actor. This was a clear marker of their desire to take the films in a new direction. Barbara Broccoli courted a reluctant Daniel Craig for some time before he agreed to accept the role. Many Bond fans were appalled by the choice, even going so far as to propose boycotts of the films. His looks had enabled him to easily inhabit the roles of villains rather than heroes in Hollywood films like *Road to Perdition* (2002) and *Infamous* (2006). In retrospect, the choice seems inspired. A shorter, blonder and craggier-looking Bond was ripe for a limited de-glamourization process. It cannot be an accident that the cover photo of the authorized *Bond on Set: Filming 007 Casino Royale* (2006) by Greg Williams has Daniel Craig in a white-tiled gents' toilet. The movie *Casino Royale* (2006) retains the producing team (Barbara Broccoli and Michael

G. Wilson) and writing team (Neal Purvis and Robert Wade, but with the addition of Paul Haggis) from the final two Brosnan Bond films. It also re-engaged Martin Campbell, who had directed the first and best of the Brosnan Bonds, *GoldenEye* (1995), so there is a strong measure of continuity. In essence, the new formula was to be the marriage of glamour with grit, fantasy with a more grounded and sequential emotion. A lot of this could be found in the original Fleming novel. But to be sure, there was a danger. The Bond franchise had never been less than a cash cow for all those with an interest in it, so the reboot of an avowedly fantasy form in favour of a more local or ephemeral sense of "relevance" might risk losing those elements that had made it a lasting success.

Perhaps the most significant achievement of the reboot was the creation of a character-driven story arc beginning with *Casino Royale* but spanning all the Craig films and achieving a degree of closure in *No Time to Die* (2021). A feature of movie Bond had always been that he had no provenance and no attachments. As Connery described him, "I had to start playing Bond from scratch ... He has no mother. He has no father. He doesn't come from anywhere and he hadn't been anywhere when he became 007. He was born–kerplunk–thirty-three years old" (cited in Bennett and Woollacott 1987, 161). When *On Her Majesty's Secret Service* (1969) experimented with a wife and depth of feeling, she was quickly killed off, for this threatened the series' weightless formula. George Lazenby as Bond was also discarded along with attempts at emotional connection, although the film has subsequently come to be highly regarded. For fifteen years, the future of the franchise lay with Roger Moore, tongue-in-cheek and ever more outlandish plots.

Taking a wider perspective, it is now possible to see that seriality had become an essential constituent of the prestigious film and drama franchises of the new Millennium, whether it was the *Lord of the Rings* trilogy (2001–2013) or the cable television sensations *The Sopranos* (1999–2007), *Mad Men* (2005–2015), *Breaking Bad* (2008–2013) and *Game of Thrones* (2011–2019). Even network shows like *House* (2004–2012) and *The Mentalist* (2008–2015) required gradual accretions of character and plot development across episodes and series to complement their traditionally self-contained mystery or crime-solving narratives. Seriality helps to solve one of the perennial problems of audience response to Bond films: the perception that the actor playing Bond is ageing. The ageing process is an asset in a narrative that can accrete and develop and a serious liability in one dependent on formulaic stasis. The more temporally compact Bourne films benefit from starting with a boyish-looking Matt Damon, and as he begins to overcome his amnesia and learns more about himself, the getting of knowledge accompanies his maturing in the role, until the point where he becomes fully aware of the springs of his nature in the movie entitled just *Jason Bourne*. It is again in this respect that the *Bourne* films could have an impact on the Bond films. Bond does not discover himself in the Craig sequence so much as he *becomes* a person with attachments and regrets for the first time. This transformation is more or less coterminous with the reinvention/recognition of the assassin as a person with a personal code and a home life (roles inhabited by Jason Statham in *The Mechanic* [2011] and other movies and later taken to an extreme in the *John Wick* films [2014–]). The film *Hanna* (2011) retraces the Bourne story with a young female protagonist.

LOCATION, ACTION, TECHNOLOGIES

Since the focus of this chapter is the concrete influence of one popular franchise on another, as it bears on the business of contemporary serial visual storytelling, the argument will focus on just three areas: (1) the choice and use of film locations, (2) action sequences and (3) the representation of advanced technologies.

The Choice and Use of Film Locations

Bond films are usually geared towards the use of glamorous settings, rich people's playgrounds and panoramic or exotic cityscapes, where the protagonist's sense of access and entitlement can be showcased. Fleming's taste is apparent, for example, in his deployment of expensive hotels, casino venues and Caribbean paradises. The films, emerging from an era of post-war rationing and limited mobility, offer the promise of liberty and abundance for an aspirational 1960s generation. This tradition is perpetuated in the waterfronts and resorts in the Bahamas, Montenegro and Venice in *Casino Royale;* scenic Italy, Haiti, Austria and Bolivia in *Quantum of Solace;* some stunning photography of Shanghai in *Skyfall;* Mexico City during the *día de los muertos* and Rome by night in *Spectre*. Fleming reflected his social class's taste, a kind of snobbery that was taken up as the Bond brand by subsequent generations, exemplified in the mantra that Martinis should be shaken and not stirred. Craig's curt rejection of the Martini recipe ("Do I look like a give a damn?") in *Casino Royale* may be seen as his smartest bid to democratize and modernize the role. In contrast, John Le Carré, who in many respects comes from a similar background to Fleming, understood that conspicuous refinement and snobbery were anathema to a professional who was tasked with operating inconspicuously. His spies are therefore grey figures or people who have failed or under-achieved in life. Bond, as an icon of excitement and entitlement, must have the trappings of success, most notably his car, a hugely important signifier in the films. As a visual medium, film can give form to glamorous locations more viscerally than literature, and the cut-and-captioning style of introducing a new setting, accompanied by lush music, was very much part of Bond's initial success. The challenge was always to make the images of the high-life consonant with the realities of covert intelligence operations.

In sharp contrast, by transposing the spy story to an American agent operating in Europe, Bourne is able to throw off all of Bond's class-grounded style and to move in the shadows. The *Bourne* films situate themselves in crowded metropolitan cityscapes and obscure resorts, where the protagonist's need for anonymity could be preserved. Bourne's characteristic milieu is the railway station, so that the two major London sequences are in Waterloo (*Ultimatum*) and around Paddington (*Jason Bourne*). We constantly see him entering and exiting trains and metros, surrounded by milling commuters. Away from public transport, we find him moving through the faubourgs in Paris in *Identity*, a street demonstration in Berlin and the dormitory suburbs of Moscow in *Supremacy*, the backstreets of London, Madrid and Tangier in *Ultimatum*, and a street riot in Athens in *Jason Bourne*. In contrast, we see Bond in carefully selected casual wear steering his motorized yacht into Venice in *Casino Royale*, or when holidaying in the historic town of Matera in Italy in *No Time to Die*. Such scenes preserve the connection with the glamour of past incarnations of Bond. Liman's original conception was to film *Identity* in just one location, Paris. He was prevailed upon, however, to open up the plot and take Bourne on a journey from Marseilles to Zurich and on to Paris. Bourne briefly hides out in the French countryside before returning to Paris for the showdown with his CIA handlers. The banks, consulates, residences and cheap hotels he visits are all filmed in the same flat understated style. And while Bourne makes his many journeys (virtually as a hitchhiker in *Identity* and a purloiner of unguarded vehicles in other films) by public transport, the Bond producers, having exhausted their product placement deal with BMW, restore the iconic Aston Martin for the various climactic showdowns in *Casino Royale, Skyfall, Spectre* and *No Time to Die*.

A curious feature of both franchises seems to be a marked preference for roof-top sequences. There are a number of possible reasons for this. One of them is the need to cater for parkour athleticism, which will be addressed in the next section of the chapter. However, there is a clear difference between how they are handled. Bond atop the buildings of Whitehall and with the skyline of London as his backdrop is seen in a classical contemplative pose. These shots recall the figure of Batman glowering at the corruption of Gotham City below him, whereas Bond appears to contemplate a threatened civilian London that needs his protection. In both cases, the contemplative gaze reflects a call to duty about to be heeded. For Bourne, the roof-top is the scene of fight or flight, mostly the latter, since he is apparently overmatched. Bourne (and Cross) are almost always pictured amid clutter, in the souks of Tangier and the slums of Manila. Clutter, crowds and confusion allow them to make a quick exit from a Consulate or a hotel or apartment or office building (like the one above Paddington basin in *Jason Bourne*). Bourne seeks high vantage points to reconnoitre a risky Parisian rendezvous in *Identity* or to spy on Pamela Landy in New York in *Ultimatum*. The roof-top further provides a canvas for panoramic action, as snipers assume their positions for taking the kill shot in multiple *Bourne* films. In the opening sequence of *Spectre*, we see Bond vacate his hotel room via the window to walk purposefully and agilely along the roofs of Mexico City to arrive at his sniper's vantage-point. The sequence foregrounds his grace and athleticism in movement, as does his scaling of the high-rise in Shanghai in pursuit of an assassin in *Skyfall*. Bourne's movements reflect efficacy, resourcefulness and a muscle-memory training he cannot consciously recall. Aerial and high-rise acrobatics have become a favoured feature of special effects teams, as roof-top and cityscape chases are the favourites of stunt teams.

There is further shared feature that deserves comment here, and which accelerates in the spy film of the new Millennium. This is the tendency to bring the story to a climax closer to home. Intelligence headquarters were the shadowy places where instructions were received, missions launched and monitored, but not where significant action took place. Dispatching agents around the world, these places took pains not to advertise themselves. Agents traditionally were in the field, potentially ambiguous figures in a double-crossing game, who occasionally needed to "come in from the cold." The greater salience of the intelligence community after 1980 made showing MI5 and MI6 headquarters in London and centres of power in Washington and Langley, Virginia, a *sine qua non* of the defence-of-the-nation movie. It is not perhaps too big a stretch to see the 9/11 attacks in 2001, particularly the one on the Pentagon, as making intelligence infrastructure itself a much more plausible target, such as we see in *Skyfall* (2012). To bring the danger in-house, the figure of the saboteur/insider becomes a constant, and plots are tied up in the Craig cycle by the realization that there has been a mega-conspiracy uniting all the various malefactors of the five films. Valued allies are killed off (Judie Dench's M, Jeffrey Wright's Felix Leitner) as the conspiracy scales up to the very top of intelligence organizations. In the manner of Bourne, who ends up fighting the very head of the CIA, Bond is left with a small team of insider helpers (Moneypenny, Q, Mallory), with the might of the organization itself ranged against him. From *Skyfall* onwards, there is a clear sense of Bond's needing to adopt the Bourne strategy, injured, retired, presumed dead, in short, of going off the grid. Being off the grid becomes a necessary precondition in the millennial spy thriller, a corollary to coming home. The offer to "come in" is used as a ploy in *Supremacy* and is the tease at the end of *Jason Bourne*; it can never happen because those who want him in, his sympathizers, could just as conveniently liquidate him. Bond also cannot come in because of the McGuffin of a techno-infection in *No Time to Die*; that, along with the invention of "loved ones," forces him to sacrifice himself in an act of self-immolation. But this is an extra-textual tease, because Broccoli and Wilson have made it public knowledge that they are looking for a new Bond and that the character, like Jon Snow in *Game of Thrones*, must come back.

Action Sequences

Perhaps the greatest influence on Bond from *Bourne* has been the reconfiguring of action sequences. This influence falls mainly in the way the fights, pursuits and car chases are filmed. But there are certain structural narrative differences that need to be taken into account. Generically, Bond is in pursuit of malefactors, with a powerful but secretive organization supporting him. The narrative drive is towards justice and punishment in protection of the public greater good (or perhaps merely the restoration of the *status quo*). In contrast, malefactors are generally pursuing Bourne, with a powerful but secretive organization abetting them. Plots turn around the need for self-protection (everyone appears to be hiding things from the protagonist and is out to get him; whatever he does is therefore a variant of legitimate self-defence). There is no very clear public good at stake. Indeed, Bourne's adversaries often claim the public good in striving for his elimination. Since Bourne is a trained assassin, it follows that identification with him is predicated on his amnesia and his status as "the little guy" with an indomitable agency arrayed against him. From this point of view, the sort of mayhem Bond perpetrates is the very reason in *Bourne* why secretive agencies have to be reined in and why black ops are cast as illegitimate. Bourne's adversaries' indifference to the collateral damage they create is why they are clearly marked "bad." Traditionally, Bond's ends justify his means, whereas Bourne's enemies' increasingly callous means ultimately invalidate their ends. There is little argument in Bond films about who exactly are the patriots.

So, with the moral landscape clarified a little, we can turn to the action. In purely technical terms, there is an issue to be resolved between CGI/visual effects and stunt coordination. The later Brosnan Bonds have outdated and fantastical visual effects that caught the attention of the critics negatively. Whilst there were (and are still) a number of critic/hold-outs who valued the excessiveness and humour of the Moore/Brosnan films, the majority have come to find these features outmoded, along with the Bond girls and the cynical quips. Indeed, the films tend progressively to include these critiques of Bond by supporting characters (starting with Judi Dench as M's denunciation of him in *GoldenEye* as a "sexist, misogynist dinosaur, a relic of the Cold War"). The reboot, at least at the level of marketing, depended on a return to "the authentic," a somewhat hazy idea in the world of movie-making to say the least. With all the peripherals around film-making—such as fan blogs and DVD extras—it is not enough to create a grittier movie; you must also show that you went to great lengths to make the scenes seem real. To this end, Daniel Craig's injuries to his teeth on *Casino Royale*, his shoulder on *Quantum of Solace*, his knee on *Spectre* and his ankle on *No Time to Die* have become grist for the publicity mill (see Esquire Editors 2019). The remaking of Bond was as much about taking the films away from the visual effects specialists (the computer geeks) and giving them back to the car and bike daredevils and those with martial arts training (the hard men). It could be said that *Bourne* very much began that process, although this transformation was, in truth, more apparent than real, since both cadres of professionals have grown exponentially over the two decades. When one looks at stunt specialists, moreover, one finds that sequences are being designed and executed by the same or related teams. For example, Dan Bradley, stunt coordinator and second unit director for the *Bourne* series after *Identity*, was hired to work on *Quantum of Solace* (2008). Many stunt personnel also worked on both franchises. Black stunt performer Marvin Campbell appears in all five Craig/Bond films, two *Bourne* movies, three *Fast and Furious* films and two *Mission Impossibles* to date. Gary Powell, who has been a lead stuntman and stunt coordinator for the Bond films since *GoldenEye*, was also the UK coordinator for both *Ultimatum* and *Jason Bourne*. Teams coordinated by Gary Powell won ensemble stunt awards for both *Ultimatum* (2008) and *Skyfall* (2013).

This struggle can be seen playing out in other film franchises as they egg each other on to greater heights of technical and stunt wizardry. Fighting and driving become fetishized in films that have little other *raison d'être*. And when there is little plot plausibility to make these films otherwise hang together, the effects teams need to step in to hyperbolize the achievements of previous productions. The *John Wick* films adumbrate a super-assassin hero with an aesthetic of fantastical gunplay and brutal martial agility. The *Fast and the Furious* franchise goes all in on taking car chases to extremes, including driving cars out of planes at altitude and between high-rise buildings. Although not different in kind, the Bourne and Bond films are comparatively restrained in comparison with these adrenaline-fuelled fantasy forms.

In addition, various websites discuss what martial arts techniques are being deployed in the films and speculate on the training the star actors have received; are we watching Krav Maga or Kali martial arts, wing chun, kung fu or plain old boxing techniques (see Kurchak 2015; Jacob 2016)? Naturally, the experiences of their stunt doubles are also of interest (Crawley et al. 2019). The blogosphere is replete with commentary on fighting styles and who has assisted with the choreography of action sequences. In many cases, the trainers and stunt performers have become online celebrities in their own right. The vehicles used in chases and stunts are also openly admired in motoring magazines (Vaughn 2021). Because of their specialist interests, online enthusiasts have been more insistent on the links between various film franchises than film critics. The contribution of fan commentary to the success of these movies is hard to calculate, but no one seriously doubts that it has provided invaluable publicity.

Action sequences were very much created in the editing studio too. Liman conceived of the characters and the setting for the action, but Paul Greengrass took the Bourne style to its full realization. Richard Pearson and Christopher Rouse edited *Supremacy* for Greengrass. Rouse edited many of Greengrass's pictures, including his three *Bourne movies*. Pearson was subsequently hired to co-edit *Quantum of Solace*. The average shot length (ASL) decreases over the *Bourne* trilogy from around four seconds in *Identity* to just over two seconds in *Ultimatum*. This is best demonstrated by the Waterloo station sequence in *Ultimatum*, where Bourne takes on the whole security state with just a burner phone and his spy tradecraft, or the Tangier sequence in the same film which combines frenetic chasing and being chased in convergent story lines. The effect of Greengrass's approach is to make both the fighting and the chasing more immersive; it also delivers many of the scenes from Bourne's point of view. Given that Bourne is frequently confounded and necessarily reactive in explosive situations, the fragmentation of the shots helps to give the action a psychological plausibility. The same applies to the car scenes where rather than celebrating speed and dexterity under pressure, the chases reflect haphazardness and Bourne's desperate improvisation. He drives what comes to hand, just as he fights with whatever implements are within reach, like his famous defensive use of pen and magazine.

The long opening action sequence in *Casino Royale* is the touchstone for the new Bourne-like Bond played by Daniel Craig. The parkour chase symbolizes a commitment to athleticism over gadgetry and trickery, even though extraordinary effects are needed to make the sequence coherent. In the blogosphere, parkour and free runner expert Sébastian Foucan is foregrounded as Bond's quarry; where he can plausibly go, Daniel Craig must follow (Highfill 2021). The sequence is crucial for launching the new Bond and re-energizing the action formula. A constituent element of this is that the speed of execution carries us breathlessly over physical implausibility, and the cost of such exertion is registered on the body. Craig's Bond is accordingly more beaten up, scarred and worn down than any of his predecessors in the role.

The Representation of Advanced Technologies

One of the centres of appeal of the early Bond films was their deployment of new technologies, often in a tongue-in-cheek fashion. The 1960s, the decade of the Space Race, was the time when British Prime Minister Harold Wilson invited people to embrace what he called "the white heat of technology" as the marker of his administration. Technology was to materially improve the conditions of life for all. This mostly played out in film culture as production design. Bond would leave M's reassuringly wood-panelled office for the secret labs where the new devices were being developed by Q. The dominant symbol of this was Bond's Aston Martin DB6, with its ejector seat, tyre-slashing blades and machine guns. It was never really germane to ask whether such a vehicle did or could exist. It was fabricated to enhance Bond's charisma and autonomy; it was also part of the films' knowing playfulness, along with Rosa Klebb's spiked shoe, Oddjob's hat or Richard Kiel's (Jaws's) teeth.

Much has been made of the underground and island lairs of Bond villains, with their banks of computers attended by henchmen and schemes for world domination. In this respect, the techno-spy film is a crude branch of science fiction, not really interested enough to pursue its premise of a world made hyper-dangerous by automated systems of information and control. The threat of extinction is reduced to a game of stopping the missile or the explosion, as the electronic display counts down to zero. Rescuing in the nick of time is the *raison d'être* of these pictures; the threat itself need never be wholly plausible.

Along with the gimmickry and the gadgetry came a certain amount of international monitoring technology, but satellites and their progeny were still an object of mystery for the public. Bond still needed to be summoned to duty reassuringly by a landline. Over the long history of the Bond franchise, the power and scope of communications technologies became harder to ignore, although it is my contention that the real dangers were hidden by the absurd grandiosity of the conspiracies represented: to obtain apocalyptic munitions or monopolize energy resources for example. *Tomorrow Never Dies* (1997) has a media mogul villain, but he needs missiles and Anglo-Chinese military conflict to gain control of the Chinese media market There is only the hint that media already possess the technology and inclination to control us. *Die Another Day* reverts to weaponized solar energy and face-exchange surgery as exemplars of future threat. Yet, *The Bourne Identity* had already suggested a few months earlier that there were more plausible ways than cutting off and exchanging faces to throw a person's identity into confusion.

Covert ops depend on the management of perceptions of what is happening at street level. The agencies arrayed against Bourne have enormous power to monitor and control urban environments. As well as their own extensive resources, they can deploy the police and border control services. They can position their adversaries as always under suspicion and always outside the law. Essentially, they control the technology of identity recognition and the enforcement arms of the security state. Bond is a part of that security state, although the narratives pursued in *Bourne* influence the writers of the Craig films to move him more to the periphery of that apparatus. Technology then becomes articulated in the *spy* fiction film by production design. And in the case of Bourne, that is fundamentally the fleeting glimpse of our protagonist on monitors and in CCTV camera footage or the rendering of his presence by tracking devices. When decisive action is represented, the jagged handheld camera effects of documentary film-making come to the fore.

All Bourne films begin and end with him being or going off the grid. Between these two points, the films concern themselves centrally with the nature of this "grid." It is even represented aesthetically in the closing credits sequences, with their network-like digital lines and shapes played over by the increasingly techno-ish rock theme "Extreme Ways" by Moby, which after *Supremacy* is remixed for each subsequent film. These sequences help to convey the idea of an aggressively technologized world and yet they persist in echoing grungy lived experience on the run. The song's lyrics express alienation:

> Extreme ways that help me
> That help me out late at night
> Extreme places I had gone
> But never seen any light
> Dirty basements, dirty noise
> Dirty places coming through
> Extreme worlds alone (Hall 2004)

The refrain carries the phrase "I would stand in line for this," reflecting Bourne's democratic appeal, the many scenes where he queues for transport or at checkpoints. In contrast, Bond sweeps through airports and into hotels with valet parking, the whole point being that you do not have to stand in line. Musically, Bond films offer both showy title sequences and accompanying orchestral or ponderous ballad theme songs by invited star performers. These projects glamourized visual interpretations of the Bond plot, working variations on the established formula of sex and violence. Although delivered with the brio of sophisticated movie effects, they rarely foreground technology as a major feature of the story. Even the most techno-centred Bond movie, *Spectre*, chooses an octopus as its governing motif. In the same vein, Bond films have traditionally favoured a widescreen *mise-en-scène* and a rich technicolour palette: filtering Bond through these at once lurid and mutedly grey surveillance technologies would work against the formula that has given the franchise its longevity. But even the bright and bold Bond formula features have to give some ground to the Millennial reality that surveillance and information technologies are more ubiquitous and threatening, having become the dominant forms by which espionage is carried out.

The Bourne films work by contrasting street-level action against CIA control-room analysis of what is playing out before us. All of Europe is a chessboard as the people in suits back in Langley offer analysis of the action while Bourne evades their traps. This is the binary division into high tech and grunge/grit mentioned earlier. Formally, the Bourne films draw upon the urgency of television successes like *24* (nine series between 2001 and 2014), with its real-time helter-skelter constraints. Bond films have a more leisurely pace, mostly confining the against-the-clock heroics to the final reel. Across the five films from each franchise, Bond films are, on average, nearly thirty minutes longer (including the unfavoured pair, *Quantum of Solace* and *The Bourne Legacy*, which are anomalously short and long, respectively).

Five distinguished actors (Chris Cooper, Brian Cox, David Strathairn, Edward Norton and Tommy Lee Jones) play versions of the same character in each *Bourne* film, as they scheme to incriminate and exterminate Bourne. These plots centre on covering up scarcely distinguishable dark ops with names like Treadstone, Blackbriar, Outcome and Iron Hand. Across the series, conspiracies inflate to make these men enemies of the people as well as of Bourne. For example, we see Tommy Lee Jones scheming to take over a social media company Deep Dream that can give him secret access to the American population's private data. This finds an echo in the weak subplot of *Spectre*, where the new MI6 Head "C" wants to integrate all espionage data internationally (and thus make it available to Spectre). Synching up Bourne and Bond's personal enemies with society's foes is one of the ways in which the plots of the franchises tend to converge. Who acquires big data and what they do with it is a favoured theme of the second decade of the twenty-first century, as are the efforts of the state to prevent leaks, as in *The Fifth Estate* (2013). In each film, Bourne is also ranged against a doppelganger operative, a CIA assassin called in to liquidate him (and anyone who abets him), someone who is referred to under a soubriquet like "the professor" and "the asset." Bond likewise has his besuited villains, but he must also be pitted against a street-level killer in fights and chases, like Hinx in *Spectre* and Primo in *No Time to Die*. The problem of foregrounding techno-espionage is that it entails scenes of worried operatives in shirt-sleeves peering into screens, whereas the mobilizable "asset" or super henchman figure keeps the form grounded in action cinema.

Doug Liman conceived the character and plot of Bourne, but Paul Greengrass made him into a franchise, perfecting the technique for filming the agent/underdog. Liman displeased his producers during the making of *Identity* with what they regarded as his lack of professionalism and control of the film and its successors fell to producers Frank Marshall and Patrick Crowley. Marshall engaged Greengrass for the second and third films because of his background in journalism and politically engaged documentary film-making, but also because he had ghost-written the best-selling book *Spycatcher* (1987) for its MI5 spy-author Peter Wright. Liman's counter-culture instincts and Greengrass's investigative grit were a perfect blend. Continuity was provided by veteran film editor Oliver Wood and writer Tony Gilroy, who worked on the entire trilogy. Once covert ops had been taken to the streets, it suited Greengrass's kinetic handheld film aesthetic. The first Bourne film had been largely shot by Liman in France with a French crew and technical support. Greengrass brought in a new team in 2003 that operated more internationally. Action is visceral and immersive in Bourne, hardly ever comedic. Violence is strictly instrumental, a rapid response to a dangerous situation; it is explosive and can be surprisingly brief, like Bourne's hunting down of the professor in *Identity*.

The uses and forms of torture in these films are also a source of interest. The Abu Ghraib scandal of 2004 and Guantánamo Bay revelations post-2006 made US use of torture a hot subject. The film *Zero Dark Thirty* (2013) openly justifies the use of torture in the aftermath of 9/11. Drawing upon these iniquities, the Bourne films begin to explore how a decorated soldier could be converted into an assassin. Special ops units are shown to deploy psychological and physical torture regimes, as well as administering mind and body-altering drugs (in *Legacy*). One of the forms of advanced technology the films showcase is the use of body implants, something the Bond films take up in detail in *Spectre* and *No Time to Die*. But just as Bourne's quest is to find out how he became a killer, the Bond franchise starts to offer an explanation for how he became a 00 operative. *Casino Royale* is a true narrative of origin: a form of *Bond Begins*.

Thereafter, both film series take an interest in un-making and humanizing the killer, whilst remaining frankly enamoured of his murderous skills.

Conclusion

The desire to make over a successful film product will always be the result of many factors coming together. The movie industry is famous for its success-copying practices, but these alone do not explain the judgements and decisions taken in the revamping of Bond. Franchises that do not adapt in their various iterations will eventually exhaust the formula, as has happened with many popular film series (cf. *Death Wish*, *Lethal Weapon*). The extraordinary longevity of Bond over 60 years already suggests a high degree of adaptability. Coming late into the field of action/espionage cinema, the *Bourne* films took a fresh look at what it meant to operate in the shadows. They also abandoned the moral polarization of the Cold War years, in favour of a deep suspicion about what goes on in Western homeland security services.

Although the changing psychology is not profound, it was enough to show interest in the spy/assassin as a developmental being. Both film franchises start looking for the origins of killer instincts and, at the same time, look for narrative strategies for mitigating these instincts. In particular, they start looking for parents, both real and substitute ones. Bourne must emerge from the mist of amnesia to discover that his father did not prepare him for the life of an assassin. The orphaned Bond discovers that he was co-opted into an Austrian family with a cuckoo stepbrother in the nest. They must pick their way amongst their handlers, some of whom like M accept a quasi-parental role. Others just wish to destroy them. They must form loose family links with professional helpers and acquaintances, understanding that their humanity depends on the connections they form, especially with women. Female CIA and MI6 operatives are distinctly more collusive with Bourne and Bond than their male counterparts.

But rest and resolution are beyond their means to achieve. The desire to "come in" is checked by the notion that they are fatal to those around them and that they cannot really trust anyone. There is a supervening paranoia in these films that institutions are corruptible and that immense power is concentrated in the heads of the security apparatus. The physical dexterity of the single agent is an apparently feeble bulwark against these forces, and yet improbably, it holds off disaster in each of the films. Going off the grid is the agents' only defence against these hegemonic forces, but the films equivocate on just how possible this is. Formally speaking, being off the grid is just the interval between sequels.

It is a moot point whether the reboot of Bond could shed the series' dependence on glamour and entitlement, or indeed whether Bourne's take on the life of the agent is not just a re-glamourization for a generation infatuated with video game combat. Bond may globe-trot in style, but Bourne gets about almost as effectively. Surveillance equipment seems incapable of detecting his border-crossings. We see him travelling a lot, but there are just as many elisions and omissions of how he actually gets from A to B. In any event, in both cases, the casting of Matt Damon and Daniel Craig were unqualified successes. The initial resistance to Craig, then the full-throated acceptance and finally the regret over his abandoning the role have created a story arc that allowed for Mark Salisbury's Daniel Craig retrospective *Being Bond* (2022) hot on the heels of his making of a *No Time to Die* book (2021). Both Bond and Bourne are fantasies of individual empowerment that draw their credibility from action/adventure conventions and skilfully feed commercial cinema's insatiable appetite for fighting sequences. The contemporary spy story seeks authenticity in narratives that foreground human physical prowess as a counter to the ubiquity of technology and weaponized surveillance. Parallel to this, readings of film production in the blogosphere seek confirmation that the deeds depicted in its plots are enacted by performers, stunt people and their supporting crew rather than being merely the result of computer wizardry.

It has to be said that the Craig films are more uneven than the Damon *Bournes*, but after all, the *Bourne* formula is much simpler. Bourne's origin story culminates in the recovery of his memory and his identity as David Webb. Despite the ramifying parallel dark ops with their catchy names, after that the story has nowhere else to go. Steve Jasmine (2016) argues that Bourne's emotional journey is effectively concluded in the first film and that all that is good about the series derives from Doug Liman. However, taking the story full circle from the waters off Marseilles in *Identity* to those of New York's East River in *Ultimatum* vindicates Damon and Greengrass's initial instinct to complete the trilogy and then stop. Brian Tallerico found *No Time to Die* to be a "greatest hits package" (2021), but also that it contains nothing that is not better done in an earlier Bond film. The same could be said of *Jason Bourne*. Ultimately, there is a degree of convergence in the way contemporary genre plots ramify, action sequences imitate each other and themes cohere around security overreach in information technologies. The lesson of the abandoned TV spin-off *Treadstone* (2019) is that there is no *Bourne* without Bourne. Whether the soon-to-be-resurrected Bond will have learnt from its generic competitor we have yet to see.

REFERENCES

Bennett, Tony and Woollacott, Janet. 1987. *Bond and Beyond: The Political Career of a Popular Hero*, 161. Basingstoke: Macmillan.

Crawley, Joana, Emer Scully, and Lara Keay. 2019. Revealed: James Bond's Hunky French Body Double Who Is Putting Daniel Craig to Shame as He Takes on 007's More Dangerous Exploits in Jamaica. *Mail Online*. April 29. https://www.dailymail.co.uk/tvshowbiz/article-6972099/Daniel-Craigs-French-body-double-sets-pulses-racing-day-James-Bond-filming-Jamaica.html. Accessed 14 Aug 2023.

Esquire Editors. 2019. Daniel Craig Does His Own James Bond Stunts: Here's Every Time He's Been Injured. *Esquire*. May 14. https://www.esquire.com/entertainment/movies/a27467433/daniel-craig-james-bond-movies-stunt-injuries/. Accessed 14 Aug 1923.

Fleming, Ian. 1953. *Casino Royale*. London: Jonathan Cape.

Hall, Richard. 2004. *Moby Lyrics: Extreme Ways* (Reprise Version). AZLyrics.com. https://www.azlyrics.com/lyrics/moby/extremewaysrepriseversion.html. Accessed 14 Aug 2023.

Highfill, Samantha. 2021. *Casino Royale* Stunt Coordinator Breaks Down That Unforgettable Opening Chase. *Entertainment Weekly*. September 22. https://ew.com/movies/casino-royale-stunt-coordinator-opening-chase/. Accessed 14 Aug 2023.

Jacob [sic]. 2016. The Lethal Martial Arts of Jason Bourne. *Mixed Martial Arts*. November 13. https://www.mixedmartialarts.com/vault/the-lethal-martial-arts-of-jasonbourne#:~:text=Jason%20Bourne%20has%20a%20knack%20for%20simply%20being,hours%20of%20brutal%20training%2C%20hard%20work%2C%20and%20discipline. Accessed 14 Aug 2023.

Jasmine, Steve. 2016. *Doug Liman's Jason Bourne: The Rise and Fall of the Jason Bourne Movies*. Amazon e-book/Kindle Edition.

Kurchak, Sarah. 2015. How Daniel Craig Developed James Bond's Streetfighting Skills. *Vice*. November 4. https://www.vice.com/en/article/wn3wzq/how-daniel-craig-developed-james-bonds-street-fighting-skills. Accessed 14 Aug 2023.

Ludlum, Robert. 2003. *The Bourne Trilogy*. London: Orion.

Salisbury, Mark. 2021. *No Time to Die: The Making of the Film*. London: Titan Books.

———. 2022. *Being Bond: A Daniel Craig Retrospective*. London: Titan Books.
Tallerico, Brian. 2021. Review of *No Time to Die*. *Roger Ebert.com*. October 8. https://www.rogerebert.com/reviews/no-time-to-die-movie-review-2021. Accessed 14 Aug 2023.
Vaughn, Mark. 2021. All the Stunts in the James Bond Thriller 'No Time to Die' are real. Autoweek.com. October 21. https://www.autoweek.com/car-life/classic-cars/a37814305. Accessed 14 Aug 2023.
Williams, Greg. 2006. *Bond on Set: Filming 007 Casino Royale*. New York: Dorling Kindersley.
Wright, Peter, and Paul Greengrass. 1987. *Spycatcher*. Melbourne: William Heinemann.

Filmography

Austin Powers. 1997–2003. Jay Roach et al. (Director). New Line Cinema.
Batman Begins. 2005. Christopher Nolan (Director).. Warner Bros.
Breaking Bad. 2008–13. Vince Gilligan (Producer). AMC/Sony Pictures Television.
Casino Royale. 1967. Val Guest, Ken Hughes, John Huston (Directors). Columbia.
———. 2006. Martin Campbell (Director). Eon Prods./MGM/United Artists
Die Another Day. 2002. Lee Tamahori (Director). Eon Prods./United Artists.
Dr No. 1962. Terence Young (Director). Eon Prods./United Artists
Fair Game. 2010. Doug Liman (Director). River Road. Entertainment.
Game of Thrones. 2011–19. David Benioff and D. B. Weiss (Producers). HBO.
Goldfinger. 1964. Guy Hamilton (Director). Eon Prods./United Artists.
GoldenEye. 1994. Martin Campbell (Director). Eon Prods.//United Artists.
House. 2004–12. David Shore (Producer). Bad Hat/Shore Z/Fox Network.
Infamous. 2006. Douglas McGrath (Director). Warner Independent Pictures.
Jason Bourne. 2016. Paul Greengrass (Director). Universal Pictures.
John Wick. 2014–. Chad Stahelski and David Leitch (Directors). Summit/Lionsgate.
Lord of the Rings. 2001–3. Peter Jackson (Director). Wingnut/New Line Cinema.
Mad Men. 2005–15. Matthew Weiner (Producer). AMC/Lionsgate.
Mission Impossible. 1996–. Brian de Palma et al. (Directors). Paramount Pictures.
Never Say Never Again. 1983. Irvin Kershner (Director). Talia film/Warner Bros.
No Time to Die. 2021. Cary Joji Fukunaga (Director). Eon Prods./MGM/Universal Pictures.
On Her Majesty's Secret Service. 1969. Peter Hunt (Director). Eon Prods./United Artists.
Quantum of Solace. 2008. Marc Forster (Director). Eon Prods./MGM/Columbia.
Road to Perdition. 2002. Sam Mendes (Director). DreamWorks/Twentieth Century Fox.

Skyfall. 2012. Sam Mendes (Director). Eon Prods./MGM/Columbia.
Spectre. 2015. Sam Mendes (Director). Eon Prods./MGM/Columbia.
The Bourne Identity. 2002. Doug Liman (Director). Universal Pictures.
The Bourne Supremacy. 2004. Paul Greengrass (Director). Universal Pictures.
The Bourne Ultimatum. 2007. Paul Greengrass (Director). Universal Pictures,
The Bourne Legacy. 2012. Tony Gilroy (Director). Universal Pictures.
The Fifth Estate. 2013. Bill Condon (Director). DreamWorks/Touchstone.
The Fast and the Furious. 2001–. Rob Cohen (Director). Universal Pictures.
The Mechanic. 2011. Simon West (Director).. CBS/Millennium Films.
The Mentalist. 2008–15. Bruno Heller (Producer). Warner Bros.
The Sopranos. 1999–2007. David Chase (Producer). HBO
The World Is Not Enough. 1999. Michael Apted (Director). Eon Prods./MGM/UA.
Treadstone. 2019. Tim Kring (Producer). USA Network.
Thunderball. 1965. Terence Young (Director). Eon Prods./United Artists.
Tomorrow Never Dies. 1997. Roger Spottiswoode (Director). Eon Prods./MGM/UA.
Zero Dark Thirty. 2013. Kathryn Bigelow (Director). Columbia Pictures.

CHAPTER 10

Monsters in Animation and Related Nightmares in Contemporary Popular Culture

Rebeca Cristina López-González

INTRODUCING MONSTERS

How often did some of us struggle in early childhood attempting to fall asleep while imagining a monster in every corner of the room or under our beds? Our fancies might run wild, personifying fear in the shape of hideous creatures unable to be faced directly. Feelings of losing control became an obstacle to making a move or even breathing. This encounter with the unknown is progressively transformed as we grow older. Fear is fought and transmuted into the courage to confront those "monsters" from our childhood memories and, as a transferable skill, those to be met throughout life. As a means for channeling these dark aspects of human nature, folk and fairy tales were first disseminated orally, and then through print, as is well known, but today they are mostly encountered audiovisually. These reworkings tend to retain their focus of tackling upsetting

R. C. López-González (✉)
University of Vigo, Vigo, Spain
e-mail: rebecalopez@uvigo.gal

© The Author(s), under exclusive license to Springer Nature Switzerland AG 2024
D. Callahan (ed.), *Visual Storytelling in the 21st Century*,
https://doi.org/10.1007/978-3-031-65487-9_10

feelings and transforming them into valuable lessons about culture and identity, as affirmed by Maria Tatar:

> Disseminated across a wide variety of media, ranging from opera and drama to cinema and advertising, fairy tales have become a vital part of our cultural capital. What keeps them alive and pulsing with vitality and variety is exactly what keeps life pulsing: anxieties, fears, desires, romance, passion, and love. Like our ancestors, who listened to these stories at the fireside, in taverns, and in spinning rooms, we remain transfixed by stories about wicked stepmothers, bloodthirsty ogres, sibling rivals, and fairy godmothers. For us, too, the stories are irresistible, for they offer opportunities to talk, to negotiate, to deliberate, to chatter, and to prattle on endlessly as did the old wives from whom the stories are thought to derive. (Tatar 2002, xix)

As Tatar points out, the conversations that arose from this form of storytelling set up loops that both reflect and feed back into individuals' and communities' values, wishes, and aspirations. With alterations in technologies of transmission, fairy tales have not become archaic remnants of older patterns of storytelling and may be mediated in any form as long as their storyline and main characters are preserved, and these certainly include evil creatures and monsters. Bruno Bettelheim raised the alarm about the perils of the absence of monster figures in tales of this nature, giving the examples of some traditional folk, and fairy tales that suppressed monsters unless they were friendly. The consequences of this decision have led to neglecting the real monster we all live with:

> they [referring to those who criticize traditional fairy tales] missed the monster a child knows best and is most concerned with: the monster he feels or fears himself to be, and which also sometimes persecutes him. By keeping this monster within the child unspoken of, hidden in his unconscious, adults prevent the child from spinning fantasies around it in the image of the fairy tales he knows. Without such fantasies, the child fails to get to know his monster better, nor is he given suggestions as to how he may gain mastery over it. As a result, the child remains helpless with his worst anxieties–much more so than if he had been told fairy tales which give these anxieties form and body and also show ways to overcome these monsters. (Bettelheim 1976, 120)

Unfortunately, Bettelheim's warning has gone unheeded until relatively recently, to the point that Janet Evans, discussing picture books in the twenty-first century, highlights the fact that:

> Many adults feel that challenging and controversial picture books are not suitable for children … In reality, many young children have to deal with troubling, personal problems on a day-to-day basis … we cannot and should not "wrap them up in cotton wool" … picture books can help children relate to, and come to terms with, troubling, disturbing and sometimes controversial issues in life. (Evans 2015, 5–6)

Despite this defense of the authentic monster, a new trend in monster representation has evolved, which seems to deconstruct and disempower or even domesticate the hideous creature and replace it with a cute image of a being that lacks the ability to threaten its creator or reader, and, therefore, impedes the identification of fears and anxious feelings with the imagined and represented creature. In this sense, Jeffrey Jerome Cohen argues that:

> Anxiety manifests itself symptomatically as a cultural fascination with monsters—a fixation that is born of the twin desire to name that which is difficult to apprehend and to domesticate (and therefore disempower) that which threatens. And so the monster appears simultaneously as the demonic disemboweler of slasher films and as a wide-eyed sickeningly cute plush toy for children. (Cohen 1996, viii)

This coexistence of a two-faced monster is precisely what triggers this study aimed at analyzing how monsters are being represented through seven twenty-first-century commercial animated films aimed at four-quadrant audiences (all of the very broad categories into which audiences are sometimes divided: men and women, over and under 25).

Exported Popular Culture and Monsters

On one measure, popular culture is about nurturing and training. It tends to use both verbal language and visual strategies, as it attempts to intensify memory and transmit knowledge. At the same time, it is defined in terms of categories that are simplified into high versus low, elite versus popular, and often associated with a mainstream of values and customs via visual media, whether legacy media or the internet. Popular culture has also been described as vernacular, folksy, earthy, and appealing to the ordinary person.

Many iterations of contemporary popular culture now seem to be globally shared, due to the reach of commercial media and the transmission of certain more recognizable products rather than others. Familiar narrative forms travel better than local festivals, for example, and such traveling is inflected by whether a product is tradable across borders. This has largely come to mean products generated either in the United States or at least in English, resonating with the premise that "the future of international civilisation depended on the spread of Anglo-American values and institutions into less fortunate parts of the world" (Campbell and Kean 2016, 304), as believed by many Americans. As Emily Rosenberg summed up, "To many Americans, their country's economic and social history became a universal model" (Rosenberg 1982, 7). Hence, the path to modernization for many other countries could only be followed through imitations or emulation of the American experience.

The American cultural model and its global repercussion tend to be exemplified through Hollywood. This industry has dominated the international cinematographic scenario since the 1920s, and although it is currently becoming more deterritorialized, that is, unrooted from American local and national contexts, it maintains its level of impact, at least within many audiovisual markets. Neil Campbell and Alisdair Kean underline the dominance of Hollywood abroad:

> American exports in the 2010s continued to dominate the international film industry with around 63 per cent of worldwide box office receipts in 2013 (*Guardian* 2013). Hollywood's share of the world market had effectively doubled between 1990 and 2000 to around 60 per cent and remained at that level for much of the next decade (Motion Picture Association of America 2010). About 70 per cent of Hollywood's annual revenue in 2013 came from international markets. Eighteen of the top twenty films at the box office in 2014 were American and the remaining two were joint productions, largely financed with US dollars ... In many European countries in the early twenty-first century the percentage of box-office takings on domestic products was in rapid decline to as low as 10 per cent in Germany and 12 per cent in Britain and Spain. (Campbell and Kean 2016, 346)

As a result of the export of Hollywood productions and their continuing success among worldwide audiences and eventual cultural dominance, motion pictures cannot be underestimated as a vehicle able to factor into the wishes (abundance, freedom, glamour) and the fears (violence, inequalities, unfairness, and monsters) of adults and children. Campbell and Kean quote Jack Valenti, head of the Motion Picture Association of America at the turn of the century, who justified American dominance as follows:

> It is a fact, blessedly confirmed, that the American movie is affectionately received by audiences of all races, cultures and creeds on all continents amid turmoil and stress as well as hope and promise. This isn't happenstance. It's the confluence of creative reach, storytelling skill, decision making by top studio executives and the interlocking exertions of distribution and marketing artisans. (Campbell and Kean 2016, 346)

Although this dominance may be attenuated now that Hollywood is resorting to even more cross-national production processes to create wider international networks, its cultural global impact prevails, and this is why John Dean's words on popular culture from the early 1990s remain as valid today, if not more so with the exponential spread of streaming services:

> People in the United States and throughout the world spend time, pay money, and take their choice of American products and simultaneously, the nation's myths, icons, dreams, ideals, legendary heroes and unwritten laws [and monsters]. It pays to think seriously about American popular culture because it has become a personal matter for all of us. (Dean 1992, 11)

Moreover, this continues to be the case no matter the level of critique of American foreign policy, the spread of consumerism, or the bullying dominance of American companies.

ANIMATION: CULTURAL DOMINANCE FOR THE YOUNG

Hollywood's scope naturally not only reaches adult spectators, but also children and adolescents in the form of animated feature films. It is widely acknowledged that with the release of *Snow White and the Seven Dwarfs* in 1937, Walt Disney was the founder of the American long animated feature film (he did not create animation though; animation has a long history that began in 1892 with Charles-Émile Reynaud at the Museum Grévin in Paris through his Optic Theatre). Disney carefully picked each of the ingredients of his audiovisual fairy tale and also retained certain features that recalled the film-noir trend, which was in vogue among the directors and producers of real-action films at the time. The ASIFA, the International Animated Film Association statutes, include a definition of animation that is concerned with more than commercial profit, focusing on values such as culture, children's education, and mutual tolerance and acceptance:

> The art of Animation is the creation of moving images through the manipulation of all varieties of techniques apart from live action methods. This independent art, whatever its manner of expression—in theatres, on television, in Education or children's films etc.—should make an extensive and important contribution to the world's cultural heritage while playing its part in the search for new ways of artistic expression. It should help to promote progress towards peace and mutual understanding between all people. (ASIFA n.d.)

This definition is open about its ideological intentions or at least about the fact that popular creative products have cultural designs on audiences beyond "simple" entertainment. Jack Zipes pays serious attention in *Happily Ever After: Fairy Tales, Children, and the Culture Industry* to Disney's model, whose influence continues to structure this century's animated production system. There Zipes summarizes a series of contexts in which Disney's influence was channeled, including the absence of women among Disney animators, the subscription to the socially conventional ideological priorities of the tales that were adapted (including gender and "race" bias), and the focus on the visual exaggeration that animation made possible (Zipes 2005, 71–72). Zipes's description of Disney's key elements highlights that what had seemed to be the visual recreation of a simple tale is much more than that, as critique has revealed about all cultural products over the last 50 years, under the tutelary influence of such texts as Roland Barthes's *Mythologies* (1957) and John Berger's *Ways of Seeing* (1972).

Much attention has accordingly been devoted to the unpacking of consciously selected and unconsciously apparent ideological aspects in texts produced primarily for children. Kate Hawkey, drawing upon the work of Kieran Egan (1997) into cognitive development, explores different facets of how curricula are designed for teaching history to children and notes that there is "an inclination towards certainties and clear-cut hierarchies; an openness to 'possibility' can leave students feeling vulnerable" (Hawkey

2007, 66). Writers on children's literature frequently return to the theme of whether writing for children contains material supporting such things as sexism, racism, colonialism, violence, or consumerism, and, as a consequence, whether it should be withheld from children (see Kohl 1995, for a level-headed summary of the issues). Children and young adults have always been exposed to clearly good and clearly evil characters, including, of course, monsters, as part of the pedagogical project of helping children to learn how to cope with certain feelings and fears. This social project naturally brings together fairy tales, children's literature, and animation to such an extent that animation must be included within children's literature, together with any other material read or listened to and of interest to children (Oittinen 2000).

Monsters: Who Are They and Why Do We Need Them?

The word "monster" comes from the Latin *monstruum* and means that which exceeds what is natural, something rare, and unique. It can also make reference to something excessively wondrous. As a verb, *monstro* means to show, to reveal, to advise, and to warn. These definitions already show a kind of dualism between good and evil, as if excess drives things into darkness, the unknown, and therefore, to being dangerous.

Heinz Mode suggested that monsters were "a new shape resulting from a combination usually in visual form but sometimes only in words of characteristic components or properties of different kinds of living things or natural objects" (1973, 7). Ruth Waterhouse describes monsters as "large in size, inherently evil, deformed, grotesque" (1996, 28–29), and Joseph Andriano straightforwardly states that they are "dangerous objects of fear (and the fear of being eaten)" (1999, 91). Nevertheless, these imaginary embodiments of terror, that it might be thought we would want to avoid, have been common elements in all fairy and folk tale traditions. Unsurprisingly, a rich seam of psychological and cultural studies has developed around the phenomenon, and it shows no signs of slowing down (Bettelheim 1976; Beaudet 1990; Carroll 1990; Warner 1998; Lauro 2015; Weinstock 2020), underlining the abundant "variety and primal power of the imaginary evil creature as a cultural metaphor and literary device in folklore, fiction, art, dreaming, and everyday fantasy" (Gilmore 2003, 1).

Such creatures are not confined to a single tradition. They constitute strongly visual metaphors in all cultures when discussing human qualities that must be confronted, repudiated, externalized, and, as tends to happen, defeated, the most important of which appear to be aggression and sexual sadism. They also serve as vehicles for the expiation of guilt, from the perspective that there is a strong sense in which monsters incarnate an urge for self-punishment connected with negative desires that we feel we should not have. This externalization and internalization of monsters contributes to their emotive ambivalence and power.

From a practical point of view, tales and narrations, in general, tend to require a structure, a plot, and a set of characters. Vladimir Propp in his *Morphology of the Folktale* (1927) analyzed Russian folk tales to identify their basic structural elements in order to categorize them as irreducible units that would always evidence the same sequence, whether all of them were present or not. His work led to several conclusions, among which was the key observation that narratives needed an antihero. Antiheroes can adopt several shapes, such as ogres, trolls, orcs, cyclops, and giants, all of which can be classified as monsters or characters who combine human and supposedly degenerated traits. These misfits represent the opposite of the hero in the dualism that characterizes tales. Yet, without antiheroes and monsters, heroes would not face their specific challenges and would not be able to achieve their personal development and growth. This means that without monsters playing evil roles, there is no need for a hero's action and forcefulness and, therefore, no adventure or quest. As Propp explains, the role that is termed the "villain" can fulfill several functions in the plot such as to interrogate their victims, to get information out of them, to fool their victims to obtain the victim's goods or properties, to make one of the victim's relatives suffer, and eventually to fight the hero (Propp 1968, 32–34.). The villain has to initiate the disruption that will lead the hero to fight evil and its embodied cause. Needless to say, the role of the villain is frequently allotted not simply to bad human beings but to figures that may be classified as monsters.

Beyond the role of monsters in the narrative structuring of classic fairy tales, a psychoanalytical reading claims that the role of monsters in fairy tales fulfills a major role in subliminally instructing children to pay attention to their unconscious. The monster can represent the fear but also how the child feels and most importantly their emotions about aspects of the surrounding environment. Seemingly paradoxically, through some form of identification with monsters, children find hope and the strength to meet the adversities of life. That is one of the reasons why childhood is considered the time when fantasy needs to be nurtured (Bettelheim 1976, 120–121).

Monsters, Violence, and Animation

Children typically spend several to many hours a week exposed to screens. Material directed at children is even more provided with unreal, fantastic, and imaginary scenes compared to material directed at adults. While adults can generally distinguish between fantasy and realism, and to a less certain degree between fiction and nonfiction, these are learned abilities. The ability of children to separate the real or possible world from that of the imagination takes place largely after the age of seven. As a consequence, it can be quite challenging for very young children to differentiate what should be copied or imitated from what they see on television, about which most research has been done (see Bonus and Mares 2019), and similar challenges exist on tablet screens, streaming platforms, and related media access points.

Despite this difficulty and the fact that children develop unevenly in this sphere, depending on family and cultural contexts, young audiences do have opinions about the reality of what they see. Celeste Lacroix recalls an experience in which a toddler excitedly anticipated watching *The Lion King* on account of having already developed a relation with characters via prior contact with merchandizing and previews (2004, 213–214). The fact that the characters were animated talking animals, which he had never seen in daily life, did not dilute the toddler's predictions of pleasure.

Children's animated films include certain amounts of supervised violence to maintain the dualism commonly found in plots. While "[e]xposure to violence in any media is an established risk factor for aggression in children and adolescents" it is "only one of many" (Furlow 2017, 91). Researcher into media violence effects Ron Bushman has long warned against conflating violence and aggression in the analysis of media effects. While viewing violent media does not turn everyone into a mass murderer, there are links between such viewing and everyday aggression. Thus, "children who observe (in the media or in the environment around them) others exhibiting a specific aggressive behavior, eg, hitting, are more likely to perform the same aggressive behavior immediately." One consequence of this is that "the more similar that children think they and the observed model are, the more readily imitation will take place, but the imitation mechanism is so powerful that even fantasy characters are imitated by young children" (Bushman and Huesmann 2006, 349). Here, it can be seen that a connection exists between children's limitations in separating what is real from fiction and the influence that the media can have over particularly young viewers.

If violence and aggression are related to character representation, this could be where monsters are identified with everyday aggression. This assumption has, however, been contested by Türkmen, who studied 23 contemporary animated box-office hits to reveal that monster-form creatures only perform 7.1% of the violent acts seen in these films (2016, 23–24). In his count, 88 cases of violence were carried out by monsters out of 1,245 violent acts. Monsters are clearly not the most violent and aggressive creatures in contemporary animation, which may partly be explained by the rise of cute monsters.

Cute Monsters, Cute Violence

"Cute" is defined in the *Britannica Dictionary Online* (n.d.) as an adjective meaning "having a pleasing and usually youthful appearance." However, if one goes on to read the rest of the entries, the positive meaning of this word changes to something appertaining to informal American usage, where the corpus under discussion and analysis was originally created, so that meanings appear such as "attractive in a sexual way," "trying too hard to be pleasant or likable," or "clever in a way that annoys people." Where does a cute monster fit into such a range of meanings?

For some, cuteness involves a certain malformation and an exaggeration of features commonly present in young children's drawings of people. That would explain why certain supposedly cute toys have huge heads and eyes. But cuteness is adjacent to monstrosity if carefully considered. Monsters, as has been mentioned, are characterized through specific traits such as being large, ugly, aggressive, and immoral creatures. Cute monsters, on the other hand, are pretty, endearing, and, most importantly, re-read through the notion of strangeness as "Other." In terms of an initial binary opposition, the classic monster is a portent of danger, whereas the cute monster appears to be nonthreatening. Things may not be so simple though, as cuteness may also operate as an efficient mask for danger, and fairy tales are well supplied with apparently sweet and nonthreatening characters who are later revealed to be the principal source of violence in the tale.

Despite this caveat, openly cute monsters have become much more prevalent in children's literature and media than monsters derived from the frightening models of the past. These new, cute, and at times ethically ambivalent creatures may help the child understand what it means to be a child in an accelerating and strange world full of contradictions and transgression. And transgression is a key word here because a connection may be established between trespassing boundaries and postmodernism in general. Postmodern culture both traffics in and explores the nature of transgression and ambivalence, through such iterations as the Other, the uncanny, and the unthinkable. In order to deal with a reality composed of such things, there is a need to valorize the paradoxical. Maja Brzozowska-Brywczyńska explains this ambivalence and how cuteness can transform into something unpleasant and violent:

> The fascinating metamorphosis of cute into anti-cute reflects the above-mentioned circularity of the cute concept–for when cute acquires wicked features it in fact goes to the excess of cuteness, exploiting and parodying the sweetness to its very limits, poisoning itself while retaining the artificially loveable texture. Cute becomes grotesque. (Brzozowska-Brywczyńska 2007, 219–220)

Brzozowska-Brywczyńska also describes the culture of *alien-nation* very much in fashion in current Western popular culture. This emerges as "a result of fascination with strangeness, freakiness, otherness and ambivalence. It is a site of combining together this, what seems to be mutually exclusive, of 'familiarising' this, what cannot be neither understood nor accepted within the existing socio-cultural frames" (Brzozowska-Brywczyńska 2007, 223). An optimistic way of reading this interest in contemporary culture could be that it reveals a greater openness to difference in general, to outsiders of all sorts, but this depends very much on the outsiders in question. As Brzozowska-Brywczyńska translates fellow Polish academic, Marek Krajewski: "Alien-nation culture is as much a political culture of general tolerance and love, as a decadent popular culture, that exploits the motif of the Other and simultaneously reduces it to the aesthetical dimension" (Brzozowska-Brywczyńska 2007, 224).

Reducing otherness to the surface, to its aesthetic dimension, does violence to those others when they, including monsters and cute monsters, become just images, representations to be devoured through the eyes of the consumer, whether child or adult. If the status of otherness is to serve

Table 10.1 Box office of selected animation movies with cute monsters

Title	Box office (Box-Office Mojo)	Year
Shrek	$488.3 M	2001
Shrek 2	$928.7 M	2004
Shrek the Third	$813.3 M	2007
Shrek Forever After	$752.6 M	2010
Monsters Inc.	$579.7 M	2001
Monsters vs Aliens	$381.5 M	2009
Onward	$141.9 M	2020

as an entertaining mixture of fascination and repulsion, and even a kind of seduction detached from the other's cultural or psychological origins, does this help young audiences to understand their inner feelings and thoughts while immersed in the type of affective relationships evidenced by Celeste Lacroix's toddler about to watch *The Lion King*? Has the avalanche of cute monsters made rereading ourselves and our cultural scripts more of a challenge?

Corpus

Seven animated films released in the twenty-first century have been chosen for examination, based on their having monsters in lead roles, as the main characters or the main antagonists: The *Shrek* saga, *Monsters Inc.*, *Monsters vs Aliens*, and *Onward*. Box-office results have also been considered, in the sense that each of them had to be a box-office hit in order to become part of the study. The reasoning behind this is connected with the fact that these productions have reached millions of spectators of all ages, including children who may be identifying themselves or developing affective relationships with characters portrayed in these films. Quite what roles these characters play will be analyzed later, but first the following chart shows the title of each production, its box-office result, and the year when each film was released (Table 10.1):

Dissecting the *Shrek* Saga

Once upon a time, there was a happy green ogre who lived in a swamp and enjoyed frightening the people from the nearby village. His fondness for dirt and mud is shown in his doubtful personal hygiene and his loneliness is synonymous with his happiness. Shrek's daily routine (wash his teeth with green slime, have a bath in mud) is part of the first images of *Shrek* (2001), something which sets off the giggles of child spectators. This parody, making fun of the monster's traits and habits, transforms Shrek into a friendly monster who we want to save Fiona, a princess under a curse. Fiona's physical appearance complies with the beauty standards required of young women, but she reveals monstrous aspects: at night she turns into a female ogre, which explains her role in the film. This provides one more example of how image can be deceiving; beauty can disguise less than beautiful traits and behavior, as fairy tales have always taught. In Fiona's case, she privileges beauty as what is valuable about her, and puts on snooty airs and graces that she believes are aristocratic. The principal monstrous character in the story, however, is not visually a conventional monster, but Lord Farquaad, a very short man who refuses to accept his physique and who believes that marrying the right princess will grant him prestige, power, and the admiration of the kingdom's inhabitants. When things do not work out, he rejects Fiona on account of her being a visual ogre underneath her attractive appearance and plots to kill Shrek. Here, the monsters actually play the positive and benign roles, whereas the principal human does not hesitate to make monstrous decisions.

Shrek 2 is a continuation of the first film of the saga, but now love between ogres is no longer problematic, although meeting the parents-in-law leads to several amusing misunderstandings. The ogre couple have been somehow accepted in the land of Far, Far, Away, except by Shrek's father-in-law, Harold, who believes that green ugliness cannot work in his perfect parodic Hollywood. That bad intentions are not perceived because of external beauty remains a theme in the film, as shown in Harold's hunting invitation aimed at getting rid of Shrek, the Fairy-Godmother's potion industry, and Prince Charming's dark ambition. In line with fairy tale narrative developments, Shrek steals a magic potion to become a handsome Prince, and this upsets Fiona who has learned to be suspicious of external appearance. Harold needs time to understand that her daughter's mind is set on Shrek, and once this is clear to him, he is willing to sacrifice his human looks and become the King Frog (another of the saga's many intertextual references to fairy tales).

Shrek the Third discusses parenthood and indirectly proposes diverse families by introducing the audience to hybrid children (half donkey, half dragon). Here, cuteness is a key element in the representation of both Donkey's as well as Shrek's babies. As discussed earlier, these baby monsters are drawn for animation with big cute eyes, dimples, and human baby features to guarantee their acceptance. Donkey's offspring are depicted in round shapes, as chubby and small baby animals. While next in the line for the throne, Shrek opposes abandoning his ogre manners, which disappoints Fiona and other members of the court. Consequently, Shrek begins a quest to place teenage Arthur on the throne, and then get his consent to Shrek's raising his three baby ogres back in his beloved swamp.

The Shrek saga ends with *Shrek Forever After*, DreamWorks' attempt to canonize its most profitable character as a settled part of children's literature and fairy tales. The plot of this fourth film deals with a tired, nostalgic ogre who wants to recover his previous monster status, before marriage and children. Socially and psychologically, this ogre is a representation of the Western middle-class father who misses his carefree bachelor years. Another monster in this film, the antagonist, but with cute human traits, is Rumpelstiltskin (Rumple). He manages to tempt Shrek by promising him a chance to be once again the horrendous ogre monster who antagonized and scared villagers for a day. Needless to say, the deal works well for Shrek at first, but as the day goes by, he starts to appreciate and miss his family life, but he is now in a parallel world, the result of the decision he had made. As a consequence, he has never met Fiona, who finds her way out of the tower guarded by Dragon and gathers an army of ogres to fight the witches and Rumple. But as fairy tales dictate, all damage must be repaired and a happy ending is a must. Shrek, the ogre, and Rumple, a human monster, confront one another. Shrek wins the fight, and as a reward, he gets his family back.

Over the three films, there is an ongoing discussion about the interface between visual appearance and ethical qualities—one which attempts to confirm the conventional valorization of good actions and healthy morality over external beauty. Throughout the narrative, the supposed monsters are never frightening, not even visually, while the figures who generate the most diegetic fear are humans whose monstrousness is not visual but arises out of their attitudes and subsequent actions in the service of their hunger for power and status.

Monsters on Duty: *Monsters, Inc.*

Pixar's 2001 film humanizes monsters in a universe filled with all sorts of creatures who are deeply afraid of supposedly toxic human children. A complete monster industry is developed based on children's screeches.

Through doors that become portals to children's closets, scarers can harvest children's screams turned into energy. Yet, energy production is scarce in the world of monsters, because children are not as scared as they used to be. James P. "Sulley" Sullivan is one of the best scarers of the company but accidently allows a human girl to sneak into Monstropolis. Things go from bad to worse when the girl is spotted by other monsters, causing chaos in a restaurant. With no other choice left, Sulley hides the girl, Boo, at his place and discovers that her laughter can generate much more energy than screams.

Most of the monsters represented in this film could be and have been transformed into stuffed animals, popular merchandizing among the young audience. Soft colors have been chosen to draw the main characters, and they have been given round shapes, while their big eyes resemble four-year-old school drawings before a full body schema can be completed, as learned by age six. These forms of "Cuteness" are ever-present in most of the creatures created by Pixar across the company's output. In daily life and away from Monstropolis, when children tend to imagine monsters in the dark, under their beds, and in closets, their imagination produces images, albeit often indistinct, that are frightening. Pixar, aware of this fact, is able to turn the tables and create a plot where those who are to be feared are usually the ones who are afraid. Apart from the fun generated by reversing narrative expectations, a pedagogical intention also seems apparent when the visuality of monsters is so severely subverted: to dilute the presence of fear in children's lives.

Monsters vs Aliens

DreamWorks combines horror fiction creatures in this homage to mid-century Hollywood science fiction. This popular genre has been intertextually rebooted through animation to create a recognition effect for the adult spectators who frequently accompany children to the cinema or watch alongside their children at home. In one example of this phenomenon, animated characters can be related to traditional popular culture monsters from previous decades. Susan, who is transformed by a meteorite into a gigantic woman, is a tribute to the film *Attack of the 50 Foot Woman* (Nathan Juran 1958); *Missing Link* reminds the experienced viewer of *The Creature from the Black Lagoon* (Jack Arnold 1954); Bob is the animated friendly remake of *The Blob* (Ivan Yeaworth 1958); Professor Cockroach is a wink to *The Fly* (David Cronenburg 1986). Finally, Insectosaurus used to be a one-inch insect, which was transformed by radiation into a 350-foot monster who attacked Tokyo before being recruited, a clear allusion to Godzilla.

These five monsters must face another traditional terrifying creature, Gallaxhar, who is determined to extract the Quantonium that Susan was exposed to through the meteorite that had recently landed on planet Earth. Physically, Gallaxhar is a squid-like alien life-form and the traitorous leader of the Earth-invading force. As expected, this squid-shaped monster was not an accidental decision made by animators, quite the opposite; Gallaxhar is a tribute to Akkorokamui, a Japanese Evil-God creature who is the lord of Uchiura Bay, according to Ainu folklore. This list of monsters is complemented by General W. R. Monger, a human who needs a flying artifact to be able to lead the monster operation against Gallaxhar. He cannot be considered a full monster, but the recruiter of the Monster Department. As a general, he yells and gives orders but also shows sympathy for the creatures he directs.

Onward

One of Pixar's most recent releases, *Onward* (Dan Scanlon 2020), could be classified as a subverted fairy tale road trip shared by two brothers who have an opportunity to meet their absent father. Barley, the eldest, is an adventurous and impulsive character who, as opposed to Ian, still remembers his late father. Ian is an insecure and shy teenager who receives a gift on his sixteenth birthday from his absent father. His personality may owe much to his father's absence and will be developed as the plot evolves. Laurel, mother of both teenagers, gives Ian a magical staff, a rare phoenix gem, and a letter. These magical items will grant Ian the chance to spend a day with his absent father as long as he is able to correctly cast the spell.

Barley and Ian live in a postmodern fantasy land or fairy tale. They are elves who every night hear naughty unicorns looking for food in the neighborhood's trash cans; magical creatures behaving like raccoons. This bathetic approach to fantasy also has its impact on role characterization. For example, Specter is a female LGBTQI+ cyclops cop who serves in the city of New Mushroomton. Her name is a portmanteau of "spectre," which added to the word "inspector" sets up a play on words. Being a monster, she is purple-colored, big-eyed with a big nose, and what the audience might consider a unicorn-like horn. As a side note, she fulfills a secondary role in the film, acting as a cop in a chase scene, but due to the line "My girlfriend's daughter got me pulling my hair out," *Onward* was banned in Saudi Arabia, Kuwait, Oman, and Qatar. On the other hand, the film was released in Egypt, Lebanon, and the United Arab Emirates after censoring the dubbing of the line, which turned into "my sister's daughter." Pixar also chose an LGBTQI+ actor to give a voice to Specter, Lena Waithe, who is openly lesbian in daily life. In fact, she was the one who improvised the controversial line.

Corey the Manticore is a monster who owns a restaurant and helps Barley and Ian begin their quest. She is a female adaptation of the myth, which explains why she resembles a lion with horns but has bat wings and the tail of a scorpion. Still, her claw nails are painted pink and she wears red high-heeled shoes, supposedly female habits. Centuries ago, this character was known for her adventurous spirit by intrepid explorers, warriors, and wizards. In her tavern, she led adventurers to begin their dangerous quests. But when magic was replaced by technological conveniences in this postmodern world, the Manticore became just Corey, and her tavern became the starting point of every adventure—a medieval-themed family restaurant. Facing business and financial troubles, she even pawned her sword, the Curse Crusher, an item that Barley and Ian later need to survive the terrifying dragon pebble sculpture.

Conclusion

Of all the cast of monsters presented in this chapter, many of them have human names, such as Fiona, Mike, Sulley, Susan, Bob, and Corey—a detail which in itself reveals a change in the way monsters are being introduced into animation. There is an intentional desire to break the barriers between the horrifying creature and the child. Monsters used to be nameless, but in the industry nowadays, these monsters not only have human traits, but human names too, converting them into less scary protagonists. Such creatures do not represent paradoxically liminal beings any more, that which lurks menacingly beyond the borders, a destabilization of the tidiness of everyday categories and life.

Physical and psychological human traits also further construct the representation of the monsters described in the series of movies discussed. As monsters, they should all be deformed, grotesque, and displaying degenerate traits, which is not the case in this corpus. Instead of being dark-colored, or unpleasantly colored, the monsters combine a soft color palette with primary colors, easily recognized as friendly by children. Even Shrek's supposed swamp green is more contiguous with the colors of healthy plants than those of slimy creatures inspiring disgust. The combination of these soft, chubby, furry, and nonthreatening visual characteristics render these protagonists cute, to be sure, but it is not the excessive cuteness or parody of sweetness that is often associated with Japanese popular culture. Neither are the putative monsters violent or aggressive. On the contrary, in some of these films, humans are those who attack monsters in the first place, inverting Propp's categories to the extent that humans are the evil beings who trigger the monsters' personal quests.

As a result of these options, now the norm in animation for children, the role that monsters have traditionally played for young children has been lost sight of. As examined here, monsters that evince extreme evil or who are frighteningly grotesque are now largely taboo, despite their usefulness in both confronting and stimulating conversation with adults around aspects of existence that children need to negotiate. This kind of protective monster banning overlooks children's need to transform troubling feelings into valuable lessons for life. The child is shown a creature who is not frightening and who cannot be identified with any of children's common fears or doubts, including their own inner monstrosity and the need to discipline it. It may be time for parents, educators, and society, in general, to "beware the cute" as Brzozowska-Brywczyńska has pinpointed (2007, 225), although it seems unlikely that commercial media companies will retreat from what has proven and continues to be a highly successful format.

REFERENCES

Adamson, Andrew, and Vicky Jenson (Directors). 2001. *Shrek*. [Animated Feature Film]. DreamWorks SKG.

Adamson Andrew, Kelly Asbury, and Conrad Vernon (Directors). 2004. *Shrek 2*. [Animated Feature Film]. Dream Works Home Entertainment and Pacific Data Images.

Andriano, Joseph D. 1999. *Immortal Monster: The Mythological Evolution of the Fantastic Beast in Modern Fiction and Film*. Westport, CT.: Greenwood Press.

Arnold, Jack (Director). 1954. *Creature from the Black Lagoon, The*. [Film]. Universal-International.

ASIFA [International Animated Film Association]. n.d. *Animation*. https://asifa.net/who-we-are/statutes/. Accessed 27 May 2023.

Barthes, Roland. 1957. *Mythologies*. Paris: Editions du Sueil.

Beaudet, Denyse. 1990. *Encountering the Monster: Pathways in Children's Dreams.* New York: Continuum.
Berger, John. 1972. *Ways of Seeing.* Harmondsworth: Penguin.
Bettelheim, Bruno. 1976. *The Uses of Enchantment: The Meaning and Importance of Fairy Tales.* Harmondsworth: Penguin.
Bonus, James Alex, and Marie-Louise Mares. 2019. Learned and Remembered But Rejected: Preschoolers Reality Judgments and Transfer from *Sesame Street. Communication Research* 46 (3): 375–400.
Brzozowska-Brywczyńska, Maja. 2007. Monstrous/Cute. Notes on the Ambivalent Nature of Cuteness. In *Monsters and the Monstrous. Myths and Metaphors of Enduring Evil,* ed. Niall Scott, 213–228. Amsterdam and New York: Rodopi.
Bushman, Ron, and Rowell Huesmann. 2006. Short-term and Long-term Effects of Violent Media on Aggression in Children and Adults. *Archives of Pediatrics & Adolescent Medicine* 160: 348–352.
Campbell, Neil, and Alisdair Kean. 2016. *American Cultural Studies. An Introduction to American Culture.* 4th ed. London and New York: Routledge.
Carroll, Noël. 1990. *The Philosophy of Horror, or Paradoxes of the Heart.* New York: Routledge.
Cohen, Jeffrey Jerome. 1996. Monster Culture (Seven Theses). In *Monster Theory: Reading Culture,* ed. Jeffrey Jerome Cohen, 3–25. Minneapolis: University of Minnesota Press.
Cronenberg, David (Director). 1986. *Fly, The* [Film]. Brooksfilms and SLM Production Group.
"Cute". n.d. *The Britannica Dictionary.* https://www.britannica.com/dictionary/cute. Accessed 27 May 2023.
Dean, John. 1992. *American Popular Culture. La culture populaire americaine.* Nancy: Presses Universitaires de Nancy.
Docter, Pete (Director). 2001. *Monsters Inc.* [Animated Feature Film].. Walt Disney Pictures and Pixar Animation Studios.
Egan, Kieran. 1997. *The Educated Mind: How Cognitive Tools Shape our Understanding.* Chicago: University of Chicago Press.
Evans, Janet, ed. 2015. *Challenging and Controversial Picture Books: Creative and Critical Responses to Visual Texts.* London: Routledge.
Furlow, Bryant. 2017. Media Violence and Youth Aggression. *The Lancet: Child & Adolescent Health* 1 (2): 91–92.
Gilmore, David D. 2003. *Monsters. Evil Beings, Mythical Beasts, and All Manner of Imaginary Terrors.* Philadelphia: University of Pennsylvania Press.
Hand, David (Supervising Director). 1937. *Snow White and the Seven Dwarfs* [Animated Feature Film]. Walt Disney Productions.
Hawkey, Kate. 2007. Theorizing Content: Tools from Cultural History. *Journal of Curriculum Studies* 39 (1): 63–76.

Juran, Nathan (Director). 1958. *Attack of the 50 Foot Woman* [Film]. Woolner Bros. Pictures.
Kohl, Herbert. 1995. *Should We Burn Babar? Essays on Children's Literature and the Power of Stories*. New York: New Press.
Lacroix, Celeste. 2004. Images of Animated Others: The Orientalization of Disney's Cartoon Heroines from *The Little Mermaid* to *The Hunchback of Notre Dame*. *Popular Communication* 2 (4): 213–229.
Lauro, Sarah Juliet. 2015. *The Transatlantic Zombie: Slavery, Rebellion, and Living Death*. New Brunswick, NJ: Rutgers University Press.
Letterman, Rob and Conrad Vernon (Directors). 2009. *Monsters vs. Aliens*. [Animated Feature Film]. DreamWorks SKG.
Miller, Chris (Director) 2007. *Shrek the Third* [Animated Feature Film]. DreamWorks Animation and Pacific Data Images.
Mitchell, Mike (Director). 2010. *Shrek Forever After* [Animated Feature Film]. DreamWorks SKG.
Mode, Heinz Adolf. 1973. *Fabulous Beasts and Demons*. New York: Phaidon.
Oittinen, Riitta. 2000. *Translating for Children*. New York: Garland Publishing.
Propp, Vladimir. 1968 [1927]. *Morphology of the Folktale*. Trans. L. Scott and L.A. Wagner. Austin, TX: University of Texas Press.
Rosenberg, Emily. 1982. *Spreading the American Dream*. New York: Hill & Wang.
Scanlon, Dan (Director). 2020. *Onward* [Animated Feature Film]. Walt Disney Pictures and Pixar Animation Studios.
Tatar, Maria, ed. 2002. *The Annotated Classic Fairy Tales*. New York: Norton.
Türkmen, Mustafa. 2016. Violence in Animated Feature Films: Implications for Children. *Educational Process: International Journal* 5 (1): 22–37.
Warner, Marina. 1998. *No Go the Bogeyman: Scaring, Lulling, and Making Mock*. New York: Farrar, Straus and Giroux.
Waterhouse, Ruth. 1996. Beowulf as Palimpsest. In *Monster Theory*, ed. J.J. Cohen, 26–39. Minneapolis: University of Minnesota Press.
Weinstock, Jeffrey Andrew, ed. 2020. *The Monster Theory Reader*. Minneapolis: Minnesota University Press.
Yeaworth, Irvin (Director). 1958. *Blob, The*. [Film]. Fairview Productions, Tonylyn Productions and Valley Forge Films.
Zipes, Jack. 2005. *Happily Ever After. Fairy Tales, Children, and the Culture Industry*. New York and London: Routledge.

CHAPTER 11

The Graphic Self of Public Intellectuals: Chinese *Tiaoman* as Digital Practices of Self-Representation on WeChat

Chen Li

INTRODUCTION

With the increasing ubiquity of digital mobile devices, the medium for comics is no longer confined to print media but has expanded to digital screens. Scrolling comics on digital screens has accordingly become the main reading experience of mobile comics. Such a global tendency can be exemplified by the burgeoning industry of Webtoons in Korea, Japan, Indonesia and Malaysia (see Jang and Song 2017; Yecies et al. 2019). In China, the year 2019 marked the high point of digital comics' content on Chinese social media. The Chinese term for the vertical scrolling comic, *tiaoman* (条漫), has drawn increasing scholarly interest and has also been

C. Li (✉)
Tilburg University, Tilburg, Netherlands
e-mail: c.li_2@tilburguniversity.edu

highly evaluated by the platform industry and the digital content market since 2019.[1]

The most prominent features of tiaoman are their efficiency and accessibility. Compared to print comics, tiaoman creates a reading experience of scrolling and sweeping that is much more efficient and convenient than flipping pages. The hyperlinks and multimodality of tiaoman create a level of accessibility that makes it possible for readers to reach diverse digital content with the least effort. Such features encourage the habit of reading tiaoman in the age of fragmented reading. In addition, in the process of constructing a persona, Chinese tiaoman has a similar function to the digital avatar, which is to build idealized self-representation for public figures (Zimmermann et al. 2023).

One significant nuance of Chinese tiaoman, compared to Japanese and Korean ones, is the development of plural publics instead of simply fan-centred publics. In recent years, more and more tiaoman works on social media platforms have paid attention to such things as public concerns and public deliberation, medical and health, gender issues and investigative news. Particularly during the pandemic, many accounts on the WeChat Public Platform posted tiaoman works to express opinions or emotional responses in public discussions (Rui 2020). For instance, the realist work posted by the *People's Daily* on WeChat during the pandemic attracted huge attention and discussion (see Fig. 11.1). This tiaoman work not only records the historical moment when the pandemic began, but it more

Fig. 11.1 The map of China's fight against the pandemic (中国抗疫图鉴). Image resource: *People's Daily*, April 15, 2020. https://mp.weixin.qq.com/s/mrljz1K7-mWQvfy9ZpehVA

---

[1] Many blogs on Chinese cyber space were discussing the popularization of tiaoman in 2019; for instance: https://zhuanlan.zhihu.com/p/99420941

significantly depicts a collective memory of how the pandemic changed Chinese people's lives. This tiaoman invites a strong emotional response among the audience. Apart from this significant historical moment, research on Chinese public spaces needs to take notice of the fact that tiaoman have now become a prominent genre in digital public spheres. They are able to document historical moments, to represent the lived experience of individuals and groups and to mobilize social actions, all via mobile devices.

The public-concern–centred content of tiaoman reveals the pluralization of Chinese public discourses. The creators and artists involved are correspondingly becoming more and more diverse. In recent years, tiaoman have become a communicative genre of self-representation and autobiographic narrative for public intellectuals in Chinese digital public spaces. For instance, in a tiaoman memorializing Allen Ginsberg, the narrator self-presents both himself and Ginsberg in the strip. Such a tendency reveals an important shift in the realm of communicative practice in digital spaces: comics as a genre reaches beyond comics fans, expanding to civic expression. Such pluralization has the potential to destabilize the easy perception of serious versus non-serious content, a feature of the wider comics world in general. Jan Blommaert reminds us that genres are hierarchical, which means certain genres are more prioritized than others in specific socio-cultural contexts (Blommaert 2008). With respect to Chinese tiaoman, it is noticeable that the scrolling comics of non-fictional content are a major genre for public participation, while fictional genres such as romance and fantasy are mostly engaged with by fans and ACGN (Animation, Comics, Games, Short Novels) communities. Such a feature of today's Chinese digital spaces deserves closer examination.

Scott McCloud defines comics as juxtaposed pictorial and other images in deliberate sequence, intended to convey information or to produce an aesthetic response in the viewer. The important element in such a definition is the communicative effects of comics. As mentioned earlier, today's Chinese digital public space features a popular genre of scrolling comics—one that has moved beyond light entertainment to the realm of intellectual expression. Relating this to McCloud's definition, we might wonder what information Chinese intellectuals attempt to articulate via comics, what aesthetic responses they create, and further, how they achieve such communicative effects. By answering these questions, we can obtain insights on the relationship among comics, intellectuals and publics in today's China.

Theoretical Outline

Practitioners and critics of comics have observed that the practice of composing autobiography implies doubling the self (Watson 2008). Such a practice of splitting the self into observer and observed is amplified in autographics, where different media of words and images offer multiple possibilities for interpreting experience and staging self-reflection. Among other possibilities, the self-reflexive practice of using cartoon drawings of the self is considered a new possibility for forging identities.

Scott McCloud is one who analyses the effects of cartoon images in relation to self-projection. In his acclaimed analysis, he explains that cartoon images of faces can invoke the responses of both self-awareness and "universal identification" (McCloud 1994, 28–36). He observes that although such images can be very distant from realistic images, we have no trouble relating to the simplified one, and sometimes it is even more acceptable than the realistic one. He gives the amusing example of how easily we can relate to a simplified version of his own face compared to one in which he had tried to capture his face in much more detail. In other words, our cultures have learnt to relate to the simplified reality of cartoons without needing to make a special effort. McCloud frames his analysis of cartoons by considering them a form of "amplification through simplification." That is, "when we abstract an image through cartooning, we are not so much eliminating details as we are focusing on specific details. By stripping down an image to its essential 'meaning,' an artist can amplify that meaning in a way that realistic art can't" (McCloud 1994, 30). In McCloud's explanation, *The Wizard of Oz* is a cinematic example of the stripping down of realistic images. He points out that simplifying characters and images towards a purpose can be an effective tool for storytelling in any medium. In his insight, cartooning is a way of visualizing things and not simply a type of failed mimesis. By highlighting the effects of simplification of cartoons, McCloud points to their ability and power to focus readers' attention. The second effect, in his view, is that the universality of cartoon imagery allows and encourages diverse understandings of a cartoon face. In his words, "the more cartoony a face is, for instance, the more people it could be said to describe" (McCloud 1994, 31). This generalizing effect aids in the process of self-identification, which is the third effect, self-projection onto cartoon faces. By making fun of himself, McCloud makes a strong point that "the cartoon is a vacuum into which our identity and awareness are pulled, an empty shell that we inhabit which enables us to travel in another realm. We don't just observe the cartoon, we become it!" (McCloud 1994, 36; Watson 2008, 29). As he points out, this does not happen when the face is recognizably someone else's face or a face that does not look anything like us. Ironically, a stylized, simplified face looks even less like us than a realistically drawn one, but its simplification makes it more generalizable, and hence easier to identify or empathize with. (McCloud 1994, 30–36).

Previous research mostly focuses on scrolling comics' communicative content and strategy. Little attention is paid to the narrator, or the avatar, presented in them. Considering participation in public debates and interpreting knowledge as intellectual practice, it can be seen that creating autographic selves has become a popular means for current intellectuals to present themselves in digital public spaces. The realm of persona studies examines the strategies of self-presentation of public individuals, including how self-presentation functions in negotiating the position of public intellectuals within institutions and the broader culture (Marshall et al. 2015). One common starting point now in researching new persona is unsurprisingly to look at the production of the presentation of the self in online environments, as in Inge Van de Ven and Ties van Gemert's work on the importance of the public performance of self-representations and media communication in the situating of public intellectuals. In recent years, several theorists have underlined this importance of performativity in analysing the impact of public intellectuals (see, e.g., Heynders 2016; Baert and Morgan 2018). It has also been pointed out that public intellectuals are relatively easily able to manage their persona by positioning themselves in line with or against certain groups or ideas (Baert and Morgan 2018). Moreover, with the development of social media, public intellectuals have become acutely aware of the constraints and possibilities brought by digital technology. If we understand the persona as indicating a way to manage the self in the social, an observation that long predates digital environments (Goffman 1956), it is important to consider the impact of digitalization on persona construction and the social environments where publics can generate responses. Resonating with McCloud's point about cartoon faces, we can explore whether the cartoonist persona of intellectuals could provide a less realistic but more universal location for public expression.

Considering tiaoman and the autographic self in cyberspace as digital practice, Rodney Jones et al. remind us that such practices "associated with certain digital technologies are recognizable by specific groups of people as ways of attaining particular social goals, enacting particular social identities, and reproducing particular sets of social relationships" (2015, 3). This also requires us to employ a sociological perspective to address the effects and consequences of digital self-representation. Danah Boyd, founder and President of Data & Society (datasociety.net), reminds us that there has developed an increasing class divide between different social networking systems, which could partially be explained by differing class aesthetics (2007). Gillian Whitlock and Anna Poletti continue Boyd's analysis, leading research in the direction of exploring how the functionality of the software, in conjunction with the cultures of usage which develop amongst the communities of users, shapes the production of specific autographic performances (2008). According to Whitlock and Poletti's discussion of Boyd's analysis, we may conclude that autographics in social media is not only a genre concerned with self-presenting but also a digitally configured strategy of communication. This diagnosis may be exemplified and expanded with respect to Chinese tiaoman on digital mobiles. By looking at public intellectuals' autographics on digital platforms, we might map out the visual communication strategy and effects of tiaoman from a sociological perspective.

Methodology

For this research, I focus on a Chinese intellectual, Xu Zhiyuan, and his tiaoman series, *Uncle Lion Diary*, which consists of 38 episodes. This choice is due to having the opportunity to observe the series closely during the COVID-19 pandemic, when Xu started his tiaoman posts. Placing the series in the context of the pandemic gives a more contextualized and synchronic understanding of its development. I employ digital ethnography to approach Xu Zhiyuan's tiaoman content and his graphic self, Uncle Lion. I also consider Xu's public presentation, which includes interviews, public speeches and published articles. Such an approach enables me to observe not only the comic content but also the contextualized digital environments of Xu's self-representation. It helps me to see tiaoman content as the interplay of Xu's intellectual persona and the audiences' response.

With such a scheme, I collected the data through three phases. The first, also the major instrument throughout the whole process, is observation. First, I watched the six seasons of the documentary, *Thirteen Invitations*, in order to get familiar with its topics and discourses. While I was observing the documentary, I also observed the comments box of each episode in order to gain the audience's responses. During the second phase, I collected the tiaoman content of *Uncle Lion Diary* that is derived from *Thirteen Invitations*. During this phase, I focus on how the scrolling content is different or not compared to the documentary itself. Similar to the first stage, I also consider the interactional communication between readers and Uncle Lion. These first two stages of data collection give me details and the main narratives of Xu Zhiyuan's public persona. In the third stage of data collection, I focus on the meaning-making of Xu's autographic self. I collected articles and interviews where Xu developed self-reflexive explanations of his role as a public intellectual. Such data may serve as an autobiographical resource for understanding Xu's graphic self.

To analyse the data, I deploy digital discourse analysis to investigate the situated meaning constructed by Uncle Lion. Situated meanings (Gee 2015) are determined by what speakers/writers and listeners/readers take as relevant aspects of context. Situated meanings are also determined by shared cultural knowledge. Such knowledge has been studied under umbrella terms like "folk theories," "cultural models," "figured worlds," "schemes," "frames" and others (Gee 2015). As is known, discourse is related to the study of cultures and social groups that share knowledge and practices with each other. Analysing the situated meaning of Xu's production implies analysing his self-representation through multiple aspects, especially how the image is understood by his publics. This leads to the investigation of the effects and functions of the communication between Xu and his audience.

Xu Zhiyuan is a Chinese intellectual who was born in the 1970s. He has written for international newspapers and magazines, which include the *Economic Observer, Life, Bloomberg Business Work* (Chinese Version), *Oriental History Review* and *One Way Street* magazine. He is also a columnist for the *Financial Times*. In 2005, Xu founded the independent bookstore OWSPACE (abbreviation for One Way Space), which now has become a famous public space in the Chinese cultural arena. Since 2016, he has been hosting the interview documentary, *Thirteen Invitations*, which has aroused a widespread response and substantial influence. In this documentary series, Xu interviews public figures within and outside China, including celebrities, humanities scholars, scientific scholars, influential entrepreneurs, etc. The six seasons have been reproduced and published in the post-pandemic years on the WeChat platform as a series of tiaoman, called *Uncle Lion Diary* (2021–2022). In the tiaoman, Xu is self-presented as Uncle Lion.

Data Analysis

The image of Uncle Lion (see Fig. 11.2) is based on the interview series *Thirteen Invitations*. Once a new episode of documentary is released on the Tencent Video platform, the *Uncle Lion Diary* will update a corresponding post on WeChat, attaching a link to the interview. In this sense, I consider tiaoman provides a differently visual transmedia setting for Xu's self-representation. Henry Jenkins says that transmedia storytelling "represents a process where integral elements of a fiction get dispersed systematically across multiple delivery channels for the purpose of creating a unified and coordinated entertainment experience" (Jenkins 2010, 944). Melanie Schiller further reminds us of the constraints arising from particular media affordances, which means that the same story told by a comic book will necessarily be different from that told by a television series (Schiller 2018, 99). In this light, it can be seen how the transmedia strategy adopted by Xu Zhiyuan benefits his public self in a platform-afforded, efficient and simplified way. On the Tencent Video platform, every episode of the interview series lasts longer than one hour. But these relatively

Fig. 11.2 One example of Uncle Lion in Xu's *Uncle Lion Diary*. Image resource: https://www.sohu.com/a/489190668_611314

time-consuming contents for an attention economy of constant flow and fragmentation are extracted and simplified in the posts of the *Uncle Lion Diary*. This simplification provides an alternative channel to consume the interviews, with less time and effort. On the other hand, the creation of Uncle Lion by Xu can be seen as what I have called the transmedia self. It can visually compensate for the detail of the interview as its after-production and expand the dimension of Xu's public persona on social media platforms in the process. In my observation, this transmedia self enables Xu to present certain scenes and ideas that are not able to be showed in the programmes. For instance, some noticeable differences between Xu's interviews and the *Uncle Lion Diary* are revealed in the episode about Chinese Produce 101, a popular competitive reality show aiming to build China's first girl group (Nvtuan, 女团) through talent shows.

The year 2018 witnessed the high peak of the Chinese idol industry. Social media platforms have one source of their energy via digital traffic generated by idol-related content and fans' digital activities. Xu did not miss this trend. For Chinese public intellectuals, interviewing entertainment idols to understand idol culture is not commonly seen in the public space, not to mention interviewing them over a three-year time span. But Xu Zhiyuan and *Thirteen Invitations* made one episode to interview three outstanding popular idols in the year 2018 and 2021. The topics of Xu's interviews are centred on the meaningfulness of being an idol. What is noticeable is that the interviews and the post-produced *Uncle Lion Diary*, although both forms of narrativizing the exploration of a person's achievements and points of view, operate very differently. The main difference lies in a characteristic at the heart of visual spectating: the relationship of the gaze between Xu and the interviewed idols.

In Fig. 11.3, we can see that Uncle Lion Xu Zhiyuan is observing from behind the stage, listening to the monologues of idols who are in the spotlight at the front of the stage. But in the tiaoman version, Xu's presentation is different from that in the interview. When these female idols are expressing their feelings of "I own the world" and "I am glowing (shining) ... I change to a completely different person," Uncle Lion is standing behind the curtain in a somewhat voyeuristic position, instead of conversing with them face to face. However, in *Thirteen Invitations*, such scenes are absent. Instead, what we see in the latter is that Xu sits beside the girl group and converses with them face to face. During these conversations, Xu often shows self-reflective awareness of his ignorance and lack of knowledge of the burgeoning idol culture and industry. Here, he is not in

Fig. 11.3 Uncle Lion observing teen idols from behind a curtain. Image resource: https://mp.weixin.qq.com/s/-uY32x9O4K3VKgWE1ZxqYQ

control. In addition, in the beginning of the programme, Xu indicated that the three-year interview period also witnessed his own changes. As he said, "when I met them again, I found my condescending gaze upon them has disappeared after three years. Such a disappearance is like the end of a stage of my life." Several similar self-reflective moments frequently appeared in the programme, indicating the self-disclosure of Xu's duality of being both a criticizer and a learner. Later, I compare the scenes when a girl group member told Xu about their motivation and desire for being on stage. As we can see in Fig. 11.4, Xu presents himself as an interviewer with his typical, casual outfit, sitting on the floor with the girl group member.

As mentioned earlier, transmedia storytelling presents different affordances, depending on each medium's narrative and visual strategies. Regarding such seemingly fictional scenes in the tiaoman, I consider the transmedia self, Uncle Lion, as a media strategy for Xu to employ tiaoman on the social media platform in order to extend dialogues with audiences and to continue a narrative of self-positioning. Although in the documentary Xu is sitting with show idols in an equal relationship, the tiaoman Uncle Lion reveals a curious distance created by Xu with respect to the interviewees. Specifically, Uncle Lion's gestures and his altered focus create a distance between Xu and the female idols. The relation between the female idols to the distanced Uncle Lion provides a supplementary

Fig. 11.4 Xu Zhiyuan speaking with teen idols on an egalitarian physical level. Image resource: https://v.qq.com/x/cover/mzc00200ql6hmqx/r32634hv8q8.html

narrative presenting Xu's condescending position as an intellectual observing phenomena to which he does not belong. It illustrates a doubled self of Xu. In the interview, he shares a platform with the female idols, evincing self-reflective moments with respect to his elite position, while in the tiaoman he conveys sceptical and judgemental attitudes towards idol culture and the industry that surrounds it. Importantly, his altered gazes modulate both the male gaze and the power distance gaze, which can be milder and more acceptable in the face-to-face interview than in the enigmatically represented cartoon. That judgement of social phenomena is central to Xu's activity is clear; he is not trying or pretending to be objective. In *Thirteen Invitations* "prejudice" is a significant and frequent keyword for Xu Zhiyuan's self-representation. At the beginning and end of every episode, Xu always leaves a final remark: "everyone sees the world with prejudices. If you have no prejudices, then you have no way of looking at the world." This statement reveals the core of Xu's transmedia self and can be seen as a rejection of absolute relativism and an awareness that ideological flows are an integral part of human beings' relation to the world. In articulating how our status as judging beings works, Xu is able to split his approach to the same phenomena through his documentary approach to his interview series and his tiaoman persona. While in the tiaoman diary, Uncle Lion repeats a similar statement about the unavoidability of prejudice, this strong insistence on the prejudiced self is softened via the visual style and narration of the cute figure Uncle Lion. The reconstruction of the images of Uncle Lion as images occurring within the protocols of comics thus sets up or at least establishes the potential for a differentiated connection between Xu's self-representation and his publics.

Xu Zhiyuan and Lion: A Cute and Relatable Self

We can see in Fig. 11.2 that the image of Uncle Lion illustrates a comic, cartoon animal image of Xu Zhiyuan. In the tiaoman *Uncle Lion Diary*, Xu is depicted as an urban wanderer in an anthropomorphic form, a lion's face with a pair of human glasses, a male body wearing a white shirt and dark jeans, a pair of flip-flops and, sometimes, a rolled book squeezed into the back pocket of his jeans. Through such a design, a simplified image of Xu Zhiyuan is presented to the audience. This simplification eliminates the details of Xu Zhiyuan's facial expressions and blemishes, leaving an abstract yet softened lion's face. Figure 11.5 may serve as an example of this portrayal of Uncle Lion. With a slight flush on his cheeks, Xu Zhiyuan renders

Fig. 11.5 The cartoon cuteness of Uncle Lion. Image resource: https://www.sohu.com/a/489190668_611314

himself as a cute and benign public self to his readers. Such an image is avowedly more cartoonish than realistic, more cute than serious. When the image was first presented to audiences on WeChat, "it is cute" was one of the most frequent responses. Some comments regard the image as "warm (wennuan, 温暖)" and "amusing (youqu, 有趣)," revealing the affective dimension of the image, kindly and entertaining. In the case of Xu's Uncle Lion, the cuteness does not simply emerge from the fact that it is a cartoon image. It is achieved through a deliberate design in order to make milder the tiaoman persona of the real Xu Zhiyuan. In other words, Xu, as a public intellectual who used to be distanced from the popular media and their audiences, is now engaged and intimate with such a public via this benign persona. As an effect, the creation of Uncle Lion becomes an intermediary, shortening the distance between the real person Xu and his audiences.

With respect to the cute, non-threatening image of Uncle Lion, the most immediate question is the choice of a lion. Despite the fact that the cuteness of the image frequently appears in audience responses, many of them agree that Uncle Lion actually looks like very similar to Xu Zhiyuan in person. In the tiaoman *Uncle Lion Diary*, readers can also find pieces of Xu's self-reflective confessions expressed through Uncle Lion's narration. This self-reflective image envisages the micropublic of Xu's audiences. David Marshall reminds us that micropublics identify a new duality: they are "the followers and friends that are connected to a range of content via a particular individual that is simultaneously a 'private' network, but regularly and publicly updated and responded to in the tradition of broadcast and print media forms, that makes it a quasi-public network" (Marshall 2014, 164). In this sense, "[t]o understand the new public persona, one has to begin looking closely at these developed and developing micropublics that are emerging around individuals" (Marshall 2014, 164). In the case of Xu and his comic persona, Uncle Lion, the creation of such a public persona helps Xu to develop his micropublics. By following updates of the *Uncle Lion Diary*, audiences can respond and discuss relevant topics via WeChat without the time-consuming efforts of watching a one-hour interview. More importantly, following Marshall's indications, we need to understand who the audiences of the creation Uncle Lion are. To answer this question, two potentially significant lines of enquiry are discussed later.

The first clue is the meaning-making of the Uncle Lion. In my research, Xu himself has not made any direct explanation of why he chose a lion as his image. However, an article posted by Onewaystreet explains the meaning of the lion in Xu's comic persona. According to this view, the image of Uncle Lion is both iconic and relatable for Xu's audiences. It directly identifies the characteristics of Xu's audiences, and, hence, the micropublics developed surrounded Xu's persona:

> Is this lion Xu Zhiyuan? ... The answer is yes and no. This lion, like you and me, is full of ideals and weaknesses, praises the brave but can't help being afraid, longs for the sublime but often gives in to the temptation of the senses, wants to experience different lives, but only has affection for the abstract world, and accept the most luxurious and the cheapest at the same time. He rebels against everything, including his own life, and he wants to be everything but himself ... We all want to be lions or get to know lions. 'I don't want to live in a world where there are no lions and no lion-like people,' said Herzog, director of *Fitzcarraldo*. In *The Old Man and the Sea*, Santiago dreamed of the lion three times. Hemingway gave the lion a new symbolic meaning, 'Man is undefeatable. You can destroy a man, but you can't defeat him.' (Available in two locations: Onewaystreet, which posted the texts on September 9, 2021, when Xu was about to open a pub branded

with his lion image; and "The Thirteen Invitations," the official account of Xu's documentary series *The Thirteen Invitations*, 12 March 2021)

In the paragraph, the meaning of the lion is constructed through three levels. On one level, it is connected to statements by the German director Werner Herzog and the American writer Ernest Hemingway. By quoting their remarks, the piece underscores the convention of lion-like men who are undefeatable. However, what the specialness of the "lion" is and what the "undefeatable man" is fighting against is not clear. While the relevance of Herzog's film *Fitzcarraldo* is not described, it is assumed that readers will know that it narrates an adventure story of a man trying to madly transport a steamship through dense jungle in order to access rubber territory in the Amazon Basin, just as they are imagined to know the connection between Hemingway and tales of conventional male bravery. A second level is provided by the iconic meaning of the lion. Sentences like "he rebels against everything" and "we all want to be lions or get to know lions" confirm the heroic and iconic image of the lion. This iconic lion "rebels against everything, including his own life." Such phrases link to a strong determination for self-reconstruction.

The makeover narrative is currently popular in the global context of neoliberalism (Lovelock 2017). In this narrative, heart-rending stories of arduous transformation are accompanied by consumer-oriented slogans of self-reconstruction, backed up by recourse to anything from off-the-shelf products to expensive procedures, along with knowledge products such as websites and books. However, similar to the understanding of the first level, the symbol of the lion functions as the result and evidence of the transformative process of building what Xu believes to be an iconic persona at the current time. The first two levels therefore provide resources for expressing a relatable self of Xu Zhiyuan in front of his audiences. They lead to the third level, the relatable self of Xu Zhiyuan itself. What is noticeable is the phrase "this lion, like you and me." This gestures to the desire to generate a relatable self to his audience. Being relatable calls for such things as authenticity and common experiences believed to be shared by members of certain groups (Gill and Kanai 2018). In line with McCloud's outlining of the empathetic potential of a stylized cartoon face, audiences are not only seeing cartoonist's persona but also identifying with it in some way. Xu's aforementioned text creates a participatory and invitational tone, which suggests a shared feeling between Xu and his audience. By beginning with "this lion, like you and me," what follows subtly invites the complicity of audiences who do the seeing and understanding. The followers are presumed to share the succession of paradoxes: "full of ideals and weaknesses, praises the brave but can't help being afraid, longs for the sublime but often gives in to the temptation of the senses, wants to experience different lives, but only has affection for the abstract world, and accept the most luxurious and the cheapest at the same time." These paradoxes illustrate Xu's diagnosis of the public's anxieties of the era. It reveals multiple uncertainties and ambivalences in the identity crisis considered characteristic of post-modernity (Bauman 1987). This strategy further desires that in confronting these uncertainties, the public will be guided by the intellectual persona, to which end an attempt is made for a process of identification to take place. The depiction of Xu the cartoon lion seems relatable and identifiable with his audiences, but it is also deliberately reinforced by the intellectual Xu Zhiyuan. The meaning-making of Uncle Lion channels Xu Zhiyuan's imagination of himself, but also of his awareness of the micropublics who are seeing it.

At the end of every episode of the comic diary, Uncle Lion leaves an open question to his audiences. Such a question is often related to the topic of the interview but allows more space for individual expression and self-disclosure. For instance, in the episode about idol culture as mentioned, Uncle Lion Xu leaves a question for his audience on WeChat: "who is your idol?" (Fig. 11.6). Unlike the Tencent Video platform, although there is a comments box under the interview programme where audiences can discuss and communicate, there is no conversation room such as the one Uncle Lion can offer via WeChat to guide audience responses. Regarding the comments posted by diary readers, I found comments mentioning American song writer Bob Dylan and English musicians John Lennon and Roger Waters. They also mentioned Chinese singer Li Jian (李健), who shares a similar artist status in the field of contemporary Chinese music. One comment also clarified that "they are epoch-making idols (shidai ouxiang, 时代偶像)." In this case, shared cultural references among Xu's audiences may be seen, but also a certain canonical hegemony of taste with respect to the musical idols of an older generation, apparently superior to the contemporary idol culture and idol industry discussed in Xu's documentary. The willingness of such commentators to participate, however, may show their affinity to and identification with Xu's attitudes towards today's Chinese idol culture rather than represent generalized perceptions.

11 THE GRAPHIC SELF OF PUBLIC INTELLECTUALS: CHINESE... 211

Fig. 11.6 In the text box, Uncle Lion asks his readers "who is your idol?" Image resource: https://mp.weixin.qq.com/s/-uY32x9O4K3VKgWE1ZxqYQ

Uncle Lion on the Move: A Commercialized Self

From the discussion, it may be seen that the *Uncle Lion Diary* not only complements Xu's public persona but also develops and gathers audiences who share similar opinions and tastes, a micropublic, as mentioned. If we see the public space as a nexus of online and offline, we can see that Xu Zhiyuan's transmedia self of Uncle Lion has a commercial dimension. This dimension specifically refers to something that is able to be sold. It is usually seen as the criteria for assessing the level of commercialization of celebrities. In the realm of Chinese intellectuals, recent years have witnessed a burgeoning trend of selling lifestyles or aesthetic values–selling goods that can contribute to a certain lifestyle or show a certain aesthetic taste. Xu Zhiyuan's Uncle Lion is no different. Based on the image of Uncle Lion, Xu and his team found an offline cultural space, called Thirteen Bar (see Fig. 11.7). The Uncle Lion image became the logo of the bar. At this point, Xu Zhiyuan's Uncle Lion image has become commercialized and separated from his intellectual positions. In other words, his intellectual persona is constructed through intellectual interventions

Fig. 11.7 A photo of *Thirteen Bar*. Image resource: https://zhuanlan.zhihu.com/p/400905411

on the platform, and, at the same time, it is commodified in both online and offline public life.

Xu's team posted thirteen posters on the WeChat account Onewaystreet (see Fig. 11.8). Each poster shows a comic self, Xuzhiyuan, accompanied by a keyword. The design is commercial and the colours are strong. The number indicates the countdown of days before the opening of the pub. Chinese readers can identify words such as the twelfth word "quiet quitting," and the seventh term *nei juan* (a comment on increased social competitiveness) had comprised two highly visible buzz words during the preceding three years. *Nei Juan* (内卷) is a term that has circulated widely in China since 2020, referring to an increase in all-round competitiveness. But given that not everybody can come out on top in such a scenario, a certain anomie and frustration can set in, whether in employment, education or social competition in general (adapted from Li 2021, 1028). They do not correspond to the global trend of public resentment towards neoliberalism, but rather to a sense of community among the customers of the

11 THE GRAPHIC SELF OF PUBLIC INTELLECTUALS: CHINESE… 213

13: Curiosity
"Every conversation is an unexpected encounter."

12: Quiet Quitting
"Slowing down is also a speed."

11: Rebellion
"Be skeptical of an over-certain answer."

10: Intellectuality
"Be a not so parochial person in the limitless world."

9: Loneliness
"I am an inopportune writer."

8: Adventure
"You can dance at any time."

7: Nei Juan
"From this nowness to the next nowness."

6: Anxiety
"The appearance is determined but the inside is full of uncertainty."

5: Sincerity
"The appearance is calm and peaceful, but the inside may be dealing with a surge of emotions."

4: Insightfulness
"Develop foresight in order to surmount the unseen."

3: Revelry
"We are having revelry with loneliness."

2: Confusion
"Discontinuation might be a new beginning."

1: Prejudice
"Those charming heretics."

Fig. 11.8 The screenshots of thirteen posters posted by the WeChat account Onewaystreet on 1 September 2021. My translation is provided below each poster. Image resource: https://mp.weixin.qq.com/s/VLQEiLUCfhB3LxjIv1F_TA

Thirteen Bar in their confrontation with changing social patterns occasioned by the hegemony of neoliberalism.

In addition, when watching *Thirteen Invitations*, one of the most frequent comments among audiences is about Xu Zhiyuan's flip-flops. "Before the production of *Thirteen Invitations*, nobody could foresee that an intellectual, wearing flip-flops, getting into a Mercedes or a Lexus could be a normalized and formalized presence for any serious interview documentary" (Onewaystreet 2019). On the WeChat official accounts of Xu Zhiyuan's OWSPACE, as well as at the beginning of every episode of *Thirteen Invitations*, audiences can easily find advertisements for cars, including luxury brands such as Mercedes Benz, Lexus and Volvo. At the same time, Xu's marketing team packages Xu's publications together with flip-flops of the same styles as Xu's (see Figs. 11.9 and 11.10). Such a juxtaposition—luxury cars, bar space, flip-flops and literary works—accompanied by the cartoon image of Uncle Lion Xu Zhiyuan appears to connect with a public who are chasing a similar lifestyle and associations with the aesthetic taste provided by Xu's public persona. In my opinion, they are often loosely identified as the newly emerged Chinese urban middle-class.

Fig. 11.9 The promotion package of flip-flops and a book written by Xu Zhiyuan. Image resource: https://www.sohu.com/a/327613569_611314

Fig. 11.10 Xu Zhiyuan's style. Image resource: https://www.sohu.com/a/327613569_611314

However, such a class still has no explicit identity demographically and politically in the current Chinese context (Dong 2018). And it is difficult to demonstrate its socio-cultural relationships to other social groups. However, the juxtapositions mentioned in the case of the commodities associated with Xu Zhiyuan may serve as an avenue to characterizing the urban middle-class in terms of quite specific consumer behaviours such as cultural product choice, preference of leisure activities and their consumption of taste. In the cultural market, Xu, through his role as cultural critic, also plays the commercial role of an influencer for consumers' decision-making process.

Conclusion

Through examination of the intellectual Xu Zhiyuan and his self-representation as Uncle Lion, this chapter has mapped out the communicative effects of Xu's Uncle Lion persona. It has been found that although Chinese scrolling comics, tiaoman, provide a seemingly non-elite medium for intellectual intervention and performance, they still imply a top-down, Pygmalion-type relationship between public intellectuals and their niched audiences.

In today's general climate of uncertainty and identity crisis, Xu creates a universal persona of a male lion who observes and comments on urban phenomena while wandering around the contemporary city. By means of affectively invitational tones and the cartoon mediation of his established public subjectivity as an intellectual, the meaning-making of the persona Uncle Lion becomes another way of acting upon contemporary audiences. Uncle Lion's visual mini-narratives identify and attract audiences who are similar to the Uncle Lion character, curating an affinity with his style and tastes. By referencing cultural texts from the non-Chinese world, the image Uncle Lion establishes gestures towards a certain assured, outward-looking style, distanced to some extent from the debilitating uncertainty of the present for many people. However, this strategy channels the long-established tradition of intellectuals cultivating or shaping their audiences, beckoning to them to identify with an intellectual as a way of shoring up their status. The depiction of a relaxed *flâneur* seems uncomplicated, but it is deliberately designed by Xu, whose role is similar to that of traditional intellectuals: securing the assent of a less-educated audience. While the constructed "commonness" in Xu's self-positioning is noticeable, it consists of multiple uncertainties and paradoxes in the realm of personal and intellectual style, not least the fusing of a supposedly unintellectual visual medium with his exploration of post-modern identity crises (see Bauman 1987). Such commonness ironically illustrates how uncommon Xu is, exemplified by his having had the idea to deploy his interests in such a medium in the first place, and then to have them matter to his audience.

From the perspective of the media strategy in Xu's self-representation, Xu's Uncle Lion creates a doubled self to complement the style of his approach elsewhere. What seems to be inappropriate in the person-to-person interview is illustrated through the *Uncle Lion Diary*. I argue that Xu creates a platform-afforded, comic, softened gaze, which combines the male gaze and a foreshortened power distance that might be unacceptable in the person-to-person interview. Xu Zhiyuan's public persona is further expanded via a less-than-refined commercial dimension through the Uncle Lion image. The juxtaposition—luxury cars, bar space, flip-flops and literary works—accompanied by the cartoon image of Uncle Lion Xu Zhiyuan, evokes a dominant public audience who are chasing a similar lifestyle and cultural style to that provided by Xu's public persona. Such a public is often loosely identified as the Chinese urban middle-class (Dong 2018), and, as has been seen here, such an identity is not normatively formed but identified through style affiliations in which Xu's use of the visual storytelling resources of tiaoman has itself been one of the signs of his contemporaneity, underwriting his authority as a witness to the present.

References

Baert, Patrick, and Marcus Morgan. 2018. A Performative Framework for the Study of Intellectuals. *European Journal of Social Theory* 21 (3): 322–339.

Bauman, Zygmunt. 1987. *Legislators and Interpreters: On Modernity, Postmodernity and Intellectuals*. Cambridge: Polity Press.

Blommaert, Jan. 2008. *Grassroots Literacy: Writing, Identity, and Voice in Central Africa*. London: Routledge.

Boyd, Danah. 2007. Viewing American Class Divisions Through Facebook and MySpace. *Apophenia blog essay*.

Dong, Jie. 2018. Taste, Discourse and Middle-Class Identity: An ethnography of Chinese Saabists. *Journal of SocioLinguistics* 22 (4): 432–453.

Gee, James Paul. 2015. Discourse Analysis of Games. In *Discourse and Digital Practices: Doing Discourse Analysis in the Digital Age*, ed. Rodney H. Jones, Alice Chik, and Christoph Hafner, 18–27. London: Routledge.

Gill, Rosalind, and Akane Kanai. 2018. Mediating Neoliberal Capitalism: Affect, Subjectivity and Inequality. *Journal of Communication* 68 (2): 318–326.

Goffman, Erving. 1956. *The Presentation of Self in Everyday Life*. New York: Doubleday.

Heynders, Odile. 2016. *Writers as Public Intellectuals: Literature, Celebrity, Democracy*. Basingstoke: Palgrave Macmillan.

Jang, Wonho, and Jung Eun Song. 2017. Webtoon as a New Korean Wave in the Process of Glocalization. *Kritika Kultura* 29: 168–187.

Jenkins, Henry. 2010. Transmedia Storytelling and Entertainment: An Annotated Syllabus. *Continuum* 24 (6): 943–958.

Jones, Rodney H., Alice Chik, and Christoph Hafner, eds. 2015. *Discourse and Digital Practices: Doing Discourse Analysis in the Digital Age*. London: Routledge.

Li, Meng-ying. 2021. 'Nei Juan' in Exam-oriented Education in China. *Journal of Literature and Art Studies* 11 (12): 1028–1033.

Lovelock, Michael. 2017. Call me Caitlyn: Making and Making Over the 'Authentic' Transgender Body in Anglo-American Popular Culture. *Journal of Gender Studies* 26 (6): 675–687.

Marshall, P. David. 2014. Persona studies: Mapping the Proliferation of the Public Self. *Journalism* 15 (2): 153–170.

Marshall, P. David, Christopher Moore, and Kim Barbour. 2015. Persona as Method: Exploring Celebrity and the Public Self Through Persona Studies. *Celebrity Studies* 6 (3): 288–305.

McCloud, Scott. 1994. *Understanding Comics: The Invisible Art.* New York: William Morrow.

Onewaystreet. 2019. Xu Zhiyuan. "Chuanzhe Renzituo Quyoudang". https://mp.weixin.qq.com/s/_1kt_SmdSqc59W4vh6I2EA. Accessed 1 June 2022.

Rui, Lai. 2020. Manhua Rannuan ye Kangyi (Zhongguo Zhan 'Yi' Xilie Baodao 16). *People's Daily Overseas Edition.* February 28. http://paper.people.com.cn/rmrbhwb/html/2020-02/28/content_1973574.htm. Accessed 27 May 2023.

Schiller, Melanie. 2018. Transmedia Storytelling. In *Stories: Screen Narrative in the Digital Age*, ed. Ian Christie and Annie van den Oever, 97–108. Amsterdam: Amsterdam University Press.

Watson, Julia. 2008. Autographic Disclosures and Genealogies of Desire in Alison Bechdel's *Fun Home*. *Biography* 31 (1): 27–58.

Whitlock, Gillian, and Anna Poletti. 2008. Self-Regarding Art. *Biography* 31 (1): v–xxiii.

Yecies, Brian, Aegyung Shim, and Jack Yang. 2019. Chinese Transcreators, Webtoons and the Korean Digital Wave. In *Digital Transactions in Asia: Economic, Informational, and Social Exchanges*, ed. Adrian Athique and Emma Baulch, 224–241. New York: Routledge.

Zimmermann, Daniel, Anna Wehler, and Kai Kaspar. 2023. Self-representation Through Avatars in Digital Environments. *Current Psychology* 42 (25): 21775–21789.

CHAPTER 12

Through Etched Glass: Representing Urban Place in Christina Fernandez's Photographic Series *Lavanderia*

Sheila Brannigan

INTRODUCTION

Photographs of urban communities have received considerable critical attention, with continuing interest in the social values such works appear to articulate. How the observing gaze of the photographer operates in such contexts, how photographers mediate lived experience in urban neighbourhoods, have accordingly drawn much investigation. In this contribution to a volume on visual storytelling, this chapter attempts to

S. Brannigan (✉)
Nova University, Lisbon, Portugal

CETAPS, Centre for English, Translation and Anglo-Portuguese Studies, Lisbon, Portugal

© The Author(s), under exclusive license to Springer Nature Switzerland AG 2024
D. Callahan (ed.), *Visual Storytelling in the 21st Century*, https://doi.org/10.1007/978-3-031-65487-9_12

219

address these concerns through an analysis of Christina Fernandez's photographic series *Lavanderia* (2002–2003).[1]

The analysis investigates the narratives *Lavanderia* constructs around the specific places of launderettes and the communities of the neighbourhoods where they were situated, in the Eastside of Los Angeles, in the early 2000s. Through this analysis, the positions Fernandez occupies in the complex interchanges of the photographs are also investigated. Stuart Hall shows that images disturb by the very way in which they exceed meaning (Hall 1999, 311), so that this chapter explores how Fernandez's photographs in *Lavanderia* exceed meaning in the narratives constructed around the act of looking from the street at night into the places of specific launderettes in the Eastside of Los Angeles, customers in their interiors, and their glass window surfaces etched with tags.

In *Lavanderia*, Fernandez portrays the strip-lit interior of launderettes seen from the street at night-time, everyday places that may be passed unnoticed by people circulating in cars or on foot. The series consists of ten photographs, the undescriptive titles of which merely contain a number, from *Lavanderia #1* to *Lavanderia #6*, and then *Lavanderia #8* to *Lavanderia #11*. Photographs depicting the act of looking into and onto glass windows in the urban landscape are prevalent in American photographic histories. For example, Lisette Model's photographs of New York City in the 1940s explore both the street-side of cities reflected and the glass window displays of shops, in which they are reflected.[2] John Pfahl's *Picture Windows* series (1978–1981) explores the act of looking and the picture window in urban and rural American places, while John Divola's *Zuma* project (1977–1979) interrogates the place of a ruined building in Southern California, exploring windows and light among the artist's own,

---

[1] Parts of this chapter will appear in adapted form in my doctoral thesis, "Outside the Inside: Shifting Views in Photographs of American Urban Places" (Brannigan, forthcoming), Nova University of Lisbon.

[2] Lisette Model's photographs exploring New York City through its reflections in shop window displays include *Reflections, New York* (1939–45). This work and a number of Model's works from this series can be viewed online on the Bruce Silverstein Gallery Web site at: https://www.brucesilverstein.com/exhibitions/self-reflections-the-expressionist-origins-of-lisette-model/selected-works

and others' interventions.[3] Fernandez references the work of another Angeleno artist, Anthony Hernandez, as being close to the aesthetic approach of her own photographs (Fernandez 2022b, 212). Hernandez's works focus on urban place, narratives of redevelopment, and the places of homelessness. For instance, the series *Landscapes for the Homeless* (1988–2007) represents urban places in Los Angeles where homeless people live.[4] Fernandez's works in *Lavanderia*, in turn, interrogate the act of looking from the street at night-time onto glass window surfaces etched with tags, and the illuminated interiors of launderettes and their customers within, as integral elements of their street environments.

In *Lavanderia #1*, the glass doors of a launderette are depicted dripping with graffiti tags etched into the glass (see Fig. 12.1). Through the etched windows, a richly coloured, blurred figure of a launderette customer is portrayed standing in front of the banks of machines and driers. She emblematizes the stillness, watching, and waiting that the mundane work of doing the laundry in the launderette demands. *Lavanderia #11* frames looking from the street into an illuminated launderette to articulate a powerful sense of place (see Fig. 12.2). The dull side of a washing machine pressed up against the etched, smudged, windows, along with a bench, are ordinary elements foregrounded in the photograph. On the other hand, above these heavy fittings, customers engaged in the work of laundry are depicted as bright, blurred presences seen through the frenetic marks of tags and in the glare of strip-lights. *Lavanderia #6* frames the illuminated interior of a launderette and the figure of a man doing his laundry through the grid of its window structure and stencilled and printed Spanish and English signs (see Fig. 12.3). Unlike the blurred presences of people visible through the glass in most of the other photographs in the series, the man is portrayed more distinctly, and seems to be looking out to the exterior of the launderette, and to the camera. In *Lavanderia #2*, tall panels of etched glass monumentally frame the everyday goings on

---

[3] John Pfahl's *Picture Windows* series includes *2637 Main Street, Santa Monica, CA, 1978*. This work and the series can be viewed online on the Joseph Bellows Gallery Web site: https://www.josephbellows.com/exhibitions/john-pfahl?view=slider#29 John Divola's *Zuma* project (1979) includes the work *Zuma #33* (1977). This work and the project as a whole can be viewed online on the Yancey Richardson Gallery Web site: https://www.yanceyrichardson.com/artists/john-divola?view=slider#4

[4] Anthony Hernandez's *Landscapes for the Homeless* series includes the work *Landscapes for the Homeless, #5* (1988). This work and the series can be viewed online on the Whitney Museum of American Art Web site: https://whitney.org/collection/works/57726

Fig. 12.1 Christina Fernandez. Lavanderia #1. 2002–2003. Archival pigment print. 76.2 × 101.6 cm (30 × 40 in.) Web. Gallery Luisotti Web site. https://galleryluisotti.com/images/lavanderia-2002/ Courtesy of the artist and Gallery Luisotti, Los Angeles

in a launderette's interior (see Fig. 12.4). It is through this surface of opaque graffiti tags that the customers in the launderette are depicted, although they are not clearly visible. Instead, like most of the customers depicted in the photographs in *Lavanderia*, they are portrayed as blurred presences seen through glass surfaces and appear not known and unreachable.

Fernandez references the influence of the works of the New Topographics group on her landscape photographs (2022a, 201). As David Campany shows, diverse artists had begun to make artworks in photography and the photographic was entering dialogues with diverse arts, from the 1960s onwards (2003, 16). Among them were artists in the United States and Europe who produced works in the medium exploring

Fig. 12.2 Christina Fernandez. Lavanderia #11. 2002–2003. Archival pigment print. 76.2 × 101.6 cm (30 × 40 in.). Gallery Luisotti Web site. https://galleryluisotti.com/images/lavanderia-2002/ Courtesy of the artist and Gallery Luisotti, Los Angeles

the geography, or topography, of places.[5] The 1975 exhibition *New Topographics: Photographs of a Man-altered Landscape* included the works of ten photographers and artists whose photographs interrogated the

---

[5] The works of Germany-based artists Hilla and Bernd Becher investigated the industrial and post-industrial landscape transnationally through depicting typologies of isolated technical buildings in photographs, such as *Pitheads* (1974). Hilla and Bernd Becher additionally had a marked influence on the development of photography through their teaching, which shaped a number of photographers at the *Kunstakademie Düsseldorf*. Andreas Gursky, whose photographs represent human interventions in the landscape in large-format colour, such as *Montparnasse* (1995), and Thomas Ruff, whose diverse works include large-format colour frontal portraits as well as interrogations of the urban and industrial landscape, such as *House no 7 I* (1988) (which can be viewed online on the artist's Web site at https://www.thomas-ruff.com/werke/hauser/#pid=6), were among their students.

Fig. 12.3 Christina Fernandez. Lavanderia #6. 2002–2003. Archival pigment print. 76.2 × 101.6 cm (30 × 40 in.). Gallery Luisotti Web site. https://galleryluisotti.com/images/lavanderia-2002/ Courtesy of the artist and Gallery Luisotti, Los Angeles

urban and industrial landscape in North America.[6] It is significant that Fernandez aligns her work portraying place with the specific developments which the New Topographics brought to photographic practice representing the American landscape. Fernandez notes the work of Lewis Baltz as a particular reference in her works, in the flatness, the use of a grid, and the

---

[6] The exhibition *New Topographics: Photographs of a Man-altered Landscape* (1975) was held at the International Museum of Photography, Rochester, New York (which is now known as The George Eastman Museum). It included works by the following photographers and artists: Robert Adams, Lewis Baltz, Bernd and Hilla Becher, Joe Deal, Frank Gohlke, Nicholas Nixon, John Schott, Stephen Shore, and Henry Wessel. The restaging of the exhibition (July 17–October 3, 2010) at the San Francisco Museum of Modern Art, which included the work of the ten photographers from the original exhibition, emphasizes the continuing importance to photography of the works exhibited.

Fig. 12.4 Christina Fernandez. Lavanderia #2. 2002–2003. Archival pigment print. 76.2 × 101.6 cm (30 × 40 in.). Gallery Luisotti Web site. https://galleryluisotti.com/images/lavanderia-2002/ Courtesy of the artist and Gallery Luisotti, Los Angeles

pared down framing (2022a, 201).[7] However, as Campany argues, in depicting California's commercial landscapes of the 1970s, Baltz's work attempted to convey neutrality, which "avoided it being caught up in any particular social or political viewpoint" (2003, 81). This chapter examines whether Fernandez's photographs representing the places of launderettes in the Eastside of Los Angeles in *Lavanderia* convey a similar neutrality or, in contrast, articulate a particular social perspective. In reading Fernandez's representation of specific places in the series, Agnew's definition of *place* proves useful, in terms of the three dimensions of place as a site where an

---

[7] Lewis Baltz's photographs of landscapes in California include *Alton Road at Murphy Road Looking toward Newport Center* (1974), from the series *The New Industrial Parks near Irvine, California* (1974).

activity or object is located, as the setting where everyday-life activities take place, and as a *sense of place* (Agnew 2011).

Filaments of Life: Histories of the Communities of the Neighbourhoods

The series *Lavanderia* portrays launderettes in streets across the Eastside of Los Angeles. Fernandez notes that the launderette in the first work in the series, *Lavanderia #1*, was located in Boyle Heights, while the other photographs portray launderettes near Nueva Maravilla Public Housing Development, on Cesar Chavez Avenue, and around the Eastside (Fernandez 2022a, 209). The Eastside area is historically considered to stretch from the east bank of the Los Angeles River in the city centre, into the neighbouring San Gabriel Valley further east, and spans the Central Los Angeles and San Gabriel Valley regions (Brightwell 2011, pars. 3, 7). As an area, it is "the social, economic, political and cultural centre" of Los Angeles's diverse Mexican American community (Dominguez 2016, 53–54). Drawing on the notion of place as above all a setting for social interaction, indicated by Agnew and also by Tim Cresswell (2004), a discussion of the histories of the Mexican American and Latino communities of the Eastside neighbourhoods of Los Angeles represented in *Lavanderia* is essential to the investigation in this essay. As Katharine Hodgkin and Susannah Radstone argue, histories of all communities are contested and critical, but particularly in regards to minority communities. This means that "[t]he meanings and narratives of the past that we live with are of critical importance in establishing our sense of ourselves and our cultures" (Hodgkin and Radstone 2003, 5). In the case of Mexican American communities, those meanings tend to privilege the struggle that they have confronted in the United States (Acuña 1981, 419).

What follows is a necessarily cursory discussion of studies into the histories of the Mexican American and Latino communities of the Eastside. In her investigation into a 1921 deportation proceeding in the US-Mexico borderlands, Natalia Molina shows the extent to which Mexican communities spanned the border areas until the US-Mexican War and the imposition of the border in 1848 (Molina 2014, 434). To the northwest of the occupied territory, the area of Alta California became simply California. Discussing the rights of minorities in the United States as citizens and the struggle to gain rights, Molina points out how the war cast a long shadow, to the extent that generations later, "it continued to serve as a lens for viewing Mexicans as perpetually foreign" (Molina 2014, 441). From the late nineteenth century to the 1950s, Rodolfo Acuña argues that the Mexican American community in Los Angeles lived through nothing less than oppression and discrimination (Acuña 1981, 117). The community confronted a legalized dual wage, with Mexican Americans and Chinese workers being paid lower than whites (Acuña 1981, 117). The Mexican-American community in Los Angeles also endured mass arrests, a lack of criminal justice, segregated housing, schools, and facilities including public swimming pools, police violence, and incidents of violence from the US armed forces (Acuña 1981, 305–29). Acuña writes of unity leagues formed in the 1950s to resist police violence against the community, violence that was particularly directed towards teenage boys and young men (Acuña 1981, 336).[8] Another form of resistance was for Chicano bureaucrats to enter state and federal positions in the 1970s, while Chicana activists also emerged in the second-wave feminist 1970s, at a time when the Mexican-American population of Los Angeles increased to over 1,200,000 (Acuña 1981, 385–87). The significant term *Chicana/o* is used in this chapter in the sense of an identity positioned by a social movement, as Armando B. Rendón argues in his *Chicano Manifesto* of 1971:

> Chicano is a unique confluence of histories, cultures, languages, and traditions... Chicano is indefinable, more a word to be understood and felt and lived than placed in a dictionary or analyzed by Anglo anthropologists, sociologists, and apologists... It portrays the fact that we have come to psychological terms with circumstances which might otherwise cause emotional and social breakdowns among our people if we only straddle cultures and do not absorb them. (Rendón 1971, 325)

Despite the advances the Eastside community achieved through political representation and activism, discrimination and oppression persisted, in the form, for instance, of police violence against the Mexican-American community, which continued throughout the 1970s (Acuña 1981, 412).

---

[8] Acuña further highlights how non-white communities in the Eastside were displaced by the building of freeways in the city and urban renewal plans, quoting Mayor Norris Poulson's statement in 1959: "If you are not prepared to be part of this greatness, if you want Los Angeles to revert to *pueblo* status ... then my best advice to you is to prepare to resettle elsewhere" (qtd. in Acuña 1981, 340–41).

In a discussion of the United States-Mexico borderlands, anthropologist Renato Rosaldo argues for a view of histories as interconnected, in which subordinated histories are a pathway, "to a renewed vison of national histories" (Rosaldo 1996, 1041). Rosaldo reasons that "[t]he inclusion of excluded and marginalized histories offers a vison of the social whole" (Rosaldo 1996, 1041). William V. Flores claims, in turn, that marginalized groups define themselves, form a community, and claim social rights, in a process of *cultural citizenship*; "Latinos, like other 'new citizens,' yearn for a space of their own in which to think, to create, and to act in a way that reflects their sense of themselves" (Flores 2003, 88). In a significant study of cultural production from Los Angeles Chicana/o musicians and writers in the 1980s, Raúl Homero Villa shows that writers, musicians, and artists critically engaged with urban development of the period. As Villa observes, urban development in the Eastside was inflicted on, and effaced, communities. He shows how urban developers, the police-judicial system, and the mainstream media "combined in conscious and unconscious fashion to culturally marginalize and spatially contain the Chicano (and now greater Latino) working-class residents of Los Angeles" (Villa 1999, 111). The term *Latina/o* is taken in the present study in the sense of referring to:

> multi-generational migrants from Latin America and the Caribbean, citizens from Puerto Rico, Indigenous citizens of tribal nations who persist in their struggle for sovereignty from nation-states, and longstanding residents and communities born in territories expropriated by the Treaty of Guadalupe Hidalgo (Fountain-Stokes et al. 2017, par. 12).

However, Latina/o is also understood in this chapter as a contested term.[9] Among the cultural texts Villa selects in his study, the lyrics of the song "Rampage" (1983) by Chicano punk band Los Illegals are a testament to

---

[9] The terms *Latina, Latino,* and *Latina/o*, with the terms *Latin@* and *Latinx* introduced to overcome the gender binary of these pronouns, have been critiqued by scholars, including José Esteban Muñoz. Muñoz suggests *Latino*, "has not developed as an umbrella term that unites cultural and political activists across different national, racial, class, and gender divides" (Muñoz 2000, 67). However, he argues, it constitutes an "identity in difference", drawing on the work of Chicana feminist Norma Alarcón (Muñoz 2000, 67). In contrast, *brownness*, in Muñoz's theory, is posited as, "a structure of feeling, as a way of being in the world, a path that does not conform to the conventions of a majoritarian public sphere and the national affect it sponsors" (Muñoz 2000, 79).

the erasing of the Mexican American communities of the Eastside through urban development (Villa 1999, 114). The song states, "Tangled in a battlefield of mortar and steel, I am witness to a lifestyle-being destroyed, it's for real!" (Los Illegals qtd. in Villa 1999, 115).

In 1998, the Latino population in the City of Los Angeles was 1,651,000, while in the wider Los Angeles County it was 4,226,000 (Valle and Torres 2000, 4). Furthermore, the significant Latino population that made up the community of the Eastside was predominately working class (Sassen 2000, ix). For instance, Valle and Torres show that in 1990, 72% of workers in the manufacturing sector in the city of Los Angeles were Latino (2000, 16). In addition, the low-wage manufacturing jobs contributed to high levels of poverty for the communities of the Eastside. The child poverty rate in the Latino community in the United States was 28.4% in 2000 (The Federal Interagency Forum on Child and Family Statistics 2021 par. 3), while this rate remained at 27.3% in 2020 (Chen and Thomson 2021, par. 2). Having briefly discussed studies into the histories of the communities of the Eastside of Los Angeles, the analysis now turns to an examination of *Lavanderia* and the narratives constructed around the places of the launderettes and the communities of the neighbourhoods where they are situated, in the complex interchanges of the photographs in the series.

Framing a Close Dialogue with Launderettes and the Communities Around Them, in *Lavanderia*

A routine place of urban life, which may ordinarily be overlooked, is rendered remarkable in *Lavanderia #1*. Framed through the window structure and dripping graffiti tags, the photograph presents a kaleidoscopic view of this mundane launderette, seen from the street (see Fig. 12.1). Julian Myers's significant examination of *Lavanderia* shows that Fernandez's process began with the making of this photograph, which she then developed into a series (Myers 2022, 138). In *Lavanderia #1*, a striking representation of this place is articulated through the depiction of particular elements. These encompass the glass etched with dripping graffiti tags; a shopping cart parked up prominently against the doors; and banks of washing machines and driers. A further impressive element depicted is the light emanating from the ceiling panels, which illuminates the tags it passes through and spills onto the street-side of the window glass. Agnew's definition of place is drawn on here, particularly the dimension defined as "identification with a place as a unique community, landscape, and moral order", termed *a sense of place* (Agnew 2011, 327). Through the arrangement of these elements, a sense of place is conveyed in *Lavanderia #1*; a sense of place which spans this particular launderette and the street just in front of its window, at night-time. Moreover, the photograph speaks to this particular launderette as a social place. The place as the setting for social interaction is conveyed in the portrayal of graffiti tags, which are an aspect of the series examined below, and also in the elements which point to the labour which is carried out in this launderette, such as the shopping cart to carry laundry home, and the banks of machines. The launderette as the setting for social interaction is additionally conveyed in the depiction of a deeply coloured, blurred image of a woman absorbed in the work of doing the laundry. The figure of this customer speaks to time spent in this place; time spent in working, waiting, and in thinking. In the portrayal of a unique coming together of place, seen from the street, in *Lavanderia #1*, the artist seems to occupy a position of recognition of a sense of place there. In contrast, at the same time, Fernandez is positioned at a place of distance from the goings on inside the launderette. This place of remove is suggested through the motif of looking through glass onto the interior, and in the distance represented from the blurred figure of the woman portrayed, absorbed in waiting, and appearing unreachable.

Lavanderia #11 is a powerful juxtaposition of a view of the heavy bulk of dull fittings of washing machines and a dynamic, edgy interior scene (see Fig. 12.2). The photograph foregrounds the shabby, dingy view of a bank of washing machines, pressed up against the glass window panes of this launderette. The frenetic interior is visible through the glare of the launderette strip-lights and the glass etched with dripping tags, through which a shopping trolley with pastel coloured detergent bottles is prominent; elements which bear similarity with *Lavanderia #1*. The customers in *Lavanderia #11* are depicted as bright traces and blurs against banks of machines; moving presences occupied in the labour of doing the laundry. Writing on the meanings which images construct, Hall argues, "we register the image's capacity to connote on a much broader symbolic field, to touch levels of experience which seem remote or 'archaic', beyond the purely rational level of awareness, and which disturb by the very way in which they exceed meaning" (Hall 1999, 311). Tracing Hall's notion, the present study reads *Lavanderia #1* and *Lavanderia #11* as photographs which exceed meaning in the narratives they construct around the specific places of these ordinary launderettes.

The shabby exterior foregrounded in *Lavanderia #11*, together with the dynamic blurs and traces of the customers portrayed involved in doing laundry, convey this launderette as a place of labour and of the everyday, urban necessity of doing this type of work (see Fig. 12.2). In this way, *Lavanderia #11* points to this specific launderette as a classed place. In the present essay, the term class is used in the sense of a vertical social grouping which circulates, as Stephanie Lawler observes, in symbolic and cultural forms (Lawler 2005, 797). Representing a place of everyday practical necessity, the photograph speaks to the working-class facet of identity of some members of the Latino communities of the neighbourhood portrayed. Kimberlé Crenshaw's seminal notion of intersectionality provides "a lens ... for seeing the way in which various forms of inequality often operate together and exacerbate each other" (Crenshaw 2020, par. 3). Inequalities for working-class Latinos in the communities represented are articulated in aspects of *Lavanderia #11*. For example, the blurred figures of customers are portrayed engaged in the work of the laundry, which is labour being carried out at night, perhaps after a long day at work; and the task of transporting laundry to and from homes nearby is indicated in the store shopping carts. These aspects are also prominent in the other photographs across the series. Additionally, the time spent waiting, which the task of doing the laundry necessitates, is a further cost for the customers which is articulated in the photographs in *Lavanderia* (with the exception of *Lavanderia #11*, *Lavanderia #2* and *Lavanderia #3*). Beneficial aspects of the working-class places of these launderettes, which emerge across the series, include the social interactions going on there, while the possibility of time spent waiting being a quiet, contemplative moment is conveyed in *Lavanderia #1*, as abovementioned. Julian Myers and Sally Stein also interrogate the classed place of the launderette in the series *Lavanderia*. Stein discusses how the series conveys the toil involved in the process of going to the launderette, and the launderette as a communal space, suggesting, "Fernandez sought to construct different parameters so as not to divert the focus of those seeking to do the most ordinary thing–cleaning–thus allowing them to maintain their self-respect" (Stein 2022, 116). For Myers, *Lavanderia* represents the time cost of working-class life, and "the lived experience of being working class" (Myers 2022, 144). What is more, Fernandez reflects on her interest in laundrettes as a social setting, noting they are, "a space both private and public, where people are washing their underwear, taking care of their kids, watching TV, having something to eat - all in this public space" (Fernandez 2022a, 210).

Among the multiple strands of her own subjectivity which Fernandez brings into the context of her work, the artist self-identifies as middle class (2022a, 203). Thus, Fernandez seems to occupy a position of distance and removal from the working-class place of the launderette and the community of launderette customers, in the complex discourse of *Lavanderia #11*. Fernandez notes, "The graffiti creates a barricade. Obscuring the figures was a way for me to address their movement and labor, as well as acknowledge that I don't know them" (Fernandez 2022a, 210). In this way, the artist is careful to state that she recognizes the position she occupies as outsider to the community of customers that *Lavanderia #11* represents, and outsider to the communities of the neighbourhoods represented across the series. Mark Sealy argues that the question of *who sees whom, and where* in photography is a matter of power, and that race is a critical factor in photography (Sealy 2019, 197). Through depicting the community members in the launderettes as blurred presences seen through glass surfaces and, thus, not known, in the series *Lavanderia*, Fernandez seems sensitive to the representations that have been historically made of the communities of the neighbourhoods of the Eastside. Ehrig, Jung and Schaffer suggest challenging the othering of neighbourhoods of multicultural and multi-ethnic people to frame the local, lived experiences of urban neighbourhoods, as "a fluid space in which various temporal and spatial axes intersect; as the locus where diverse trans/cultural practices can engender togetherness as well as differences and conflict" (Ehrig et al. 2022, 12). By mediating aspects of working class and Mexican American and Latino lived experience in the neighbourhoods, in the early 2000s, in representations of the places of the specific launderettes and their customers, *Lavanderia* raises questions, acknowledges struggles, and leaves space for differing ideas of identity.

The rectangles of a glass window free of tags frame the interior of a launderette in *Lavanderia #6* (the works *Lavanderia #5*, and *Lavanderia #8* also depict launderettes with windows of clear glass). The illuminated interior of this place of labour centres on a bank of steel, shining machines, and lines of strip-lights (see Fig. 12.3). A male customer who is waiting for his laundry to finish is portrayed, observing the exterior. Foregrounded in the photograph is a stand of laundry baskets, and signs in the interior appear prominent. Using Spanish and English, the textual elements comprise a partial message in the word *clean* stencilled in paint over the door, a printed sign in the interior which provides *Instrucciones*, and a paper sign attached to the window glass displaying the opening times in both languages. The specific characteristics of the place, rendered significant in the view from the street in *Lavanderia #6*, seem more settled and certain than those in the other photographs in the series. In depicting the man indirectly, through signs and glass, a subtle exchange is mediated between this customer contemplating the exterior and the camera. The exchange locates the launderette as a specific place, as do its regulated, organized features, with the prominent signs pointing to Spanish and English-speaking customers and a multilingual neighbourhood. Like the other photographs which make up the series, *Lavanderia #6* speaks to the specificity of this launderette: in the discernible portrayal of the customer, in its regulated, organized fittings, and in the prominent signs indicating both Spanish and English-speaking customers and a multilingual neighbourhood, rendered significant in the representation of a view from the street.

The Spanish and English signs and notices in *Lavanderia #6* point to the multilingual Latino communities of the neighbourhood of the Eastside where the launderette was situated. Moreover, multilingualism is not only present in the textual elements depicted in *Lavanderia #6*, but in the title of the series and of each of its photographs. Joanna Szupinska examines how the Spanish word *lavandería* is altered in the title of the series *Lavanderia*, and demonstrates that Fernandez intentionally left out the accent as a play on the way Spanish is used in signage in Los Angeles and to highlight "hybrid cultures and multilingual neighbourhoods" (Szupinska 2022, 15n2). In a study on Latino writers' use of code-switching, a term taken in the present study in the sense of speakers / writers shifting between two languages whether in speech and written text, Lourdes Torres argues that

> code-switching in literature is not only metaphorical, but represents a reality where segments of the population are living between cultures and languages; literary language actualizes the discourse of the border and bilingual/bicultural communities. (Torres 2007, 76)

The multilingualism of communities, the "reality [of] ... living between cultures and languages," that Lourdes Torres discusses, is articulated in the prominence of the Spanish and English signs and notices in *Lavanderia #6* (2007, 76). What is more, in its portrayal of the visibility of the signs and notices in the launderette viewed from the street at night, the photograph articulates Spanish and English multilingualism embedded in the visual environment of the street where the launderette was situated (see Fig. 12.3). In the representation of multilingualism through the visibility of the launderette signs and notices as part of the visual environment of the street, *Lavanderia #6* expresses a sense of place of this neighbourhood as, as Cresswell writes, "a rich and complicated interplay of people and the environment" (Cresswell 2004, 11). It is significant that Fernandez is also a member of the multilingual discourse community that is represented in the photograph, a facet of the artist's own subjectivity as insider to the community, embodied in the complex discourse of *Lavanderia #6*. At the same time, the artist occupies a contrasting position at some removal from the place and community represented in this photograph, both through the motif of looking through glass onto the launderette interior, and in the indirect, distanced exchange between the depicted customer and the camera.

Fernandez brings multiple strands of her own subjectivity into the context of her work in a number of ways. The term subject is understood here in the sense of what Hall argues is an entity which is not fully formed, "but something which is produced, through complex and unfinished processes which are both social and psychic–a subject-in-process" (Hall 1999, 311). Moreover, a contemporary view of concepts of identity informs the approach employed here: a view which encompasses the notions of hybrid identities, diasporic identities, and what José Esteban Muñoz identifies as, "multiple modes of being, feeling and knowing in the world" (Muñoz 2014, 250).[10] One aspect of the artist's subjectivity is clearly her Mexican American identity. A substantial number of her works articulate and question aspects of Mexican American identity, while Fernandez brings this facet of her own subjectivity into the context of some of these works. For instance, the mixed-media work *María's Great Expedition* (1995–1996) is an exploration of Mexican-American migration and identity, shaped by her great-grandmother María Gonzales' migration across Mexico and California (Fernandez 2019, par. 1). It is additionally significant that Fernandez does not refer to herself as a Chicana artist, nor a Mexican

[10] Paul Gilroy describes how the notion of diaspora was, "imported into Pan-African politics and black history from unacknowledged Jewish sources" (Gilroy 1993, xi). Petra R. Rivera discusses the African diaspora of Latin America, which, she demonstrates, incorporates Brazil and Cuba, as well as Puerto Rico, Costa Rica, Ecuador, Argentina and Venezuela, and points to the Afro-Latina/o contribution to culture in the United States (Rivera 2011, 157).

American, an American, or a Latina artist. This is a point which Joanna Szupinska explores in the recent monograph published on the photographer: "We refer to the artist as Latinx with her permission, though she herself would not use the term" (Szupinska 2022, 15). While Fernandez resisted the United States art establishment bias of a one-dimensional view of Chicana artists, her oeuvre presents works in photographic and mixed media series with a social, gendered, and political slant, particularly addressing Mexican-American migration and identity as well as the themes of ecology, and labour.

An additional strand of the artist's subjectivity which she discusses is the significance of Los Angeles to her identity and to her work. Fernandez notes, "I'm a native Angeleno, born and raised in the San Gabriel Valley" (Fernandez 2022b, 212). The County of Los Angeles is where Fernandez was born, studied, lives and teaches, and where she is based as an artist (Benton Museum of Art 2023, pars. 1–4). Myers demonstrates the artist had lived in the Boyle Heights neighbourhood (the community where the launderette in *Lavanderia #1* was situated) and was a resident of Monterey Park in the San Gabriel Valley region, around the time *Lavanderia* was made (Myers 2022, 138). Discussing the significance of the place of Los Angeles as a subject in her work, Fernandez notes:

> I need to do something about where I am and what I know, to find a pathway to address this landscape question–for me, and for this space ... My whole attitude in photography–and what I talk about, what I care about, what I teach–is embedded in my identity as an Angeleno. (Fernandez 2022a, 211)

In this statement, Fernandez clarifies the intersection of the place of Los Angeles and notions of identity in her own subjectivity. She discusses the importance of articulating questions about the landscape of wider Los Angeles in her photographic practice precisely because, she argues, it is the place where she is from.

The ordinarily banal features of window panes, strip lights, and banks of washing machines create powerful lines leading into and across the luminous interior in *Lavanderia #2* (see Fig. 12.4). Framed through the tall structure of the windows, the photograph conveys a monumental sense of the interior space of this launderette, viewed through graffiti tags scattered across the glass. Through these tagged identities etched into the surface of the window, two customers in the launderette are depicted as they are bent into the work of loading and unloading machines. Carried out in a public place, the toil of laundering that *Lavanderia #2* portrays echoes the historical use of water in the city of Los Angeles, and the contested and crucial issue of water supply to its history.[11] The Zanje Madre was a principal channel built in 1781 to bring water from the Los Angeles river to the Pueblo of Los Angeles and was also the site of a wash-house where communities laundered (its course is historically documented today in Olvera Street, in the city) (Water and Power Associates Corporation n.d.).

As the launderette was traditionally a gendered place of women's work, *Lavanderia* unexpectedly presents men and women carrying out the labour of the laundry. The customers bent into the work of loading and unloading machines in *Lavanderia #2* seem gender neutral figures. What is more, in *Lavanderia #1*, the figure portrayed standing facing banks of machines seems to be a female customer (see Fig. 12.1), while in *Lavanderia #6*, what appears to be a male customer is depicted, standing and peering towards the camera (see Fig. 12.3). Fernandez notes that, prior to making the work, she had anticipated she would be photographing women in the launderettes but found that there was actually a balance of genders in the resulting photographs, a fact that she considers a challenge to notions of Latino machismo (2022a, 210). In *Lavanderia #2*, the blurred figures of the two customers working to load and unload machines depict identities that are not known, paralleling the figures in *Lavanderia #1* and *Lavanderia #11* The indecipherable figures contrast with the emphatic identities signified in the many graffiti tags *Lavanderia #2* depicts.

Each photograph in *Lavanderia* portrays the luminous, strip-lit interior of its launderette seen from the street at night-time. Fernandez notes that the series was inspired by the work of the American painter Edward Hopper, which she had viewed in 2000 at the Musée d'Art Américain, Giverny, France (Fernandez 2022a, 209).[12] The artist reflects, "I started thinking about doing things at night, the solitary quality of his work, and the light emanating from the buildings that he was painting. I saw a laundromat and I thought, that's Hopper's light, and I had to photograph it"

---

[11] A historical description of the supply of water to Los Angeles can be found on the site of the Water and Power Associates corporation: https://waterandpower.org/museum/Water_in_Early_Los_Angeles.html

[12] The exhibition Fernandez refers to was *L'Amérique et les Modernes, 1900–1950* (*American Moderns, 1900–1950*) (July 25–October 31, 2000) at the Musée d'Art Américain, Giverny, France, which was open from 1992 to 2008. (Fernandez 2022a, 209n5).

(2022a, 209).[13] *Lavanderia* realizes a close dialogue with the places of the launderettes and the neighbourhoods around by their portrayal at night.[14] The motif of looking through the glass etched with graffiti tags onto the luminous interior in *Lavanderia #1*, *Lavanderia #2* and *Lavanderia #11* (see Figs. 12.1, 12.2 and 12.4) could only be achieved by photographing the launderettes through their window panes at night-time. Furthermore, photographing at night allowed for the use of the lines of strip-lights in the launderettes as a powerful compositional device in some of the works, such as in *Lavanderia #2* (see Fig. 12.4). Above all, in portraying looking in to the launderettes at night-time, through etched window glass or signs onto illuminated interiors in which people are engaged in the labour of laundering, the series evokes powerful senses of place of these specific streets in neighbourhoods in the Eastside.

In *Lavanderia #2*, and in four of the other photographs in *Lavanderia*, graffiti tags etched into the glass create a disturbance in the representations of looking in onto illuminated launderettes at night-time.[15] The photographs *Lavanderia #1*, *Lavanderia #2* and *Lavanderia #11* foreground graffiti tags (see Figs. 12.1, 12.2 and 12.4). Discussing how the series came about, Fernandez has explained how taggers in Los Angeles began to experiment with using etching liquid instead of spray paint: "At the time, there was an explosion of this drippy graffiti… it can't just be scraped off the glass… So the graffiti stays for a long period of time, which of course is the goal" (Fernandez 2022a, 209). She notes: "I'm attracted to the beauty of the graffiti and the oppressiveness of it as well" (Fernandez 2022a, 210). Myers explores the graffiti as a prominent framing device in the series, with the tags playing a formal role in the work, "as a lyrical screen radicalizing everyday life" (Myers 2022, 145). According to his findings, the significance of the graffiti in the series is read through the context of the political climate of the United States in the early 2000s,

---

[13] While Fernandez uses the term *laundromat* in interviews, in this chapter I use the UK word *launderette*.

[14] For a detailed analysis of the process through which Fernandez arrived at the frontal composition for the works in the series *Lavanderia* (2002–3), see Myers (2022).

[15] The photographs in the series in which graffiti tags etched into the glass create a disturbance in the representations of looking in onto illuminated launderettes comprise *Lavanderia #1*, *Lavanderia #2*, *Lavanderia #4*, *Lavanderia #10* and *Lavanderia #11*. In the photographs *Lavanderia #3* and *Lavanderia #9*, the launderette glass is scratched, which indicates an attempt to clean tags off the glass. *Lavanderia #5*, *Lavanderia #6* and *Lavanderia #8* portray launderettes with clear glass, which is free of tags.

with tagging considered "visible evidence of disorder," and linked to subsequent serious crime (Myers 2022, 145). However, Myers' analysis does not rule out other readings of the role graffiti plays in the photographs. The foregrounding of tagging in *Lavanderia* can be read as mediating a sense of place of the neighbourhoods of the Eastside of Los Angeles portrayed, and the historical and social legacy of tagging in the city, and, particularly, in these neighbourhoods.

Tagging has been a component of the visual culture of the neighbourhoods of the Eastside of Los Angeles depicted in *Lavanderia* dating back to the 1960s, while tags have also been found dating from earlier in the century. Gary Ayala's news photograph from 1976 portrays a community outreach project in the Eastside, with graffiti tags visible and prominent across a street wall in the image (see Fig. 12.5). Susan A. Phillips' research has found graffiti in Los Angeles in messages written in grease pencil by hobos from 1914 as well as in an early gang mark from 1931, found under the Spring Street Bridge (over the Los Angeles River, which marks the western boundary of the Eastside) (2019, 13). Phillips theorizes that marginalized people have left these messages across the city since then: "notes from the subaltern, the wanderers, the vilified, the vandals, the workers–from people who have broken the social contract of public space by actually inserting themselves into it" (Phillips 2019, 8). In Phillips' theory, tags can be read as messages left for others by the marginalized as a counter-narrative. For Phillips, "[t]respass is a rejection of the values embedded in private property. Graffiti is a key artifact of that rejection" (Phillips 2019, 10). Defining tagging as a social practice, Laurie MacGillivray and Margaret Sauceda Curwen state that to tag is a literacy event and practice (MacGillivray and Curwen 2007, 367). They argue that taggers "throw up a tag, their carefully selected subculture nickname, with the intention of connecting to a particular social community" (MacGillivray and Curwen 2007, 367). Tags indicate a message left for someone else, conveying that a person was present in a place and left their nickname, or a mark. The photographs *Lavanderia #1*, *Lavanderia #2* and *Lavanderia #11* negotiate the identities which the graffiti tags given prominence in these works signify (see Figs. 12.1, 12.2 and 12.4). The three photographs in the series articulate a reading of *the messages left by others* of graffiti tags, and Fernandez's visual response to these messages, in the form of photographs. In this way, the entangled identities and left messages of tagging enter the discourse of these three works.

12 THROUGH ETCHED GLASS: REPRESENTING URBAN PLACE IN CHRISTINA... 239

Fig. 12.5 Ray Torres of Victory Outreach program speaking with youths in East Los Angeles. August 9 1976. Photograph by Gary Ayala from black and white 35mm negative. University of California, Los Angeles, Library, Department of Special Collections Web site. https://digital.library.ucla.edu/catalog/ark:/21198/zz0002r153 The Regents of the University of California. Licensed under Creative Commons Attribution 4.0 International License. https://creativecommons.org/licenses/by/4.0/

Conclusion

This chapter has attempted to show that the accumulated images of *Lavanderia* assemble narratives in representing the places of specific launderettes and the neighbourhood communities around them, in the

Eastside of Los Angeles. In constructing this view, Agnew's definition of *place*, in which he defines place in terms of three dimensions, has been drawn on. This understanding of place highlights the importance of the histories of the Mexican American and Latino communities of the Eastside neighbourhoods to investigating *Lavanderia*. The analysis has shown that *Lavanderia #1* portrays a unique coming together of place, seen from the street, and that the artist appears to occupy a position of interiority and recognition of a sense of place there and, at the same time, a position at a removal from the customers portrayed as well as the goings on inside the launderette (see Fig. 12.1). By mediating aspects of working class and Mexican American and Latino lived experience in the neighbourhoods, in the early 2000s, the series *Lavanderia* raises questions about belonging, acknowledges struggles, and leaves space for differing concepts of identity.

Furthermore, the investigation has also suggested that Fernandez carries out the complex visual discourse of *Lavanderia #11* (see Fig. 12.2) while occupying a position of distance and removal from the working-class place of the launderette and the community of its customers. Fernandez herself notes that she recognizes the position that she occupies outside the community of the neighbourhoods around the launderettes, represented across the series. In addition, the analysis has shown that the blurred figures of the two customers working to load and unload machines imply identities that are not known in *Lavanderia #2*, paralleling the figures in *Lavanderia #1* and *Lavanderia #11*. What is more, I suggest that the representation of multilingualism through the visibility of the launderette signs and notices as part of the street environment in *Lavanderia #6* articulates a sense of place of this neighbourhood, particularly its richness and complexity (see Fig. 12.3). The analysis has proposed that Fernandez occupies an unsettled position as both insider to the multilingual discourse community, while also existing at some removal from the place of the launderette and the neighbourhood community, in the complex interchange of *Lavanderia #6*. Tagging has been considered a further facet of meaning, bringing its entangled identities and left messages into the complex discourse of the series. It has been argued that when Fernandez made *Lavanderia* in 2002–3, tagging had been a presence for decades in the visual culture of the neighbourhoods the series represents, as Phillips shows (2019) and as Ayala's news photograph demonstrates (see Fig. 12.5). Accordingly, in these works in *Lavanderia*, tagging as a historic element of visual culture in the Eastside is noticed, acknowledged, and responded to.

This analysis has shown that Fernandez's *Lavanderia* is in close dialogue with the specific places of the launderettes and the neighbourhoods in which they are located, with the photographs articulating filaments of everyday life while leaving space for differing ideas of identity and community. What *Lavanderia* does is to construct image narratives around largely indecipherable figures, along with the emphatic identities signified in graffiti tags, spilling out into the street environment at night-time and seen through etched glass. In portraying looking in to the launderettes at night-time, through etched window glass or signs onto illuminated interiors in which people are engaged in the labour of laundering, the series tells eminently visual stories of daily resilience, without accompanying verbal narration, not even descriptive titles, providing a somewhat enigmatic but powerful sense of place of these specific streets in neighbourhoods in the Eastside of Los Angeles.

REFERENCES

Acuña, Rodolfo. 1981. *Occupied America: A History of Chicanos*. 2nd ed. New York: Harper & Row.

Agnew, John A. 2011. Space and Place. In *The Sage Handbook of Geographical Knowledge*, ed. John A. Agnew and David N. Livingstone, 316–330. Thousand Oaks, CA: SAGE.

Benton Museum of Art, Pomona College. 2023. *Christina Fernandez: Under the Sun*. https://www.pomona.edu/museum/exhibitions/2022/christina-fernandez. Accessed 9 Feb 2023.

Brannigan, Sheila. Forthcoming. *Outside the Inside: Shifting Views in Photographs of American Urban Places*. PhD thesis. Nova University of Lisbon.

Brightwell, Eric. 2011. *California Fool's Gold–An Eastside Primer*. March 30. https://ericbrightwell.com/2011/03/30/california-fools-gold-an-eastside-primer/. Accessed 9 Mar 2023.

Campany, David. 2003. *Art and Photography*. London: Phaidon Press Limited.

Chen, Yiyu, and Dana Thomson. 2021. Child Poverty Increased Nationally During COVID, Especially Among Latino and Black Children. *Child Trends*. June 3. https://www.childtrends.org/publications/child-poverty-increased-nationally-during-covid-especially-among-latino-and-black-children. Accessed 15 Mar 2023.

Crenshaw, Kimberlé. 2020. She Coined the Term 'Intersectionality' Over 30 Years Ago. Here's What It Means to Her Today. Interviewed by Katy Steinmetz. *Time*. February 20. https://time.com/5786710/kimberle-crenshaw-intersectionality/. Accessed 12 Sept 2021.

Cresswell, Tim. 2004. *Place: A Short Introduction*. Oxford: Blackwell.
Dominguez, Laura. 2016. Este lugar sí importa: Identity and Heritage Conservation in East Los Angeles. *California History* 93 (3): 52–74.
Ehrig, Stephan, Britta C. Jung, and Gad Schaffer. 2022. Exploring the Transnational Neighbourhood: An Introduction. In *Exploring the Transnational Neighbourhood: Perspectives on Community-Building, Identity and Belonging*, ed. Stephan Ehrig, Britta C. Jung, and Gad Schaffer, 9–34. Leuven: Leuven University Press.
Federal Interagency Forum on Child and Family Statistics. 2021. America's Children: Key National Indicators of Well-Being, 2021. *The Federal Interagency Forum on Child and Family Statistics*. https://www.childstats.gov/americas-children21/eco1.asp. Accessed 15 Mar 2023.
Fernandez, Christina. 2019. Christina Fernandez's *María's Great Expedition*. Interviewed by Lucy Gallun. *The Museum of Modern Art*. May 31. www.moma.org/magazine/articles/75. Accessed 14 May 2023.
———. 2022a. In Conversation with Roberto Tejada. In *Christina Fernandez: Multiple Exposures*, ed. Rebecca Epstein and Joanna Szupinska, 199–211. Los Angeles: UCR ARTS and the UCLA Chicano Studies Research Center Press.
———. 2022b. In Conversation with Susanna V. Temkin. In *Christina Fernandez: Multiple Exposures*, ed. Rebecca Epstein and Joanna Szupinska, 212–214. Los Angeles: UCR ARTS and the UCLA Chicano Studies Research Center Press.
Flores, William V. 2003. New Citizens, New Rights: Undocumented Immigrants and Latino Cultural Citizenship. *Latin American Perspectives* 30 (2): 87–100.
Fountain-Stokes, Lawrence La, Nancy Raquel Mirabal, and Deborah R. Vargas. 2017. *Keywords Latina/o Studies NYU Press*. NYU Press. https://keywords.nyupress.org/latina-latino-studies/introduction/. Accessed 27 July 2022.
Gilroy, Paul. 1993. *The Black Atlantic: Modernity and Double-Consciousness*. London: Verso.
Hall, Stuart. 1999. Looking and Subjectivity: Introduction. In *Visual Culture: The Reader*, ed. Jessica Evans and Stuart Hall, 309–314. Thousand Oaks, CA: SAGE.
Hodgkin, Katharine, and Susannah Radstone. 2003. Introduction: Contested Pasts. In *Contested Pasts: The Politics of Memory*, 1–21. London: Routledge.
Lawler, Stephanie. 2005. Introduction: Class, Culture and Identity. *Sociology* 39 (5): 797–806.
MacGillivray, Laurie, and Margaret Sauceda Curwen. 2007. Tagging as a Social Literacy Practice. *Journal of Adolescent & Adult Literacy* 50 (5): 354–369.
Molina, Natalia. 2014. The Long Arc of Dispossession: Racial Capitalism and Contested Notions of Citizenship in the U.S.-Mexico Borderlands in the Early Twentieth Century. *The Western Historical Quarterly* 45 (4): 431–447.
Muñoz, José Esteban. 2000. Feeling Brown: Ethnicity and Affect in Ricardo Bracho's 'The Sweetest Hangover (And Other STDs)'. *Theatre Journal* 52 (1): 67–79.

———. 2014. Wise Latinas. *Criticism* 56 (2): 249–265.
Myers, Julian. 2022. Nightcleaners Revisited. In *Christina Fernandez: Multiple Exposures*, ed. Rebecca Epstein and Joanna Szupinska, 135–147. UCR ARTS and the UCLA Chicano Studies Research Center Press.
Phillips, Susan A. 2019. *The City Beneath: A Century of Los Angeles Graffiti*. New Haven: Yale University Press.
Rendón, Armando B. 1971. *Chicano Manifesto*. London: Macmillan.
Rivera, Petra R. 2011. Triple Consciousness. *Transition* 105: 156–163.
Rosaldo, Renato. 1996. Foreword. *Stanford Law Review* 48 (5): 1037–1045.
Sassen, Saskia. 2000. Foreword. In *Latino Metropolis*, ed. Victor M. Valle and Rodolfo D. Torres, ix–xiii. Minneapolis: University of Minnesota Press.
Sealy, Mark. 2019. *Decolonising the Camera: Photography in Racial Time*. London: Lawrence and Wishart.
Stein, Sally. 2022. Outside in, Inside Out. In *Christina Fernandez: Multiple Exposures*, ed. Rebecca Epstein and Joanna Szupinska, 111–122. Los Angeles: UCR ARTS and the UCLA Chicano Studies Research Center Press.
Szupinska, Joanna. 2022. Multiple Exposures. In *Christina Fernandez: Multiple Exposures*, ed. Rebecca Epstein and Joanna Szupinska, 13–15. Los Angeles: UCR ARTS and the UCLA Chicano Studies Research Center Press.
Torres, Lourdes. 2007. In the Contact Zone: Code-Switching Strategies by Latino/a Writers. *MELUS* 32 (1): 75–96.
Valle, Victor M., and Rodolfo D. Torres. 2000. *Latino Metropolis*. Minneapolis: University of Minnesota Press.
Villa, Raúl Homero. 1999. Ghosts in the Growth Machine: Critical Spatial Consciousness in Los Angeles Chicano. *Social Text* 58: 111–131.
Water and Power Associates Corporation. n.d. Zanja Madre: LA's Original Aqueduct. *Water and Power Associates.* https://waterandpower.org/museum/Zanja%20Madre%20(Original%20LA%20Aqueduct).html. Accessed 31 Mar 2023.

CHAPTER 13

The Artwork in Geological Time

Roger Davis

INTRODUCTION

This chapter examines three future-oriented conceptual or artistic projects that struggle with the problem of representing human experience and human existence through geological time measured in centuries, millennia, and beyond. Before considering the future, the analysis will begin with Edward Burtynsky's documentary photographs and films that illustrate how human industrialization has visually marked or scarred the Earth itself. Humans have not only altered the surface of the planet but also mined its depths and influenced its regulatory systems. After using Burtynsky to establish the visual history and traces of industrialism, the chapter considers Cedric Blaisbois' short film *Autocannibalism* (2018) as a mixed-media and temporal pivot from the past to the future. Framed as if viewed on a cellphone, the film contrasts local nightlife with geopolitical tensions during an evening in Caracas, Venezuela. The chapter then analyzes three projects concerned with the uncertainties of our human future. First, perhaps the shortest-term project is Katie Paterson's *Future Library* (2014), which is collecting 100 texts from 100 different artists over 100

R. Davis (✉)
Red Deer Polytechnic, Red Deer, AB, Canada
e-mail: roger.davis@rdpolytech.ca

© The Author(s), under exclusive license to Springer Nature Switzerland AG 2024
D. Callahan (ed.), *Visual Storytelling in the 21st Century*,
https://doi.org/10.1007/978-3-031-65487-9_13

years, with plans to publish them all at end of the project in 2114. Second, *Earth's Black Box* (2022) is a nascent project that will attempt to catalogue nearly all ongoing and future digital publications and data about climate change and environmental science. Third, the Onkalo facility in Finland plans to bury, to seal off, and to forget Finland's nuclear waste.

These three projects are all concerned with how humanity will manage, document, and visually represent its current history to the future: through art, through data, through half-life decay of waste. Moreover, the projects are all situated in supposedly geologically stable locations to ensure their endurance into the future: Norway, Tasmania, and Finland, respectively. The argument is that the conceptual principles of these projects rely on the artwork–broadly conceived–to do the difficult labour of recognizing, understanding, interpreting, and acting on climate change, yet they defer the labour into the future. Functioning almost like time capsules, these projects are repositories of information that will be opened (or not) at some future point for consideration and analysis. In this way, they are projects that defer judgement, whether final or provisional, to the future, while simultaneously inviting speculative judgement from the contemporary audience about the purposes and potential effects of the projects. As humanity struggles with political questions around practical action on climate change, these projects stand back as relatively disinterested observers that collect, manage, and represent–in multiple ways–the often-frenetic anxieties surrounding the anticipated catastrophes of the Anthropocene.

These works engage in visual storytelling because they attempt to narrate or to represent the present human situation to some imagined future audience, often through conventional forms like the novel or through alternative modalities like visual symbols or data sets. They struggle with or question the appropriate forms for expression. The projects participate in what Mahlu Mertens and Stef Craps call "prospective archaeology" as a defining feature of the Anthropocene: "it will only be detectable as a geological stratum after humans have ceased to exist" (Mertens and Craps 2018, 135). The imagined future audience may be human, inhuman, or even non-existent. The artworks face an existential crisis in that they may not even be perceived, thereby embodying humanity's own existential crisis. While Mertens and Craps choose novels for their analysis of the Anthropocene and geological time, they are aware of the constraints of the form, much like Amitav Ghosh's arguments in *The Great Derangement*. According to Ghosh, the contemporary novel struggles to render accurate representations of climate change precisely because the usual punctuations of major events like storms or droughts overshadow or obfuscate the very incremental and barely perceptible environmental shifts of the ubiquitous changes of climate and environment (Ghosh 2016). In other words, despite the novel's formal abilities to render the seemingly most minute details of human history and human psychology, it has yet to find, according to Ghosh, consistent or noticeable ways to register the slow creep of geological time and climate change. Despite Katie Paterson's possibility for contributors to include the novel genre in her *Future Library*, none of the projects under analysis in this paper is novelistic in form, and each work functions as a repository of deferred information.

Mertens and Craps note that their "prospective archaeology" will occur "after the total destruction of the archive" (Mertens and Craps 2018, 135), yet the works discussed here aim to persist into the future despite knowing the potential future destruction of the archive: they hope to escape destruction. In acknowledging and perhaps overcoming their denial of the collapse of civilization, these artworks move from denial and into deferral. Unable to find convincing ways to solve current problems and survive in the present, these works invest their energies into creating ways to archive their knowledge and defer its analysis until some specified or unspecified time. The great repressed hope is that the future archaeologist will be able to explain why humanity failed, despite most critical and scientific minds already having the understanding that humanity's problems likely exist in a nexus of insatiable energy needs, irresponsible resource extraction, and compromised political will.

Imre Szeman has identified three primary strategies that facilitate a lack of action: strategic realism, techno-utopianism, and apocalyptic environmentalism. Strategic realism largely accepts a status quo future of industrial capitalism with the bleak recognition that life will become more difficult and resources will become more scarce. Techno-utopianism believes that technology will save the day with a "just in time" (Szeman 2019, 103) intervention in the near future. Apocalyptic environmentalism is perhaps the most realistic, but it paints a grim future picture of pollution, conflict, and disease. For Szeman, none of these perspectives offers hope for the radical change that is needed, such as a complete transformation of the energy economy. Rather than working on the necessary changes that Szeman calls for, the projects in this chapter catalogue their accomplishments–good or bad–for some future archaeologist to unpack. While Szeman argues that our thinking should likely change now, these artworks arguably reserve some of their contents and capacity for change to future archaeologists.

Edward Burtynsky: From *Manufactured Landscapes* to Uncertain Timescapes

Edward Burtynsky is a Canadian photographer who documents large-scale human industrial projects such as open pit mines, hydroelectric dams, oil fields, and agricultural regions. He uses the term "Manufactured Landscapes" to describe the ways in which human activity has altered the face of the Earth, the face of nature. He states that he works with an inverted notion of the Romantic sublime. Burtynsky himself comments in a filmed interview: "Now, Nature's been diminished… We've released another kind of sublime, the industrial sublime… We are dwarfed in our own creation, of industrial creation. So, we are… small workers in a massive theatre." He continues, "We are now the force of nature to be feared" (Burtynsky 2014, "Photographer Spotlight"). Where the Romantics saw nature as a threatening and wondrous force stronger than humanity, Burtynsky's photographs show how humanity has since come to dominate and alter the natural landscape in almost incomprehensible ways. Moreover, not only has humanity extracted natural resources, but it has also usurped nature's sublime power. The mechanical and chemical transformations of the landscape hold a sublime beauty based not in nature but as a result of human industrial development, and many critics have observed this in Burtynsky's work. Ann Donar has attributed Burtynsky's sublimity to "Aesthetic Openness" (Donar 2010, 63) to reflect the vast scale of the landscapes. Rod Giblett says Burtynsky's sublime represents "an empty now and a terrifying prospect" (Giblett 2009, 786) to draw out the awe-inspiring effect of the sublime. Cynthia Haveson Veloric has noted how Burtynsky's photographs fit into a subgenre of "the *toxic sublime* or the *industrial sublime*" (Veloric 2021, 30, emphasis in original), moving it away from natural origins and towards manufactured product. Borrowed from Jennifer Peeples, the term "toxic sublime" clarifies the problems of these industrial landscapes because it aestheticizes the very real hazards of the wastelands in Burtynsky's photographs (Patchett 2012, 145). Moreover, it engages in the aesthetic disinterestedness that defines the sublime in Kant's *Critique of Judgment* (Kant 1987). Partly, it is the tension between disinterestedness and awe that facilitates the thesis of this chapter: stunned by the magnitude of the scale of the Anthropocene, some artworks register an aesthetic engagement, but defer it into the future, often to a disappearing horizon beyond the human.

Three documentary films have been made about Burtynsky's work by the team of Jennifer Baichwal, Nicholas de Pencier and Burtynsky himself (*Manufactured Landscapes* 2006, *Watermark* 2013, and *Anthropocene: The Human Epoch*, 2018, the latter of which which will not be discussed here). The opening scene of the first film, *Manufactured Landscapes*, has a roughly nine-minute pan shot of an assembly line plant in China that shows row after row of near-identical workers. The insistent repetition of sameness invokes a sense of tedium for the viewer who may wonder just how far the factory can stretch. After cutting from the pan shot, the film shows two photographs for contrast: one of the rows from inside the factory; one of assembled workers from outside the factory. The photograph of the assembly plant mirrors the photograph of the assembled workers outside, blurring the distinction between mechanical production and human organisms. The factory itself requires the assembly of the biological, organic workers outside, waiting to begin their work shifts: workers assemble for assembly work. Yet, Burtynsky frames these atomized workers as part of an almost incomprehensible globalized supply chain system, where the contrast between worker and system is vertiginous. About his work on the landscapes, Burtynsky says, "This is what it is" (Burtynsky 2014) to reinforce the documentary and artistic elements rather than positive or negative judgments he or others may make about these places and projects. Burtynsky frequently refrains from overtly politicizing his work, preferring to leave it up to the viewer to draw conclusions. Perhaps he is also careful to remember that his work generally requires permission to access these industrial sites.

In the second documentary film, *Watermark*, Burtynsky asks: "How does water shape us? And, how do we shape water?" The work is about reciprocal human—ecosystem interaction, and it opens with images of thunderous, cascading waters through Xiaolangdi hydroelectric dam in China (Munteanu 2014). It then abruptly cuts to a scene of dry, cracked earth. The location is the Colorado River Delta in Mexico that has run dry because the US has diverted the water at multiple, upstream points. The contrast between the immense energy of the dam and the barrenness of the dry delta encourages the viewer to imagine the human infrastructure of water diversion, damming, extraction, or irrigation. It suggests that the fate of the full Xiaolangdi is perhaps similar to the mighty and once-full

Hoover dam on the Colorado River, which has been depleted over decades through hydroelectric generation, agricultural irrigation, human consumption, and droughts resulting from climate change. The film also offers some brief contrasting examples of generally sustainable harvesting practices that have existed for centuries, such as rice paddies in the Yunnan province and some examples of relatively egalitarian fishing villages.

The awesome spectacle of Burtynsky's photographs shows how the history of human industrial projects reveals an ever-increasing burden on the environment. For example, he photographs twelfth-century water wells in Rajasthan that have run dry because of climate change and aquifer depletion from more modern wells. He documents the receding glaciers in the Stikine River Watershed in northern Canada and the United States (Alaska). He explains the ecological and political problems associated with the diversion of water from the Owens River for the needs of Los Angeles. The non-linear and exponential growth of many industrial projects requires that increasingly extractive projects be built to satisfy human needs. Burtynsky's photographs and films capture the waste, depletion, and other consequences of industrial progress.

Cedric Blaisbois's *Autocannibalism*

Burtynsky comments that "if we destroy nature, we destroy ourselves," which sets up a transition to Cedric Blaisbois's short film *Autocannibalism*. *Autocannibalism* is an appropriate metaphor for human industrial progress, where we devour and exhaust all the accessible resources on the planet. When we have no more natural resources, in Malthusian fashion we may turn on each other in cannibalistic hunger. After we have devoured each other, there is nobody else to devour but ourselves. The insatiable hunger of human progress appears to inevitably turn in on itself. After all, the original taboo of cannibalism, really, is the fear of eating our own species, the fear of eating ourselves.

Autocannibalism is a 19-minute short film that presents itself as if viewed on a cell phone, confined by the frame of the handheld device. Shot as a real-time movie represented on or through the cell phone screen (not shot through the cell phone camera), multiple cell phone applications interrupt the expected formal conventions of film. While the opening image of the film is an idyllic tropical beach photo of Cayo de Agua in Venezuela—something perhaps reminiscent of a holiday getaway where one might disengage from phones and the labour of daily life—the film itself is a frantic depiction of the violent life in Caracas, Venezuela. The stock image of the peaceful beach invokes our imagined spaces of relaxation and safety, and it freezes these holiday-goers in an idealized place forever, one which many people may never experience. A close examination of the photograph reveals that every group in the photograph has a person holding a camera. The stock image—as background, as wallpaper—suggests the deceptive ease with which cell phone users can escape to an imaginary and constructed paradise while simultaneously being immersed in the real, daily life of a violent urban environment. The bulk of the film displaces our comfortable expectations of passive film viewership with a barrage of competing messages, notifications, application changes, keyboard screens, service lags, dying battery warnings, and device shut-offs that are meant to remind of us our frenetic lives mediated through our phones.

The film's general trajectory begins with a group of youthful partygoers who experience a kidnapping of one of their female members and a subsequent probable murder of one of their male members. We see the intimacy of Noeli, the filmmaker's girlfriend, sending erotic photos and invitations to him against the unfolding violence of the night and the interruptions of globalized life, the conditions that prohibit, disrupt, or destroy these familiar and intimate spaces. Moreover, the images are gestures toward internet pornography, and they challenge the legitimacy or authenticity of the intimacy. The screen of the cell phone transmits media images of street violence, political violence, and sexual violence that can be read against going to a party, a night of friendship and camaraderie, and a call from your partner. This raises further questions about the qualities of friendships that exist on online social media platforms.

The film ends with an encounter with corrupt police who stop the group for routine questioning and harassment, only to end up murdering them, including the diegetic filmmaker. The now-cracked cellphone screen shows the policeman levelling a gun at the filmmaker alongside the pleading Whatsapp message from Noeli to her lover, apologizing that "todo es mi culpa" or "everything is my fault." The totalizing statement of Noeli is meant to be understood in the intimate space of two lovers trying to reconcile a disagreement, but when represented over the brutal murder of her lover the viewer cannot help but recognize the tensions between these intimate spaces and the larger urban and globalized world. Blaisbois' setting choice of the cell phone screen emphasizes technology's ability to compress the expanse of geopolitical conflict and intimate conflict into the few square centimeters of a screen. It is as if every action—whether foreign, domestic, public, or intimate—carries the same importance or weight. Even the construction of cell phones themselves represent the increasing global needs for diminishing rare materials: they are a symptom of the ubiquity of personal cellphone use contrasted with the globalized extraction of natural resources. Where Burtynsky documents the broad accumulation and slow violence (Nixon 2011) of industrialism through expansive photographs about landscape, Blaisbois captures the immediate violence of the "now" with all its competing demands for attention, desire, survival: the claustrophobic space of a screen of multiple subjects and applications. Burtynsky is the slow accumulation of the past manifesting in sublime scarring; Blaisbois is the immediate release of the present manifesting in chaotic destruction.

While the contrast between Blaisbois' immediate "now" and Burtynsky's centuries-long documentary view is meant to create a sense of temporal scale, the contrast collapses when considered alongside geological time. Modern human history of two-hundred thousand years barely registers in the scale of geological time that spans roughly 4.5 billion years. The three projects that constitute the remainder of the analysis for this chapter invoke timelines that project into the future. The timelines range from a century to hundreds of millennia, yet none of them explicitly tackles the genuine scale of geological time of billions of years. This limitation points to the human struggle to conceptualize the sublime timescape of an open-ended future. While modern science informs us that the Earth will eventually be destroyed, these projects compress human imagination into conceptually manageable timeframes. As humans wrestle with questions of climate change and the Anthropocene, the terrifying edges of the sublime perhaps inevitably limit the imaginative horizon to human problems, and these artworks are arguably unable to grapple meaningfully with a non-human future. However, they nonetheless attempt to engage with questions of how human artworks might conceivably interact with a non-human sentient future or even simply with time and land themselves.

All of these projects are geographically located in geologically stable locations. These locations speak to each project's desire to endure through time as a physical entity. That is, faced with climate change and human extinction, these projects manifest their anxiety about the longevity of the artwork. They want to persist, to be visible, for some future imagined audience, whether or not that audience is human or even possible. If William Butler Yeats wrote about art building "monuments of its own magnificence," these projects—as products of the toxic sublime or, more generally, the Anthropocene—we might read as "monuments of our own malfeasance." Faced with the prospect of the collapse of civilization, these projects ask whether or not they can endure beyond any future catastrophic events.

THE FUTURE LIBRARY

Begun in 2014 and located in Oslo, Norway, Katie Paterson's *The Future Library* solicits a single, written manuscript from a different notable author annually for 100 years. The manuscripts are housed at the Oslo Public Library (completed in 2019) in "The Silent Room," where select viewers can sit quietly and contemplate the project. However, no one knows anything about the works other than the authors and the titles. A forest of trees has been planted outside of Oslo, and these trees will be harvested at the end of the century, pulped for paper, and used to publish the manuscripts. In doing so, the project attempts to appear to be ecologically sustainable by growing its own resources for production. The project invites speculation about the future of our planet and its readers in a hundred years and whether or not artists of the present day have anything to offer through their works. The project is a visual paradox because it simultaneously announces and displays the physical holdings of its texts, yet it prohibits any detailed knowledge of them and delays their unveiling to a future date. One of the primary functions of the project is to delay the transmission of the texts' written messages. Simultaneously, it generates a wealth of speculative writing about both the texts' and the project's effects.

Formally, *The Future Library* is similar to at least three familiar modes of communication: a message in a bottle, the time capsule, and the safety deposit box. First, a message in a bottle is frequently (although not exclusively) a hopeful plea to be rescued, and this is one ecological motivation for the project. Paterson has commented that "Norway has a futuristic long-term view of climate change and environment: this was one of the key reasons to create this project there" (Leuzzi and Sbrilli 2018, 77). Stressing the hopeful nature of the project, Paterson is well aware that almost nobody currently living will be around to be saved from climate change in a hundred years. Rather, she hopes one effect of the project will serve to remind people that the entirety of the planet—like a globalized version of the desert island castaway—is in need of saving. Resources are becoming scarce, and there appears to be no clear means of escape.

Understood as a message in a bottle, *The Future Library* might provide a glimpse into the final moments and location of a civilization that finds itself beyond saving.

Second, and perhaps most obviously, this project functions like a time capsule, and it invites future judgements about its contents. Given that Margaret Atwood was the first author to contribute to the Library, it is worth noting that she has published a short story called "Time Capsule Found on the Dead Planet" that chronicles the broad stages of the collapse of civilization (Atwood 2011). William E. Jarvis explains the scope of time capsules as ranging from a few artifacts for a short duration to comprehensive overviews of a civilization sealed off for a significant period of time. While many time capsules may be simple cornerstones of buildings containing only a few curiosities, Jarvis points to Thornwell Jacob's ambitious *Crypt of Civilization* that attempts to catalogue human history up to the twentieth century. It was completed and sealed in 1940 and is not set to be open until 8113, some 6000 years in the future (Jarvis 1992, 284). *The Future Library* lies somewhere in between, with a relatively short lifespan but a potentially rich deposit of artworks. Yet, as Jarvis points out: "Even archives must be interpreted, however, and one can do so in an endless variety of ways" (Jarvis 1992, 290). Not only is there a robust discussion of art, politics, and climate change today, but also this project speculates about how the future of a likely climate-ravaged planet will respond to our contemporary actions and inactions, our selections and omissions, our successes and failures. As Jeffery R. Di Leo points out, a contemporary view back at the 1914 zeitgeist reveals that James Joyce was a marginal figure and D. H. Lawrence was about to be banned for obscenity. He asks whether or not these artists would have been included in a similar project during that era. He also notes that many popular authors at that time have faded into obscurity or irrelevance. Paterson also addresses this, stating that "[w]e hope that the project encompasses many different languages and cultures, established and younger authors" (Leuzzi and Sbrilli 2018, 75). Much of this project rests on hope, and nobody can predict how current commitments to diversity, equity, and inclusion will persist or transform in the next century.

Di Leo introduces the third formal comparison to a safety deposit box. Working from his interpretation of the value of artworks, Di Leo points out that deposit boxes exist in the context of banking, economics, and capitalism. Just as one cannot reasonably predict the market forces of capitalism, the same argument holds for selecting *bankable* writers that may have a meaningful voice in a hundred years. Even if the artistic or other cultural values are unknowable now, there are features of Paterson's project that undoubtedly participate in capitalist practices. For example, Di Leo notes that people can purchase a future copy of the 1000 first editions of *The Future Library*. Not only does this fund the project (which perhaps speaks to the lack of sufficient public or other funds to see the project through), but it also trades in the economic investment in art. Purchasing a first edition speculates on the value of this rare commodity, fetishizes the first edition, and secures a hereditary token for a future generation to claim (a token likely stored in a safety deposit box). This project participates in canon formation of a particular kind (the notoriety of being included in this project) as well as the potential academic opportunities of accessing, assessing, and studying these works. It seems that authors are not financially compensated for their labour in producing a book for the project. According to Merve Emre, the texts are a "donation" (Emre 2018) to the project. Yet, if we imagine a worst-case scenario of climate change in a century, the trees meant to be pulped for printing may be more valuable as fuel to be burned, logs for building shelter, filters for the air, or material for some other purpose in 2114. People's attitudes towards natural resources such as subsequent growth forest may be radically different than what Paterson imagines for the library.

The Future Library establishes a curious relationship between the artwork and time. As Di Leo mentions, what would the current state of our contemporary literature be if some of the great texts like "The Love Song of J. Alfred Prufrock" or *Metamorphosis* were never published but deferred for a century? (Di Leo 2015, 30) Some artists are often characterized as being "ahead of their time," yet this project makes that literally true in a somewhat melancholic or even tragic way: nobody will experience these particular works for decades to come. What artist wilfully silences their work, especially an emerging or unknown artist? Do we not need to hear our artists now, in this moment? For an emerging author, is their inclusion in this project a legitimizing move for their career? Is the delay of an artwork akin to the stories of authors ordering their manuscripts and letters burned upon their death or locking up their estate for one or two generations? And, while some artists intentionally create works to be destroyed as part of their *raison d'etre*, *The Future Library* is a monumental exercise in delayed gratification. It is tempting to re-write Ozymandias's famous proclamation: "Look on my Works, ye Mighty, and despair" that you did not know of them sooner. The view, at least of the cultural monuments, will not be "boundless and bare" but bountiful and bookish. The physical environment may well have arrived at the same desolation as in Shelley's poem, however (Shelley 1818).

Earth's Black Box

If the *Future Library*, in part, promises a creative surplus in the future, *Earth's Black Box* offers a future forensic analysis of our collective failures (Earth's Black Box 2023; Glue Society 2023). Managed and promoted by Australian media and advertising agency Clemenger BBDO, in collaboration with the University of Tasmania, an artist collective called the Glue Society (Thompson 2022), and the groups Room 11 and Revolver, *Earth's Black Box* is named after the flight recorder that all aeroplanes carry (and which was invented by David Warren, who went to school in Tasmania), but that only becomes of social interest when an aeroplane crashes. The function of this Black Box is to record geophysical data about climate change as well as news media relevant to our changing planet. It is both an open and sealed time capsule. Open to schools and universities to facilitate learning about climate breakdown, as a repository of data, it is also meant to persist through time, indefinitely, for any future lifeform to discover and interpret our moment in cultural and geological history. With no set date for opening, the project assumes its relevance after the catastrophic collapse of our present civilization and may offer insight as to why the plane crashed. Unlike the well-wrought urn approach of a great artwork sealed in a library vault, *Earth's Black Box* relies on vast amounts of available data to function as a cumulative record of 500 metrics related to human and planetary health (Glue Society). The hypothesis is that future generations will be able to sort and to analyze the data to map the decline and collapse of civilization. This is predicated on the assumption that any future generations have the sensory, intellectual, and technological capabilities to read and decipher the data. However, in the frame of anthropocentric or geological time, there may not be humans around to experience this monument. Whether or not other lifeforms may experience the monument is simply part of the unknowable, speculative nature of this project.

The visual appearance of the project resembles the monoliths from Stanley Kubrick's *2001* (Kubrick 1968), which invokes the question of two types of intelligence: that of the primates and that of the aliens, except the "alien" knowledge here is from a past, failed society. Or, if the *Voyager* spacecraft is humanity's message in a bottle to communicate with alien species across space and time, *Earth's Black Box* is the terrestrial equivalent of *Voyager*, except to communicate with a future time and community on Earth. But, unlike a message in a bottle or a time capsule, it is more of a conceptual art piece because it functions solely to collect data. It does not participate in the creative genius of the Romantic artist tradition like *The Future Library*, nor does it house any artistic masterpieces or contemporary objects (other than its own construction and technology). It speaks to the transition between the third and fourth industrial revolutions between data and creativity, as if enough data and connectivity will yield unforeseen creative explanations to the questions humanity cannot currently answer. Or, perhaps given enough time with a practically limitless set of data, human primates will pound out not the works of William Shakespeare but a solution to, or explanation of, climate catastrophe. It embodies Szeman's techno-utopianism but only in retroactive understanding of our failed human civilization; it does not save us as much as explain us: Mertens and Craps's "prospective archaeology." The primary drawback is the project's reliance on the promise that enough data will reveal insight into the human and ecological conditions of our time, so that it does not engage in the difficult qualitative work of analysis in order to find a solution. The problem is supposedly political, not statistical or theoretical. The project seems already to draw its conclusion: like a crashing plane, there is little to be done at this point except to hope that the flight recorder is operational in order to facilitate post-mortem analysis.

Earth's Black Box differs from a time capsule in one other very important way: rather than offering a carefully curated set of representative items, the Box's data gathering functions more like a tool of surveillance. Given that the box is both closed and open, the designers hope that it will serve as a contemporary resource of information, much like any university library system with books and periodical subscriptions, yet it remains unclear from the online publicity materials how this particular approach is different or preferable from existing systems of data gathering and information analysis. As already stated, it performs aggregation rather than analysis. Moreover, the box does not necessarily *conceal* any information like *The Future Library*. Both projects store information: the *Box*'s contents are known, while the *Library*'s contents are unknown, yet both are on display as closed and concealing storehouses. Although the *Box* briefly suggests that humanity may steer away from climate catastrophe, it makes the statement that "[o]nly one thing is certain, your actions, inactions, and interactions are now being recorded" (Earth's). This somewhat ominous statement implies that the forensic post-apocalyptic capabilities of the *Black Box* are a manifestation of repressed human knowledge about the Anthropocene: we are killing off the Earth's systems, but only a future analysis will reveal how humanity allowed this to occur. Again, such is "prospective archaeology."

One final comparison is in order. *Earth's Black Box*, as a large monolith in the Tasmanian wilderness, bears a peculiar resemblance to the black boxes many people carry around daily: the cell phone. Cell phones have similar data gathering and access abilities in real time, yet they lack the storage capacity of the Black Box. In this way, *Earth's Black Box* shares similarities to Blaisbois' *Autocannibalism*. Where Blaisbois' film focuses on the immediate experience of clashing global data sets in real time, *Earth's Black Box* stores these interactions across a longer timeframe but without Blaisbois's critical sensibilities. However, when measured in geological time, both *Autocannibalism* and *Earth's Black Box* are reduced to ephemera. *Autocannibalism* recognizes this self-consciously through its own performative self-destruction at the film's conclusion; *Earth's Black Box* wishes to persist through time indefinitely.

Onkalo: *Into Eternity*

As reported by the Australian Broadcasting Corporation (Kilvert 2021), Earth's Black Box began its archival mission to coincide with the COP26 conference and its principles in Glasgow in 2021. One of the commitments of the conference was "to rapidly scale up our deployment of clean power generation and energy efficient measures in our economies" (Japan Beyond Coal 2021). The link between energy and economy is one of the defining features of the Anthropocene crisis. Fuels for human use have become increasingly energy intensive: from wood, to coal, to oil, to nuclear. With each successive stage, however, the harmful waste products are equally intensive, from CO_2 emissions, to methane, to nuclear waste. The age of renewables and "clean power" mark humanity's attempt to change this trajectory of waste production, and it comes with a similar reduction in energy intensity. Michael Madsen's film *Into Eternity* (Madsen 2010) documents the construction of Finland's nuclear waste storage facility, Onkalo, and ponders the very distant future in terms of nuclear half-life decay. More than *The Future Library* or *Earth's Black Box*, *Into Eternity* imagines a radically altered human future—even a non-human future—on the scale of 100,000 years or more. Exponential human consumption of energy is creating a similar exponential era of long-term waste. The cost of immediate energy abundance is millennia of waste management.

The rationale for Onkalo is to protect future generations from the danger of nuclear radiation by building a subterranean tunnel system that will house nuclear waste in the bedrock for over one hundred thousand years. Two of the film's central debates are whether or not to mark or even to remember the site and whether or not anyone will (or should) ever open up the vault. Unlike a time capsule or a safety-deposit box, Onkalo is, arguably never to be opened because of its toxic contents. Where *The Future Library* holds creative work and *Earth's Black Box* holds supposedly objective data, Onkalo holds nothing desirable but toxic waste. Katie Paterson has discussed the *Library* in terms of the gift economy (Leuzzi and Sbrilli 2018), yet Onkalo operates more like a curse.

The various governmental, policy, engineering, and cultural offices that contribute to Onkalo generally assume that it has little to no identifiable future value. Perhaps future beings could find in it some value that humans cannot understand or realize. For example, the film asks whether or not the toxic radiation can be harnessed as an energy source. The film explains that this is theoretically possible, but humans have no technology to do so now. It is worth noting that the technology to harness nuclear energy emerged only in the mid-twentieth century, and future technology may be able to accomplish this. This speaks to the contemporary era's general assumption that the future will be more technologically advanced than the present, which may not be the case, given climate change and environmental degradation. Moreover, the supposition is that nuclear waste can still be used for energy production, which likely says more about contemporary energy needs than about any future value system around nuclear waste. Or, as Brent R. Bellamy has pointed out, there may be future creatures who perhaps can coexist with nuclear radiation, beings for whom it is not toxic and possibly benign or even productive (Bellamy 2014). The film also suggests that future beings may simply be curious about Onkalo, much as humans are curious about the pyramids of Giza or other archaeological sites, and both future beings and contemporary humans may simply ignore the warnings of curses posted at these burial sites, a testament to the failure of communication across millennia.

The film wrestles with the possibility of creating a symbol system that can communicate across such a long time. The various professionals consider physical "markers" like obelisks as well as symbolic representations like thorns, chaotic scenes, and even Edvard Munch's *The Scream*. But, when faced with non-human entities, the possibilities for visual storytelling become highly problematic. How do we communicate with something that may not even recognize our symbolic systems? What are the perceptual systems and capabilities of a non-human future across geological time? Modern humans have existed for roughly 200,000 years, and our oldest discovered examples of human art supposedly date as far back as Neanderthal cave paintings from 60,000 years ago (Hoffman et al. 2018). While this gives some hope for the ability of visual art to persist through time and even across humanoid species, it reveals little about the interpretive possibilities of future encounters for a nuclear waste facility. While Onkalo imagines a future timeframe that is roughly equivalent to the entirety of modern human evolutionary history, it is more likely that our undesirable waste products will persist with greater success than our symbolic or communicative enterprises. Our desires may be to communicate the remarkable monuments of human magnificence, but the ultimate communication will be made of persistent nuclear radiation, ubiquitous plastic, and a carbon-choked atmosphere. This marks a return to Burtynsky's artistic documentaries of human waste.

Ironically, Onkalo is also a story about forgetting and invisibility. If nuclear power is desirable precisely because it is a carbonless alternative for fossil fuels, the Onkalo story is decidedly grounded in our energy crisis. Although carbon dioxide and other gases have created our atmospheric climate crisis, the nuclear radiation from uranium constitutes a different ecological crisis, one not manifested in climatic storms and sea-level rise. Rather, it potentially rests in biological disease, poison, and genetic mutation and degradation. Yet both greenhouse gases and nuclear radiation are invisible to the human eye. Our only registers of these threats are in the technological devices designed to measure them and in the climatic or human effects of catastrophe, disease, and breakdown. For how long can we ignore invisible things we know to exist? Will we be able to forget those forces that threaten to remain with us for millennia? Will our efforts to forget force us to include traces of these effects in our oral and visual traditions of storytelling? Perhaps the most we can hope for is that Onkalo's best story is the story it never tells. The visual story of Onkalo is essentially about industrial infrastructure as it relates to the energy economy. Onkalo is a sophisticated mine that returns the transformed material to its terrestrial origin. If Burtynsky's photographs document the damage of industrial extraction, Onkalo attempts to redress or reclaim this damage, despite burying a toxic secret below the surface. By contemplating the potential stories we do or do not tell to the future, is it a gift to the future that this story attempts to remove from visual access what it is telling us, a story so destructive that it may only be pointed to but not shown?

Conclusion

These three projects are all future orientated. They are all in geologically stable locations, and they all rely on different types of information to be communicated in differing forms to the future: Paterson's artworks, the Black Box's data, Onkalo's waste and silence. It is perhaps unsurprising that in a time of geopolitical turmoil and climate crisis, conceptual artists turn to the stability of geology and art to find a sense of place for humans in the future. Yet these projects all work with the concept of delay, where the works themselves are not completed at this point in time: they require a future time of completion, even if that future time is uncertain, due to environmental crisis. Similarly, the most energy-intensive nuclear project is the one that may require the greatest effort to contain it; the youngest source of energy may have the longest geological footprint. If the greatest energy benefit comes with the greatest risk, reflecting on this should inform us about how to view our excessive reliance on energy and resources.

As the term "Anthropocene" suggests, humans have fundamentally altered the geophysical balance of the planet. These projects mark a variety of attempts to grapple with our own existence within the frame of our relatively recent discovery of the scale of geological time. Our seemingly insatiable uses and misuses of energy have transformed the planet into something unfamiliar and threatening, and the sublime has returned not as natural beauty but as industrialized catastrophe. I suggest that these artworks all leave a considerable amount of energy and labour to the future to discover and interpret, partly because humans struggle to comprehend geological time. The artworks become the hopeful, if precarious, visual and aesthetic traces of our exhausted, or more accurately insufficient, attempts to alter the course of human cultural and industrial progress.

As artistic projects that consider past, present, and future events of ecological damage and environmental collapse, the works discussed in this chapter engage in at least two types of visualization: first, an imaginative visualization of a speculative future that cannot be known; second, a visual rendering of that future in the contemporary artwork. Although Burtynsky works partially within familiar documentary conventions, his photographs' sublime affects compel the viewer to consider not only the past and present visual markings upon the landscape but also the planetary ecological impacts of future actions at the limits of human imagination in spans of geological time. These works do not follow normal or familiar artistic conventions, which gestures to their ongoing struggle to find visual and narrative forms to represent the uncharted terrain of global climate change. Blaisbois's filmic inventiveness showcases the overabundance of visual imagery that bombards us daily, which highlights both their quotidian banality and their geopolitical urgency. The projects of Paterson, Earth's Black Box, and Madsen attempt to organize the proliferation of images and information into coherent maps for some future "prospective archaeology" that may never materialize. Notwithstanding the catastrophic and apocalyptic contexts of these artworks, they all encapsulate the human impulse to continue to create meanings through narrative and visual responses to the questions that demand responses and actions. Whether or not anyone or anything is present to view, to experience, or to interpret them in the future remains to be seen.

REFERENCES

Atwood, Margaret. 2011. Time Capsule Found on the Dead Planet. In *I'm with the Bears: Short Stories from a Damaged Planet*, ed. Mark Martin, 191–193. London: Verso.

Baichwal, Jennifer (Director). 2006. *Manufactured Landscapes*. [Film]. National Film Board of Canada.

——— (Director). 2013. *Watermark*. [Film]. Mongrel Media.

Bellamy, Brent R. 2014. *Into Eternity*: On our Waste Containments and Energy Futures. *Paradoxa* 26: 145–158.

Blaisbois, Cedric (Director). 2018. *Autocannibalism*. [Short Film]. Cineburo.

Burtynsky, Edward. 2014. Photographer Spotlight: Edward Burtynsky. [Short Film]. *LA Review of Books*. April 25. https://www.youtube.com/watch?v=6Guy90qPKCU. Accessed 25 Mar 2023.

Di Leo, Jeffery R. 2015. Future Readers. *American Book Review* 36 (5): 2–30.

Donar, Ann. 2010. An Appreciation and Analysis of Edward Burtynsky-*Manufactured Landscapes*: A Film by Jennifer Baichwal. *Canadian Review of Art Education–Revue canadienne d'éducation artistique* 37: 57–71.

Earth's Black Box. 2023. *Earth's Black Box*. [Website]. https://www.earthsblackbox.com/. Accessed 22 Mar 2023.

Emre, Merve. 2018. This Library Has New Books by Major Authors, But They Can't Be Read Until 2114. *New York Times*. November 1. https://www.nytimes.com/2018/11/01/t-magazine/future-library-books.htm. Accessed 22 Mar 2023.

Ghosh, Amitav. 2016. *The Great Derangement: Climate Change and the Unthinkable*. Chicago: University of Chicago Press.

Giblett, Rod. 2009. Terrifying Prospects and Resources of Hope: Minescapes, Timescapes and the Aesthetics of the Future. *Continuum: Journal of Media & Cultural Studies* 23 (6): 781–789.

Glue Society. Earth's Black Box. 2023. https://web.archive.org/web/20220216063506/; https://gluesociety.com/work/ebb1-earths-black-box/. Accessed 22 Mar 2023.

Haveson Veloric, Cynthia. 2021. Aesthetic and Industrial Rupture in the Work of Edward Burtynsky and Justin Brice Guariglia. *Afterimage* 48 (1): 28–36.

Hoffman, D.L., et al. 2018. U-Th Dating of Carbonate Crusts Reveals Neanderthal Origin of Iberian Cave Art. *Science* 357 (6378): 912–915.

Japan Beyond Coal. 2021. COP 26: Global Coal to Clean Power Statement. *Japan Beyond Coal*. November 5. https://beyond-coal.jp/en/news/global-coal-to-clean-power-transition-statement_20211104/. Accessed 5 Nov 2023.

Jarvis, William E. 1992. Modern Time Capsules: Symbolic Repositories of Civilization. *Libraries and Culture* 27 (3): 279–295.

Kant, Immanuel. 1987 [1790]. *Critique of Judgment*. Trans. W.S. Pluhar. Indianapolis: Hackett Publishing.

Kilvert, Nick. 2021. Earth Is Getting a Black Box to Record Our Climate Change Actions, and It's Already Started Listening. *ABC News* [Australia]. December 16. https://www.abc.net.au/news/science/2021-12-06/climate-change-earth-black-box-recorder/100621778. Accessed 5 Nov 2023.

Kubrick, Stanley (Director). 1968. *2001: A Space Odyssey*. [Film]. MGM.

Leuzzi, Laura, and Antonella Sbrilli. 2018. 2114, Future Library: A Conversation with Katie Paterson. *KronoScope* 18: 72–79.

Madsen, Michael (Director). 2010. *Into Eternity: A Film for the Future*. [Film]. Films Transit International.

Mertens, Mahlu, and Stef Craps. 2018. Contemporary Fiction vs. the Challenge of Imagining the Timescale of Climate Change. *Studies in the Novel* 50 (1): 134–153.

Munteanu, Nina. 2014. Watermark. *thealiennextdoor*. November 17. https://themeaningofwater.com/2014/11/17/watermark/. Accessed 22 Mar 2023.

Nixon, Rob. 2011. *Slow Violence and the Environmentalism of the Poor*. Cambridge, MA: Harvard University Press.

Patchett, Merle. 2012. Reframing the Canadian Oil Sands. *Imaginations* 3 (2): 140–169.

Paterson, Katie. [Website]. 2014. *Future Library.* https://katiepaterson.org/artwork/future-library/. Accessed 1 Apr 2023.

Shelley, Percy Bysshe. n.d. [1818]. Ozymandias. *Poetry Foundation.* https://www.poetryfoundation.org/poems/46565/ozymandias. Accessed 22 Mar 2023.

Szeman, Imre. 2019. *On Petrocultures: Globalization, Culture, and Energy.* Morgantown: West Virginia University Press.

Thompson, Joanna. 2022. *Earth's Black Box Warns of Planet's End Due to Climate Change.* January 12. https://science.howstuffworks.com/environmental/conservation/issues/earths-black-box-news.htm. Accessed 22 Mar 2023.

Index[1]

A
Aagerstoun, Mary Jo, 112
Abu Ghraib, 169
Activism, 74, 75, 111–113, 125, 136, 139, 140, 147, 148
Acuña, Rodolfo, 227, 227n8
Adams, Robert, 224n6
Adaptation, 48, 91, 93, 94, 102, 105
Agamben, Giorgio, 37
Agnew, John, 225, 226, 230, 240
Alarcón, Norma, 228n9
Almodóvar, Pedro, 75
Alt, Matt, 39
Andriano, Joseph, 181
Anthropocene, 246, 249, 252, 253, 258, 261
Apperley, Tom, 18
Artivism, 111, 112, 118–120, 122, 124, 125, 136
Atkison, Paul, 34

Atwood, Margaret, 91–94, 105, 106, 254
The Handmaid's Tale, 91, 93, 102, 103
Auther, Elissa, 112
Autobiography, 3, 198
Ayala, Gary, 238

B
Bacholle, Michèle, 81, 83
Baichwal, Jennifer, 249
Bak, Meredith, 39
Baltz, Lewis, 224, 224n6, 225, 225n7
Barlow, Sam, 35
Barthes, Roland, 180
Bateman, Chris, 48
Becher, Hilla and Bernd Becher, 223n5, 224n6
Berger, John, 2
Bettelheim, Bruno, 176

[1] Note: Page numbers followed by 'n' refer to notes.

Bhabha, Homi, 95
Blaisbois, Cedric, 245, 250–252, 258, 262
  Autocannibalism, 245, 250, 258
Blake, William, 17
Blommaert, Jan, 197
Boyd, Danah, 200
Bradley, Dan, 164
Briedik, Adam, 92
Broccoli, Barbara, 157, 162
Brosnan, Pierce, 154, 157, 158, 163
Brubaker, Rogers, 5
Brzozowska-Brywczyńska, Maja, 185, 192
Buckland, Warren, 82
Burtynsky, Edward, 245, 248–250, 252, 260, 262
  Manufactured Landcapes, 248, 249
  Watermark, 249
Bush, George W., 155, 156
Bushman, Ron, 183
Byrne, Deirdre, 17n2

C

Campany, David, 222, 225
Campbell, Martin, 154, 158
Campbell, Marvin, 164
Campbell, Neil, 178, 179
Carlisle, Belinda, 97, 99, 105
Cassara, Joseph, 74
Children's literature, 181, 185, 188
Cholodenko, Alan, 37, 38
Churchill, Winston, 147
Clancy, Tom, 155
Clark, Nicole, 23
Climate change, 246, 247, 250, 252–256, 259, 262
Clune, Michael W., 30
Coghlan, Simon, 30
Cohen, Jeffrey Jerome, 177

Colonization, 92, 95, 101–103, 106
Comics, 8–10, 56, 58, 61, 67, 109–118, 111n1, 116n4, 116n5, 124, 125, 195–199, 206, 215
Connery, Sean, 154, 156, 158
Cooper, Chris, 168
Cooper, Jonathan, 37
Cote, Amanda C., 21
Cousins, Mark, 46
Covid-19, 196, 197, 200, 201
Cox, Brian, 168
Craig, Daniel, 157–159, 162–165, 167, 171
Craps, Stef, 246, 247, 257
Crenshaw, Kimberlé, 231
Cresswell, Tim, 234
Crowley, Patrick, 169
Curwen, Margaret Sauceda, 238
Cuteness, 184, 185, 187, 189, 192, 207
Cyberpunk: Edgerunners (Anime), 45

D

Damon, Matt, 156, 159, 171
Deal, Joe, 224n6
Dean, John, 179
Dench, Judy, 154, 162, 163
Derrida, Jacques, 16
Di Leo, Jeffrey R., 254, 255
Dickens, Charles, 26
Dickinson, Emily, 73, 75
Disney, Walt, 179, 180
Divola, John, 220, 221n3
Donar, Ann, 248
Donnelly, Kevin, 94
Duffy, Carol Ann, 79, 85
Dunye, Cheryl, 73, 74, 88
Dyer-Witheford, Nick, 29
Dylan, Bob, 210

E

Earth's Black Box, 246, 256–259, 262
Ehrig, Stephan, 232
Elleström, Lars, 8, 117
Emre, Merve, 255
Environmentalism, 56, 59, 246, 247, 250, 259, 261
Evans, Janet, 177

F

Fairy tales, 175, 176, 181, 182, 184, 187, 188
Fan culture, 164
Fanon, Frantz, 95
Feldman, Charles K., 157
Fidalgo, Pedro, 136, 137, 140, 142–145, 147, 148
Finney, Albert, 156
Fleming, Ian, 154, 155, 157–159
  Casino Royale, 154, 157
Flores, William V., 228
Foucan, Sébastian, 165
Fragmentation, 2, 5–10, 36, 111, 122, 124, 125, 134, 196
Freccero, Carla, 80
Freeman, Elizabeth, 81
Frei, Michael, 42
Fujishima, Kosuke, 43
  Oh My Goddess!, 43

G

Gallagher, Shaun, 68
Gaudreault, André, 39
Genre, 9, 13–16, 23, 29, 56, 59, 62
Ghosh, Amitav, 246, 247
  The Great Derangement, 246
Giblett, Rod, 248
Gilroy, Tony, 156, 157, 169
Ginsberg, Allen, 197
Globalization, 138, 249, 251–253

Gohlke, Frank, 224n6
Goldie, Peter, 61, 62
Gordon, Avery, 80, 85
Gore, Lesley, 96, 105
Graffiti, 10, 132–139, 141, 143–145, 148, 221, 222, 229, 230, 232, 235–238, 237n15, 241
Grampp, Sven, 8
Graphic novels, 75, 109–111, 111n1, 116n5
Greenberg, Raz, 48
Greengrass, Paul, 157, 164, 165, 169, 171
Groensteen, Thierry, 109, 110
Guantánamo Bay, 169
Gunning, Tom, 39
Gurnah, Abdulrazak, 17
Gursky, Andreas, 223n5

H

Haggis, Paul, 158
Hall, Stuart, 220
Harris, Brandon C., 21
Hawkey, Kate, 180
Hemingway, Ernest, 208, 209
Hernandez, Anthony, 221, 221n4
Herzog, Werner, 208, 209
Hirsch, Marianne, 78n2
Hisaishi, Joe, 44
Hodgkin, Katharine, 226
Holloway, Miles, 17n2
hooks, bell, 81
Hopper, Edward, 236
Hybridity, 33, 93, 95, 101, 104, 105, 111, 114, 124

I

Intermediality, 38, 56, 58, 59, 94, 95, 100, 103, 105, 106, 110

Intersectionality, 75, 80, 120, 120n7, 123, 124, 124n10, 231
Isbister, Katherine, 29
Italian comics creators
    Zerocalcare, Sio, Cristina Portolano, Leo Ortolani, Zuzu, Silvia Ziche, Altan, 114

J
Jacob, Thornwell, 254
    Crypt of Civilization, 254
Jagoda, Patrick, 24
Jagose, Annamarie, 82
James, Michael, 14
Järvinen, Aki, 34, 45
Jarvis, William E., 254
Jenkins, Henry, 122n9, 202
Johnston, Ollie, 37
Jones, Chuck
    Duck Amuck (Looney Tunes), 48
Jones, Rodney H., 199
Jones, Tommy Lee, 168
Joyce, James, 254
Jung, Britta C., 232
Juul, Jesper, 34, 48

K
Kahlo, Frida, 84n3
Kant, Immanuel, 248
    Critique of Judgment, 248
Kean, Alisdair, 178, 179
Kiel, Richard, 166
King, Geoff, 34
Krajewski, Marek, 185
Krzywinska, Tania, 34

L
Lacroix, Celeste, 183, 186
Lawler, Stephanie, 231

Lawrence, D. H., 254
Lazarus, Neil, 103
Lazenby, George, 158
Le Carré, John, 160
Lee, Francis, 81
Lennon, John, 210
Lessing, G. E., 119
Levine, Caroline, 7, 13, 14, 16, 19–22, 24–26, 28, 30
Levitt, Deborah, 38
LGBTQ+, 80, 124, 190, 191
Li Jian, 210
Liman, Doug, 156, 160, 164, 169, 171
Love, Heather, 80, 85
Lucha y Siesta, 112–119, 114n2, 114n3, 124, 125
Ludlum, Robert, 155, 156
Lynch, David, 17

M
MacGillivray, Laurie, 238
Madonna, 154
Madsen, Michael, 258, 262
    Into Eternity A Film for the Future, 258
Malkowski, Jennifer, 29
Marshall, Frank, 169
Marshall, P. David, 208
Martín Núñez, Marta, 34
Matrioske parlanti, 112, 120, 121
McCloud, Scott, 197–199, 209
McNeely, Juanita, 84n3
Mertens, Mahlu, 246, 247, 257
Mikkonen, Kai, 117
Miller, Bruce, 91
Mirzapour, Narges, 92
Moby, 167
Mode, Heinz, 181
Model, Lisette, 220, 220n2
Molina, Natalia, 226

INDEX   269

Montero Plata, Laura, 44
Moore, Roger, 154, 158, 163
Moss, Elisabeth, 92, 93, 100
Mosselaer, Nele van der, 34
Movies, 1, 4, 5, 9
   Ammonite, 74, 75, 77–79, 83, 86, 87
   Attack of the 50 Foot Woman, 189
   Austin Powers, 154, 157
   Away, 36
   Batman Begins, 155
   The Blob, 189
   The Bourne Identity, 154–156, 160, 161, 164–166, 169, 171
   The Bourne Legacy, 156, 157, 168, 169
   The Bourne Supremacy, 160, 162, 165, 167
   The Bourne Ultimatum, 156, 160, 161, 164, 165, 171
   Casino Royale (1967), 157–161, 163, 165, 169
   The Creature from the Black Lagoon, 189
   Death Wish, 170
   Die Another Day, 154, 155, 157, 166
   Dr No, 154
   Fair Game, 156
   Fast and Furious, 164
   The Fifth Estate, 168
   Fitzcarraldo, 208, 209
   The Fly (1986), 189
   The Flying Luna Clipper, 36, 43
   GoldenEye, 158, 163, 164
   Goldfinger, 154
   Hanna, 159
   Infamous, 157
   Jason Bourne, 159–162, 164, 171
   John Wick, 159, 164
   Lethal Weapon, 170
   Let the Record Show, 75
   The Lion King, 183, 186
   Lord of the Rings, 155, 158
   Matrix, The, 25
   The Mechanic, 159
   Metal Gear Solid 3-Existence, 36
   Mission Impossible, 154, 164
   Monsters Inc., 186, 188–189
   Monsters vs Aliens, 186, 189–190
   Never Say Never Again, 156
   No Time to Die, 158, 160–163, 169, 171
   120 Battements par Minute, 74
   On Her Majesty's Secret Service, 158
   Onward, 186, 190, 191
   Parallel Mothers, 75
   Paris is Burning, 74
   Portrait of a Lady on Fire, 74–79, 81–86
   Pride, 74
   Quantum of Solace, 159, 163–165, 168
   Road to Perdition, 157
   Shenmue The Movie, 36
   Shrek, 186, 187
   Shrek Forever After, 186, 188
   Shrek the Third, 186, 187
   Shrek 2, 186, 187
   Skyfall, 156, 159, 161, 162, 164
   Snow White and the Seven Dwarfs, 179
   Spectre, 159, 161, 163, 167–169
   Spiderman, 157
   Star Wars, 3, 155
   Thunderball, 156
   Tomorrow Never Dies, 166
   2001 A Space Odyssey, 256
   The Watermelon Woman, 73, 88
   Wild Nights With Emily, 75
   The Wizard of Oz, 198
   Zero Dark Thirty, 169
Munch, Edvard, 260

Muñoz, José Esteban, 228n9
Myers, Julian, 229, 231

N
Nakazawa, Kazuo, 44
Narrativity, 57, 59, 61–64, 110, 111, 115, 116, 118, 119, 122–125
Neoliberalism, 209, 212, 214
Neumann, Brigit, 94, 95
9/11, 155, 162, 169
Nixon, Nicholas, 224n6
Nochlin, Linda, 78
Nolan, Christopher, 155
Non una di meno, 112, 120, 120n6, 121n8, 122–125
Norton, Edward, 168
Novels, 4, 8, 246

O
Oihra, Shinya, 44
Okri, Ben, 94, 100, 101, 104–106
  The Famished Road, 94, 100–104
  Infinite Riches, 101
  Songs of Enchantment, 101
Otherness, 95, 185

P
Pallant, Chris, 33, 35
Parsayi, Farzad, 34
Paterson, Katie, 245, 247, 253–255, 259, 261, 262
  The Future Library, 245, 247, 253–259
Pearson, Richard, 164
Peeples, Jennifer, 248
Pencier, Nicholas de, 249
Petruccioli, Rita, 113, 114, 116
Peuter, Greig de, 29

Pfahl, John, 220, 221n3
Phillips, Susan A., 238
Photography, 3, 4, 46, 86, 110, 144, 145, 248–250, 262
Playable images
  After Dark, 41
  Flipnote Studio, 43
  Flipnote Studio 3D, 43
  Johnny Castaway, 41
  Kids, 42
  My Exercise, 42, 43
  Plug & Play, 42
  Stray Sheep, 42
Poletti, Anna, 200
Postcolonial, 92, 94, 95, 101–103, 105, 106
Powell, Gary, 164
Prinz, Jesse, 68
Propp, Vladimir, 182, 192
Purvis, Neal, 158

Q
Queer, 74, 87

R
Radiohead, 99, 100, 103, 105
Radstone, Susannah, 226
Rancière, Jacques, 134
Reed, Aaron, 35
Rego, Paula, 84n3
Rendón, Armando B., 227
Renner, Jeremy, 156
Reynaud, Charles-Émile, 179
Rickenbach, Mario von, 42
Rosaldo, Renato, 228
Rosenberg, Emily, 178
Rouse, Christopher, 165
Ruff, Thomas, 223n5
Russworm, TreaAndrea, 29
Ryan, Marie-Laure, 110, 115, 118

S

Sadeghi, Zahra, 92
Salisbury, Mark, 171
Sarkeesian, Anita, 25
Scateni, Ren, 85
Schaffer, Gad, 232
Schiller, Melanie, 202
Schott, John, 224n6
Schreier, Jason, 21
Schulman, Sarah, 75
Sciamma, Céline, 74, 80–84
Science fiction, 3, 15, 166, 189
Sealy, Mark, 232
Shimizu, Yasuyuji, 44
Shklovsky, Victor, 57, 66
　defamiliarization, 57–59, 66–69
Shore, Stephen, 224n6
Sicart, Miguel, 21
Social media, 1, 9, 10, 25, 76, 113, 114n3, 117, 148, 168, 195, 196, 199, 200, 203, 205, 251
Stacey, Jackie, 76
Statham, Jason, 159
Stein, Sally, 231
Steinberg, Marc, 44
Stevens, Benjamin, 87
Stilwell, Robynn J., 98, 99
Storytelling, vii, 1, 3–5, 7–9, 11, 14, 19, 23, 24, 26–29, 36, 41, 56–65, 67–69, 86, 91, 94, 98, 102, 105, 106, 110, 111, 114, 119, 123, 125, 159, 176, 179, 198, 202, 205, 217, 219, 246, 260
Strathairn, David, 168
Street art, 10, 111, 114, 124, 132–135, 137, 139, 140, 148
Stuart, Keith, 6, 7
Studio Ghibli, 35, 44
Szeman, Imre, 247, 257
Szupinska, Joanna, 233, 235

T

Tallerico, Brian, 171
Tatar, Maria, 176
Taylor, Adam, 93, 94
Television
　Agents of S.H.I.E.L.D, 8
　Blind Spot, 7
　Borgen, 25
　Breaking Bad, 158
　Coronation Street, 8
　Game of Thrones, 158, 162
　General Hospital, 8
　The Handmaid's Tale, 91, 97, 102–106
　House, 158
　It's a Sin, 74
　Mad Men, 158
　The Mentalist, 158
　Pose, 74
　The Sopranos, 158
　The Walking Dead, 7
　The Wire, 26, 28
　Treadstone, 172
　24, 168
　Vinyl, 7
Tencent, 202, 210
Thomas, Frank, 37
Tiaoman, 10
TikTok, 1, 4
Titlestad, Michael, 17n2
Tlostanova, Madina, 95
Toriyama, Akira, 43
　Dragon Ball, 43
　Dr Slump, 43
Torres, Lourdes, 233
Tosca, Susana, 47
Transmediality, 2, 5, 8, 35, 44, 93, 94, 105, 110, 111, 116–119, 121n8, 122n9, 125, 202, 203, 205, 206, 211
Türkmen, Mustafa, 184

U

Unten, Wayne, 43
   Toadal Disaster, 43

V

Valenti, Jack, 179
Van de Ven, Inge, 199
Van Gemert, Ties, 199
Veloric, Cynthia Haveson, 248
Video Games
   After Dark, 41
   And the Sun Went Out, 36
   Asura's Wrath, 44
   Bloodborne, 15n1
   Castlevania, 15n1
   Catherine, 44
   Chuchel, 48
   Cuphead, 35
   Cyberpunk 2077, 45
   Dark Souls, 15n1
   Deathloop, 24
   Death Stranding, 36
   Demon's Soul, 15n1
   Dragon Quest, 43
   Elden Ring, 6
   Far Cry V, 18
   Florence, 6
   Gobliiins, 48
   God of War-Ragnarök, 24
   Gumboot Glory, 23
   Hitman, 25
   Horizon-Forbidden West, 14
   Kirby's Dream Land, 49
   The Last of Us, 18
   The Last of Us Part II, 6, 26, 27
   The Legend of Zelda-Ocarina of Time, 14
   Life is Strange, 26
   Life Is Strange 2, 35
   Mass Effect, 23
   Metal Gear Solid 3-Snake Eater, 36
   Metal Gear Solid 3-Subsistence, 36
   Metroid, 15n1
   Mortal Kombat, 46
   Ni No Kuni-Wrath of the White Witch, 44
   No Man's Sky, 20n3
   Papers, Please, 29
   Ratchet & Clank-Rift Apart, 24
   Red Dead Redemption 2, 46
   Resident Evil 4, 24
   Rogue, 15n1
   Shenmue, 36, 47
   Sonic the Hedgehog, 48
   Tales, 44
   Telling Lies, 36
   TMNT-Shredder's Revenge, 36
   Tux and Fanny, 46
   The Walking Dead-A New Day, 23
   Wattam, 49
   What Remains of Edith Finch, 7
   Yonder The Cloud Catcher Chronicles, 6
Villa, Raúl Homero, 228
Visual culture, 33–35, 38, 41, 45, 50, 240

W

Wada, Atsushi, 42
Wade, Robert, 158
Walder, Denis, 92
Walker, Jill, 123, 124
Waterhouse, Ruth, 181
Waters, Roger, 210
WeChat, 196, 201, 202, 207, 208, 210, 212, 214
Wessel, Henry, 224n6
Weston, Kate, 75n1
Whitlock, Gillian, 200
Williams, Greg, 157
Wilson, Harold, 165
Wilson, Kyle, 14

Wilson, Michael G., 157–158, 162
Wolf, Werner, 118, 121
Wood, Oliver, 169
Wright, Jeffrey, 162
Wright, Peter, 169

X
Xu Zhiyuan, 217
 Thirteen Invitations, 200–203, 206, 209, 214

Uncle Lion Diary, 200–203, 206, 208, 211, 216

Y
Yeats, William Butler, 252
Yorke, Thom, 100

Z
Zipes, Jack, 180

9783031654862